A Moveable Feast

Don George is the editor of four previous Lonely Planet literary anthologies: *A House Somewhere* (co-edited with Anthony Sattin), *The Kindness of Strangers*, *By the Seat of My Pants* and *Tales from Nowhere*. He is also the author of the *Lonely Planet Guide to Travel Writing*. Don is Contributing Editor and Book Review Columnist for *National Geographic Traveler*, and Special Features Editor and Columnist for the popular travel website Gadling.com. He is also the Editor in Chief of the online literary travel magazine Recce: Literary Journeys for the Discerning Traveler (www.geoex.com/recce) and the creator and host of the adventure travel site Don's Place (www.adventurecollection.com/dons-blog). In thirty years as a travel writer and editor, Don has been Global Travel Editor for Lonely Planet and Travel Editor at the *San Francisco Examiner and Chronicle;* he also founded and edited Salon.com's groundbreaking travel site, Wanderlust. He has received dozens of awards for his writing and editing, including the Pacific Asia Travel Association's Gold Award for Best Travel Article and the Society of American Travel Writers Lowell Thomas Award. He appears frequently on NPR, CNN and other TV and radio outlets, is a highly sought-after speaker, and hosts a national series of onstage conversations with prominent writers. Don is also co-founder and chairman of the annual Book Passage Travel Writers and Photographers Conference.

A Moveable Feast

LIFE-CHANGING FOOD ADVENTURES AROUND THE WORLD

EDITED BY
Don George

LONELY PLANET PUBLICATIONS

Melbourne • Oakland • London

A Moveable Feast:
Life-Changing Food Encounters Around the World

Published by Lonely Planet Publications

Head Office:
90 Maribyrnong Street, Footscray, Vic 3011, Australia
Locked Bag 1, Footscray, Vic 3011, Australia

Branches:
150 Linden Street, Oakland CA 94607, USA
2nd floor, 186 City Rd, London, EC1V 2NT, UK

Published 2010
Printed through Toppan Security Printing Pte. Ltd.
Printed in Singapore

Edited by Janet Austin
Designed by Christopher Ong
Cover Design by Christopher Brand

National Library of Australia Cataloguing-in-Publication entry

A moveable feast : life-changing food encounters around the world / edited by Don
George.

1st ed.

978 1 74220 229 7 (pbk.)

Food--Guidebooks.
Voyages and travels.
Travelers' writings.

George, Donald W.

641.3

Contents

Introduction

DON GEORGE

I had ventured way off the beaten track, into a weather-beaten fishing village on a foggy spit of land that slides into the Sea of Japan. Because I spoke Japanese and was the first foreigner who had passed that way in decades, I became the town's guest of honour, and I was taken with great ceremony to what I gathered was the local equivalent of El Bulli or Chez Panisse.

I was feted with the usual bottomless cups of sake and glasses of beer, and the endless succession of little indescribable delicacies artfully arranged on thimble-sized plates. Then, for a moment, the whole restaurant seemed to pause as a dish was carried regally to the table and set before me. It was a whole fish, arranged with its head and tail twisted to look as if it were still leaping. Its flank had been cut open to reveal thin-cut slices of glisteningly fresh flesh.

All eyes were on me as I picked up my chopsticks and brought them to the fish. I reached in to choose the most savoury-looking slice – and the fish jumped. Thinking this was some bizarre reflex reaction, I reached in again. Again the fish jumped. This was when I looked at the fish's eye – and realised it was still alive! This was the village's delicacy: the rawest raw fish in all Japan.

What could I do? Whatever discomfort – piscitarian or gustatory – I was feeling at that point, and however much I identified with that fish, there was no turning back.

On my third try I steeled myself, pincered the desired slice and brought it to my tongue. I closed my eyes, intensely aware that every other eye in the room – including the fish's – was on me. Suddenly ocean-fresh flavour leapt inside my mouth. My eyes shot open and a rapturous smile lit my face. The entire restaurant burst into cheers and applause.

———————◀

Travel and food are inseparably intertwined, and sometimes, as in that Japanese restaurant, the lessons their intertwinings confer are complex. But one truth is clear: wherever we go, we need to eat. As a result, when we travel, food inevitably becomes one of our prime fascinations – and pathways into a place. On the road, food nourishes us not only physically, but intellectually, emotionally and spiritually too.

I've learned this countless times all around the globe. In fact, many of my finest travel memories revolve around food. The *biftek-frites* I would always order at the six-table sawdust restaurant around the corner when I lived in Paris the summer after I graduated from college, where the proprietor came to know me so well that he would bring my carafe of *vin ordinaire* before I could say a word. An endless ouzo-fuelled night of shattered plates and arm-in-arm dancing at a taverna in Athens, and the Easter feast my family was invited to share with a Greek family in the rocky hills of the Peloponnesus, where the host offered me the singular honour of eating the lamb's eyeballs. The Sachertorte an American couple I met on the train kindly treated me to when we arrived in Vienna. My first fleshy-seedy taste of figs at a market in Istanbul.

I remember a time-stopping afternoon on the sun-dappled terrace at La Colombe d'Or in St-Paul-de-Vence, feasting stomach and soul on *daurade avec haricots verts* and artwork by Matisse, Picasso, Chagall and Miró. I think of a post-wedding sake and sushi celebration on the island of Shikoku, an Ecuadorian version of Thanksgiving with my family on a life-changing expedition in the Galápagos, freeze-dried *bœuf bourguignon* under the stars on a pine-scented Yosemite night, *huachinango* grilled with garlic at a seaside restaurant in Zihuatanejo, proffered by the laughing parents at the next table as their children led ours sprinting into the sea and my toes sighed into the sand. So many meals, so many memories.

This book presents a thirty-eight-course feast of such memories, life-changing food adventures, big and small, set around the world. Selected from among hundreds of edifying stories submitted for this anthology, these tales vividly illustrate the many roles food plays in our lives on the road. It can be a gift that enables a traveller to survive, a doorway into the heart of a tribe, or a thread that weaves an indelible tie. It can be a source of frustration or a fount of benediction, the object of a timely quest or the catalyst of a timeless fest. It can be awful or ambrosial – and sometimes both at the same time. Whatever its particular part, in all these cases, and in all these tales, food is an agent of transformation, taking travellers to a deeper and more lasting understanding of and connection with a people, a place and a culture.

As the host of this literary feast, I am delighted that chefs, food critics, poets and travel writers – some of them bestselling, some never published before – are sitting together at this table, spicing the air with their idiosyncratic perspectives, adventures and voices. And I am astonished and humbled by the spectrum of settings, themes and emotions embodied in these tales, robust proof that food offers a plethora of life-enriching gifts on the road, if only our minds and hearts – and stomachs – are open to them.

I am also delighted that, quite unexpectedly, this literary feast has been an agent of transformation in another way for me. As I have been working on this book over the past few months, I have found myself singing in the kitchen as I was preparing a simple salad, exulting without even realising it in the texture, scent and taste of tomato, lettuce, carrot and feta cheese. I have discovered a new-found fascination with the produce section of the local market, hefting cantaloupes and smelling them, relishing the smooth solidity of mushrooms, savouring the nutty tang of kale. I have made a one-hour pilgrimage to pick strawberries straight from the field, and when I eat out, I have been taking the time to taste, really *taste,* the grilled king salmon, garlic potatoes, and roasted asparagus with truffle oil on my plate. Even at home, I chew more intently and more intensely, and wherever I am, I cherish more mindfully the camaraderie that food convenes.

I hope this humble meal will have the same effect on you.

Food delights us, food unites us, food embodies the soil, the sea and the weather, the farmer's sweat and the fisherman's toil. But as these tales and my own edible adventures reveal, food is only part of a feast. Every meal, whether a single mango or a multicourse molecular masterpiece, is really a communing of spirit: just as important are the setting and the situation, the effort, attentiveness and intention that infuse and inform what we share. We feast on the love behind and within the offering, love for a moment, a lesson, a gift, for companions and connections, that will never be repeated and can never be replaced. For me, this revelation has been the last course in this literary bacchanal of risk, embrace and care: the exquisite beauty of the moveable feast is its savoury serendipity – as on that long-ago day in rural Japan, it can leap into your life when you least expect it, anywhere.

Now, let the feast begin. *Bon appétit!*

Food on the Hoof

JAN MORRIS

Jan Morris, who was born in 1926, is Anglo-Welsh and lives in Wales with her partner, Elizabeth Morris. She has published some forty books of history, travel, biography, memoir and fiction, most notably the 'Pax Britannica' trilogy about the British Empire; major studies of Wales, Europe, Venice, Hong Kong, Sydney and Trieste; the historical fantasy *Hav* and the autobiographical *Conundrum*.

I am a shamefacedly self-centred and often blinkered writer. Although, in the course of a long travelling life, I must have eaten several hundred thousand meals on the hoof, I have never taken food very seriously or bothered to consider the seminal contributions it has made to every aspect of history down the ages. From mammoth meat to foie gras, from the composition of Elizabethan banquet madrigals to the strategies of blockading navies, from rocket rations to genetically modified cereals – I have ignored them all.

Too late to change! Food's contribution to my historical or aesthetic thinking remains minimal to this day. But, of course, there are some foods that I decidedly prefer to others. Life without bitter Seville orange marmalade would not be worth living, but torturers could not make me eat another forkful of the Lithuanian delicacy called a *capelinas,* which is made of potato dough soaked in bacon fat, with a sausage in the middle. By and large, however, it is not the edible ingredients of travelling food that I remember, for better or for worse, but the circumstances in which I ate them.

Like most of us, I enjoy eating while actually in motion. An Indian curry is best of all when it has been thrust urgently through your compartment window at Hooghly Station the very moment before your great train leaves for Mumbai, and I remember with intense pleasure gobbling a pot of self-heating noodles on a lurching sampan on a wet and dismal dawn *en voyage* from Hong Kong Island to Tai Po in the New Territories. When I boarded the last frail remnant of the original *Orient Express,* in the absence of a restaurant car I was delighted to be handed a paper bag containing an apple, a hunk of cheese and a half-bottle of excellent white wine – what could be a better munch while we laboured across Europe?

On the other hand, eating *en avion* has generally been a disappointment to me, especially when, in more spacious times, I used to travel first class. This was chiefly because of the ridiculous hyperbole of airline menus, the preposterous sham Frenchness of them, the absurd lists of celebrated chefs who were alleged to have selected the ingredients, and the gigantic menu cards, like nightmare wedding invitations, which you were obliged, with extreme difficulty, to extract from among your magazines and Duty Free catalogues when a supercilious stewardess suddenly turned up and demanded your choice.

I do make an exception, though, for meals on the short-lived Concorde, during the brief heyday of its service between London and New York. Who could honestly complain about poached apple chatelaine (a whole apple filled with redcurrant jelly and coated with kirsch and cream) or a wine list that numbered five champagnes, six burgundies and half a dozen clarets, to be enjoyed as the cabin speedometer gently told you that you were now travelling faster than the speed of sound?

Often it is the place that bewitches me, far more than the food. For example, the food is marvellous at the Grand Hotel in Stockholm, but it doesn't compare with the welcome of the setting when I check in on a summer evening and toddle down for a jet-lagged early supper on the hotel terrace. All around me, the spires and jagged rooftops of the old city are silhouetted against the twilight – the little steamers puff by, the royal palace looks stately over the water, scores of flags are still bravely flying, and as I hear the slapping of their ropes against their flagstaffs, and breathe in the cool clear air of the North, I hardly bother to notice when my victuals arrive.

In any case, simplicity is my criterion of good food on the hoof. I love to stop off for a snack at one of the tumultuous outdoor marketplaces of Asia, anywhere east of Suez. In Hong Kong there used to be such a place bang in the centre of the city waterfront, not a hundred yards from one of the grand hotels. It would amuse me, as I sat on a bench amidst the market hubbub, eating some delightfully organic sustenance, to think that just over the way I might be having a crab soup not half as good as mine, and ten times as expensive.

O, simplicity's the thing, plus serendipity! 'Here, try one,' cried a cheerful girl to me, passing by in the back of an open truck among the orchards of Andalucía, and the kumquat she threw me, I swear, was the food of Paradise – along with baked potatoes from an open fire among the Sherpas, or the raw fresh herrings sold as snacks in the coastal streets of Holland, or Dungeness crabs among the tourists at Fisherman's Wharf in San Francisco, or the fried whitebait they have been serving for a couple of centuries at the Trafalgar Tavern beside the Thames at Greenwich, or blinis somewhere off Nevsky Prospekt, or big juicy asparagus fresh from a Lüneburg garden, or oysters on a trestle table down the road from Galway, or Guinness and prawns beside the sea in the Isle of Man, or classic fish and chips, the real thing, at Harry Ramsden's at Guiseley in Yorkshire, where they will give you a free pudding if you manage to get through the mammoth platter called Harry's Challenge …

Simple foods every one, the food of the countries I'm passing through. The very best meal I ever eat – and I have eaten it a hundred times – is simple food served with extreme sophistication. They serve it at Harry's Bar in Venice, which I have frequented since the end of the Second World War, when it used to be cooked by the proprietor's wife, Signora Cipriani. Now in her honour they call it Scampi Thermidor alla Cipriani, and it consists of prawn tails cooked in oil under a parmesan-flavoured sauce, with a little green salad and a rice pilaf on the side. I have a glass or two of the local pinot grigio, and if I ask nicely they might do me a warm zabaglione to polish it off.

Travel the world over, from the Ritz to McDonald's to a street-stall in Chiang Mai, and you won't do better than that.

Daily Bread

PICO IYER

Pico Iyer is the author of many books of travel, among them *Video Night in Kathmandu, The Lady and the Monk* and *The Global Soul*. A gourmand of experience, he prefers to consume the entire world, and not just its meals and its restaurants.

The quiche is as soft as hope itself, and the long spears of asparagus are so elegant on the plate that to pick one up feels like messing with the symmetry of a Klee. There are bowls of lettuce in our midst, and the chunky vegetable soup alone would make for a hearty meal. Bottles of salad dressing crowd the blond-wood table, large enough for six of us, while early-spring sunlight streams into the window-filled refectory, so that it feels as if we're tasting radiance and taking a long draught of the sun.

The man next to me, his white hood down, springs up to cut the fluffy long fingers of quiche for an older neighbour, who lives now with Parkinson's. Then he comes back and tells me about the nine-hour drive he just took to an ashram in southern India, and the forest fire that wiped out a colleague's place in the hills of Santa Barbara. I ask him if he saw the movie about the monks of the Grande Chartreuse and we talk about the Dalai Lama, Tanzania, how best to die. One of the men who's just left this place – for Jerusalem, to work for peace – used to zealously keep the Sabbath in the midst of all these Catholics.

'I suppose monks are the only ones who don't keep the Sabbath,' I say to my friend Raniero.

'The inner Sabbath only,' he says, his cheek dimpling as if he were not the prior.

In the corner there are two large tubs of green-tea ice cream and Italian spumoni dessert; next to them, two plates of peach pie with fruit so fresh I wonder if it's been airlifted over from the Garden. In another corner is a thermos of hot water and all the teas, fancy and a little less so, that modern California can devise. We talk of common friends – Berkeley, Shanghai, LA – and I hear from a beaming monk how all the miles collected on the monastery credit card are sending him this summer – first class! – to Rio.

Then Raniero gets up and rings a little bell. 'Dear God,' he says, quickly, without fuss, 'thank you for this food and the friendship around these tables. Special blessings to Benedict, for preparing this excellent meal. As we go forth from this room and back to our duties, may we always see that light that shines in others and in ourselves.'

'You free for some washing-up, Pico?' the man next to me, in an apron, says. Seconds later, I am standing next to the former prior, in his eighties, and the current one, working briskly, as we chat, to make all the plates shine again.

What in the world am I doing here, you might ask? I sometimes ask myself. I'm not a Catholic, and nine years of enforced chapel twice a day at British boarding school (with Latin hymns on Sunday nights) seemed to satisfy more than a lifetime's quota of religion. I respect those people who have the groundedness and selflessness that faith often brings – the alertness to compassion and a larger view of things – but I'm not quick to call those virtues mine.

Yet what I am is a traveller, whose life is about trying to occupy shoes – and lives and hearts – very different from my own; and a human being, who cannot fail to be washed clean and opened up by silence. So I come to this Benedictine hermitage, tucked into the central coast of California, and sit in a little cell looking out on the great blue plate of the Pacific, 1300 feet below, scintillant in the sunshine, blue-green waters pooling around rocks, filling the horizon from one end of my deck to the other, and think about what travel really means, and why these men in hoods seem like the most fearless and spirited adventurers I've ever met.

A monk wants to be clear and undistracted in his journey, so he doesn't have too much to eat (in theory), or too little; there's nothing uncomfortable about this place, and sometimes I feel almost embarrassed at how well treated we visitors are. In my little trailer – 'Hesychia', it's called, meaning 'spirit of stillness' – there's a large pot of Extra-Crunchy Skippy peanut butter ('Fuel the Fun!') above the stove, next to a bag of Swiss Miss Milk Chocolate. In the communal kitchen, the ten or twelve people staying here on retreat can help themselves to 'Very Cherry' yoghurt and extra-virgin olive oil, Colombian coffee and kosher salt. Someone has contributed pineapple salsa from Trader Joe's to the communal refrigerator, and one large bottle is always filled with oatmeal raisin cookies.

Every day, at 12.30, bells ring – as they do for Mass – and a monk drives down in a cracked blue hatchback, no licence plate on it, dust swirling up behind him as he accelerates out of the

Monastic Enclosure, and brings us a tureen of hot soup, a main dish, some vegetables and often extras, from which each of us collects a lunch to eat in silence in our rooms. One day it is carrot soup, flecks of Bugs Bunny's favourite floating on the surface so it looks like strawberry yoghurt. Another day there are egg rolls, and pasta shells with salmon in them (fish the only ingredient to disrupt the monks' vegetarianism). One year every dish came with a sprig of mint, or some basil, courtesy of a chef from a four-star restaurant in San Francisco who was spending a year here on retreat, getting himself in order. *'Buon appetito!'* the monk always says as he leaves the glass trays on the counter, to come and collect them again an hour later.

———————◗

If I wanted mere food, I realised some years ago – steaks and sorbets and spicy panang curry with strong chillies – I could find them almost anywhere these days, ten minutes from my home or across the world in some fairy-tale palace; if I wanted a meal to remember, I could go back to Aleppo or Buenos Aires or Hanoi. But after seventeen years of criss-crossing the globe, I came to think that it was only the food I couldn't see that really sustained me and only inner nutrition that made me happy, deep down. A meal I grabbed in a Paris McDonald's, to keep me walking through the streets of the 6th *arrondissement*, left me hungry ten minutes after I'd finished it; a richer, fancier lunch left me so replete that all energy for exploration was gone for the day.

Here I just get into a car and drive up a winding mountain road along the sea, three hours from my mother's house, and find that I am perpetually full and hungry for more with every breath – the way, in love, you thirst for the other's company, yet know that even years together will never be enough.

Now, as the bells ring and ring – time is so slowed down here that I explore every moment as I would the crevices and soft spots in a new lover or a simple honey-flavoured candy exploding in my mouth like caviar – I can reach in my little trailer for the rice and bean chips (with adzuki beans) I've brought up or (as I've smuggled in here on more than fifty retreats now over nineteen years) the jumbo bag of chocolate chip cookies. In the monastery bookstore they're selling Chocolate Fudge Royale and Special Gourmet Mocha Mix in hazelnut flavour. Pieces of the hermitage's celebrated moist fruitcake are available, free of charge, by the cash register, and bottles of Monastery Creamed Honey sit among the Tibetan prayer bowls and rosaries.

But mostly what I do here is think about daily bread, and what communion means in the context of the traveller's daily lifelong companions: restlessness and solitude. In silence the day stretches out and out till sometimes it feels as if yesterday were an eternity ago. I wake up as the first light begins to show above the hills, and make toast and two cups of tea for myself in my little kitchen. I take long walks along the monastery road, stopping at the benches set around every turn to watch the sun sparkle on the water and the coastline to the south slough off its coat of early-morning fog. I read and read – Patti Smith, Marcus Aurelius, Werner Herzog, Thomas Merton – and attention becomes so sharpened that every snatch of perfume, scuffling rabbit or echo hits me like a shock.

The day itself becomes my fuel. I reach for some 'simply cashew, almond and cranberry' trail mix from my suitcase. I stop by the kitchen to pick up an apple. I handwrite letters to friends far away, make plans for the summer, watch the colours turn above the ocean as the darkness falls.

Not having anywhere to go or anything I have to do – no telephone or laptop or television – makes each hour feel as nutritious as a Christmas feast. And spending so many hours in silence, all emptied out, gives new meaning to community when the monks invite us to share in their lunch after Sunday Mass (I go to lunch though I skip the Mass).

Sometimes, when I don't intend to, or am just walking down the road, or reading a biography of the incorrigibly licentious Lord Rochester, I think about what I seek at mealtime. It's not the tastes I savour (I was born and grew up in England, so my taste buds were surgically removed at birth); it's the setting, the circumstances, the company. I would rather, as Thoreau might have muttered, eat a hunk of bread with a friend over good conversation, in a place of beauty such as this, than suffer through a multicourse opera at El Bulli. The food is a means to happiness, a sense of peace; and the true meaning of happiness, as Socrates told me yesterday morning, is not to have more things but to need less. I've never been in a restaurant where people seem so much themselves – which is to say at home – as at the Sunday lunches with the monks.

It's really just a story of love and attention, I come to think – and not even caring which is which, or where one ends and the other begins. I've been lucky enough to eat *injera* bread at Lalibela on New Year's Eve, and to step down into a basement kitchen in Lhasa, where red-cheeked Tibetan girls were cooking up a feast. I've had $300 French kaiseki meals along the red-lanterned lane of the Pontocho district, near my home in Kyoto, looking out on the Kamo River and the eastern hills of the old capital beyond, a moon above the temple spires. I've relished vegetarian meals in a blue restaurant painted over with the lines of Neruda in Easter Island on the first day of the millennium.

But I don't think any place has taught me what a meal is – not just food and not just fuel – so much as here. 'Get up and eat, else the journey will be long for you!' was the topic of the week's sermon at St Anthony's church, in the middle of modern Istanbul, when I looked in on it seven months ago. Now I reach into my bag of Reduced Guilt white corn tortilla chips, and pull out of a drawer one of the 'sweet-hot soft ginger candies' a friend gave me on the way up here. The journey doesn't seem long at all. At the very best restaurants I've visited, my body changes a little when I'm through, and my mood lifts a bit too. Here, when I'm finished with my lunch, I feel as if my life has been transformed.

Communion on Crete

RHONA McADAM

Rhona McAdam is a Canadian poet and food writer who has eaten well in many countries. She has a master's degree in Food Culture from the University of Gastronomic Sciences (Slow Food's university in northern Italy), writes a food and poetry blog (the Iambic Cafe), and teaches an online course in urban agriculture and food security for St Lawrence College in Ontario. Her most recent full-length poetry collection, *Cartography,* was published in 2006, and two delectable chapbooks of her food poems *(Sunday Dinners* and *The Earth's Kitchen)* are soon to be published. She is a Europhile who lived for many happy years in London, but currently lives, writes and cooks in Victoria, British Columbia.

I do not honestly know how many church dinners I have attended in my lifetime, but I know there have been many. My mother's platters still bear our family name written in felt tip on the bottom, and I have memories of those modest, long-tabled spaces, the serving hatch with its retractable wooden shutter behind which the church ladies wove their footsteps, the steam, the heat, the aromas.

So the setting for the meal offered us by the village of Vistagi, in central Crete, was and was not familiar. In the company of my twenty-three classmates at Slow Food's University of Gastronomic Sciences, I had travelled to Crete on one of the several stages – field trips – we were to complete in the course of our master's degree in Food Culture. We'd had an exhausting, uncomfortable, confusing – and exhilarating – time of it, criss-crossing the narrow mountain roads in three minivans, learning about such diverse matters as biodynamics, foraged foods, winemaking, irrigation management and small-scale food production on this rocky island.

We'd been on Crete several days already. Our arrival at Vistagi had been preceded by a wander up a mountain slope to gather wild greens; a dinner in a village taverna where we were individually pressed into song; a tour of a mountain village women's baking collective; and a lesson on the making of baklava and those exquisite Greek donuts, *loukoumades*. We'd had a boggling run of boiled goat, wild onion and artichoke dinners; we'd had fava-potato purée at the start of every meal, a sweetish drink akin to church wine with our meal, and Cretan firewater (raki) at the end. But that, said Kostas, was the point: seasonal eating means repetitive eating. It means a cycle of menus where the variety occurs over the course of a year, not the span of a week.

The day of Vistagi had opened, as they all had, with thick, fresh yoghurt and honey, soft crusty bread with homemade jam, and coffee with milk from the goat tethered at the bottom of the garden. We piled into our minivans and followed Kostas' nimble white Panda up the mountain. Literally. The track we were to follow intersected the road at a near-vertical angle, then twisted its way up to the mountain-top milking parlour in that uniquely vertiginous manner of Cretan roads. The springtime vistas across the valleys were almost breathtaking enough to keep our eyes lifted from the shocking drops below our windows.

At the milking parlour, we watched a pair of shepherds swiftly divest their flock of the morning milk and release them to their grazing, scattering with the sounds of their bells down the hillside. Afterwards we stood together in the warming breeze, dutifully drinking raki and eating pastries, biscuits and fresh cheese – *mizithra* – with walnuts that the old shepherd cracked on a stone. While we ate, he talked about the life of a Cretan shepherd: the cooking and sewing and shoemaking skills each man had to take into the mountains when he travelled with the flock. The platter he thrust towards each of us time and again was heaped with cheese and we were told we had to eat it all. We ate and we ate, the raki curdling in our bellies.

Finally we were done, and gratefully decamped for the next destination: the cheesemakers' hut at the bottom of the mountain. We hurtled down the dirt track, ears popping, giddy with raki and too much cheese, eyes fixed on the blue sky and the wildflowers that blurred in our wake. Down and down we sped, until we spilled out of the vans and into the shed, where the barrels of milk were being unloaded and poured into stainless-steel vats, while the earlier batches were strained into baskets and the cheesemakers in their white aprons and boots laughed and chatted through the steam.

It was a scene we'd seen played out a number of times already, for one of the specialisations in our course was cheese technology. But this humble building was a world away from the high-ceilinged Parmigiano-Reggiano *caseificio*, or the industrial steel-and-glass facility we had yet to visit in Burgundy. The ceiling was low; the room's concrete floors were damp; the fittings functional, but occasionally improvised, like the shopping cart that held some of the equipment.

We stepped outside to the shade of an awning and another breathless view across the valley. A table had been generously spread with rusks *(paximathia)* and raki and – more cheese. This time it was *gravura,* the dense mountain cheese whose nearest cousin is gruyère. It was delicious, and we tried to put duty before hunger, but after a wedge or two I could hardly face another mouthful.

We did what we could and then Kostas, after one of the endless consultations on his cell phone, hustled us back to the vans. Lunch, he said, was waiting for us. I thought he said 'forty dishes have been prepared', but I knew that couldn't be right; I must have misheard.

More twisting mountain roads, more stunning vistas, more dips and rises, and we reached the village, quiet in the noonday sun. We parked the vans and started on foot up the narrow road, where blue doors and pots of flowers lined the way. In one alcove, a donkey was tethered. In another, a flock of chickens sheltered from the heat behind a wired opening. The distant tinkling of goat bells was the only sound we could make out. There was no-one about.

Or so we thought, until we rounded the last bend and looked up to find the town hall, where twenty or thirty villagers of all ages were gathered on the top step, waving and beckoning. Just below them was a fire pit, where the men were sitting on a stone wall, smoking and keeping an eye on the meat that was trellised on sticks, its fragrance stirring something that might once have been appetite, had it not been smothered by cheese.

We approached the crowd, and one woman, Popi, stepped forward. 'She is going to read you a poem of welcome,' said Kostas, and she did: the kind of four-line poem the Cretans engrave on the daggers the men tuck into their belts. She welcomed our tribe of students, and we – from Canada, the US, China, Taiwan, Germany, Australia, Denmark, Spain, Japan,

Austria and Korea – stepped into the group of villagers, with no more to offer in return than our greetings.

Honoured and welcomed, we entered the hall. This is where I recalled the church hall dinners: long tables lined three walls, laden with food. Behind each table were the women, waiting to explain what they had prepared for us: the snails, the ash-cakes, bread, pastries of wild greens, wild onions, artichokes. Potatoes, lemons, fava beans, omelettes. Rabbit, chicken. The men were piling platters with the meat off the charred bones from the fire.

Kostas led us round the room, translating, as the women spoke quietly about their dishes. It was a humbling experience, for these were the most personal of gifts. Each had not only prepared her dish, she had grown or cured or foraged its ingredients. The men had raised the animals, and seen to their deaths.

At the end of the trail of tables, we came to the wine: 12 different kinds, according to Kostas. Made from village grapes, these wines were presented in old and new plastic bottles of all shapes and sizes, including gas cans, and we drank from plastic cups while we ate. Afterwards, someone pulled their car near to the building and blasted folk music from the stereo so the men could dance, in their black boots and brown trousers, their Cretan daggers tucked into their belts.

Replete doesn't describe our state by the end of this day. The feeling was more of a cultural satiation: Vistagi's table had been lavishly laid just for us, twenty-four strangers who could barely pronounce our local thank yous, but we'd become, however briefly, part of the village by sharing in its food. In the words of Popi's poem: 'We are all brothers when we eat'.

Of Boars, Baskets and Brotherhood

DAVID DOWNIE

David Downie is an American author and journalist based in Paris. For the last twenty-five years he has been writing about European travel, culture and food for magazines, newspapers and websites worldwide. David's writing has appeared in a dozen anthologies. His nonfiction books include *Enchanted Liguria: A Celebration of the Culture, Lifestyle and Food of the Italian Riviera*; *Cooking the Roman Way: Authentic Recipes from the Home Cooks and Trattorias of Rome*; *The Irreverent Guide to Amsterdam* and *Paris, Paris: Journey into the City of Light*. David's latest books are *Paris City of Night*, a political thriller; and three critically acclaimed regional travel, food and wine books: *Food Wine the Italian Riviera & Genoa*, *Food Wine Rome* and *Food Wine Burgundy*. He is married to photographer Alison Harris (www.alisonharris.com). His website is www.davidddownie.com.

Alison rolled me on my side. But I wasn't snoring. The grunts and squeals came from the garden, and they had awakened me long before dawn.

Lifting the flaps of the dark green shutters, we peered down, blinking. The sky was clear, the air already too hot for May, even on the Italian Riviera. Below us, olive trees and spiky artichoke plants were silhouetted against the spreading pinkness of the Gulf of Genoa. We could hear waves lapping at a promontory, and the spluttering of a solitary fishing boat. Then the ruckus started up again, followed by the crack of a breaking branch, the scurrying of cloven hoofs, a cacophony of terrified oinks, and a series of half-suffocated human imprecations. *Porca* was the only word we made out, delivered by a gruff voice. The rest was easy to guess.

Safe behind our shutters, we watched a shadowy figure untangle itself and slide down the trunk of a tree beyond the terraced garden. Muttering, it swished open a path between the artichoke fronds, stooped under a vine-draped trellis and crossed a creek to a nearby cluster of pastel-hued village houses. A light went on in one of them, and the figure reappeared on a top-floor balcony. The scene looked suspiciously picturesque, lifted from an operetta set.

'Boars,' Alison whispered. I nodded, wondering how much damage they'd done. The vegetable patch was the pride and passion of a reclusive man whose name we knew to be Oreste. His wife shouted it several times daily across the olive groves.

Though we had glimpsed Oreste planting and weeding in the bright light of day, he – like most craggy residents of the rocky Riviera – had remained in chiaroscuro, unknowable among the high-colour masses of day-trippers, long-term sojourners and sometime-residents. Outnumbered ten-to-one, the locals rarely mixed with outsiders.

Our coffee cups in hand, the sun now scorching, we stood in the pocket-sized garden above Oreste's vegetables. The Mediterranean lolled a thousand feet below, its jagged shore covered by fantasyland villas and hotels. The moment you climbed away from them onto the steep, terraced hillsides, things changed. Many mountain hamlets were abandoned, others depopulated, and armies of wild boars descended from the Apennines to feast in gardens and orchards like Oreste's.

A clump of calla lilies lay toppled at our feet. I hoped the owner of the house did not blame us. Immediately below, at the base of a stone wall, luxuriant zucchini plants had been mangled. A tree limb dangled.

'It broke under my weight,' said a baritone voice. Oreste loomed up, carrying a wicker basket and shears. 'I wanted to scare them,' he added, approaching with caution. 'I hope you were not awakened?'

'No,' Alison lied. 'But what a shame about your vegetables. They're so lovely, and you work so hard.'

Oreste waved the shears. I noticed his white teeth under a white moustache, and his blue eyes, rare in this part of Italy. They flashed. 'One moment,' he commanded. I realised he had been speaking English, his apparent caution evaporating like the dew. With a deft gesture he snipped off a zucchini, its flower attached, then another and another. He rummaged among the artichokes, snipping and yanking, before turning to a lemon tree hung with yellow orbs. Soon the basket was bursting, its contents carefully arranged. He handed it up to us.

'How gorgeous,' Alison said. 'May I take a photo of it?'

'Please,' he replied. 'Take the vegetables. They're for you.'

'But we couldn't deprive you,' I protested unconvincingly.

'You will be doing us a favour,' Oreste insisted.

Leaving us to talk about the garden, the unseasonable heat and the pestiferous boars – Oreste said they symbolised the death of local traditions – Alison rushed upstairs, returning with a brace of cameras. She moved the basket and shot it, pulling it to the left and the right, raising a zucchini flower here, a sprig of herbs or chard there, then changing cameras, lenses or both.

'What will she do with all those pictures?' Oreste asked, lifting his hat.

'You'll see.'

We reached down and he reached up to shake hands.

It was several days later when we heard Oreste digging in his orchard again as dawn broke over Genoa. Alison darted into the garden with the basket, now empty, and a large manila envelope. I watched through the half-shuttered window as she handed them down. Oreste slipped on a pair of reading glasses, which opened like scissors. Perched on the bridge of his broad nose, they instantly transformed him from rustic peasant to unlikely yuppie.

'*Bello,*' he exclaimed. '*Bellissimo!*' He turned to face his house. '*E-o!* Maria-Antonietta!' he shouted. 'Come and see!'

On the balcony across the creek, a neatly dressed woman of middle age appeared. She yelled back, stared for a few seconds into the rising sun and then vanished through a beaded curtain. A minute later, Maria-Antonietta was beaming as she held the photograph at arm's length. She plucked the glasses off Oreste's nose.

'*Il cestino di Orestino,*' I heard her remark. Her powerful voice pierced the stillness, rising to where I stood two storeys above. 'I call him Orestino, because we've known each other since we were children.' She wiggled her palm a yard above the ground. 'How beautiful you've made Orestino's basket and zucchini look,' she continued. 'Oreste, why not fill another? How about some field greens? I'll teach them to make a vegetarian meatloaf ...'

When next we heard the boars of dawn and glanced down at the garden wall, atop it sat the basket. This time it contained cherries and a jar of Maria-Antonietta's pesto, made, Oreste told us later, with olive oil pressed from the fruit of these trees, and basil grown here, in the half-shade of the vegetable garden. 'Basil grows best like this,' he insisted, mopping his brow. 'In full sun it is too strong and tastes of mint.' Vegetables and pesto were an obsession of seafaring folk, he added, rattling off a recipe. People who eat fish every day and stare at the waves crave greenery, and Oreste was no exception.

He lifted the basket and offered it up. From a plastic bag I pulled out a book and handed it down. Oreste seemed surprised. He thanked us lavishly, flipping through the pages, admiring the photos and reading our names aloud not once but twice. He remarked, as if in an after-thought, that he had worked in the port of Genoa for something like thirty years. Now he was preparing to retire. It was the end of an epoch, and he would like to immortalise it in some way. Since we appeared to enjoy the dawn, and food and photography, he wondered if we would consider joining him on the docks one day soon, followed by lunch at a trattoria we surely did not know.

'I think you might enjoy yourselves,' he concluded in fluent, euphonically accented English.

We accepted with pleasure. Between exchanges of the basket, we had learned a few things. Oreste had been born and brought up in a humble house in this tiny hamlet on the hillside, but he was no village hayseed. As his Homeric name suggested, he was a distinguished captain, the head pilot of the harbour pilots who shepherded the giant container ships and ferries into one of Europe's busiest ports. He had lived most of his life on ships, but his true love was growing vegetables and cooking.

'The guards will let you in. Look for the tall, glassy tower.' He pointed. 'You can see it from here. Everyone knows where the *piloti* are found.'

———————⟨

At precisely 4.45am we left the house, pausing on the path to watch as three white-striped baby boars trotted south into the underbrush. We walked in the opposite direction, counting the 1057 steps of the zigzag staircase that lowered us through olive groves to a sleepy resort town by the sea. The moon illuminated an inky blue sky, dotted with stars veiled by wispy high clouds. The songbirds kicked in at 5am. Panting, we clambered onto a battered commuter train. The station's dusty clock showed 5.17am.

We got off at Genova Brignole, a handsome hulk from the nineteenth century, apparently unmolested by modernity. Stoplights flashed as a pair of Fiats raced each other along the six-lane boulevard to the harbour. Cranes and funnels rose in the distance. After twenty minutes we had passed through the security gate and were shaking hands with Oreste. In his sporty uniform, he seemed taller, younger. From nowhere, thimbles of espresso appeared, and focaccia still warm from the oven, glistening with olive oil.

Inside the control room, high above the port, we stood spellbound as the sun spilled around the Portofino peninsula, a sudden, blinding beam. The air-conditioning kicked on. A radar antenna spun, humming and throbbing. Oreste introduced us to his colleagues, their eyes glued to screens, or the horizon. They joked about *il capitano* retiring, and wondered how the port would survive.

'At least we will have photographs to remember him by,' laughed one radar man, watching Alison at work.

More coffee and focaccia arrived. The sun raked around, striking the thousand-year-old black-and-white tower of a church, then a series of frescoed townhouses, and the medieval, castellated walls that ran like a roller coaster around old Genoa. I had never seen the city from this angle, or at so early an hour. The tall stone buildings merged with the light and seemed unnaturally white, bleached by centuries of sun. They stood out against the gentle green of the hills, hills that cupped Genoa, a fortress city within the bastions of the boulder-strewn Apennines.

Amid the container ships, cruise boats and cranes on the opposite side of the harbour rose La Lanterna, Genoa's symbol, a lighthouse built nearly 700 years ago. Giant oil tanks marched up the grade behind it. Hovering on a ridge above stood the sanctuary of the Madonna della Guardia, protector of sailors.

'That is where the best basil comes from.' Oreste pointed. 'Not from the Madonna, but from Prà, at her feet. Of course, my basil is better, but Prà's is more famous, with protection. Over the hills, in Piedmont, where my wife is from, my real kitchen garden and vineyard grow.' Oreste smiled. 'But the boars, Mother of God, the boars are even worse there. No-one is left. The villages are empty.'

He excused himself to consult with a colleague, then spoke in French over a crackly radio. A Belgian ship wanted to dock but the port was full. 'Try Savona,' Oreste continued, 'repeat, try Savona.'

All communications were repeated in a clear voice, Oreste told us, just like in the movies.

'*Capitano!*' the radar operator barked. '*La Superba* is arriving.'

Oreste peered through binoculars then put them down. 'They will insist I have breakfast. All this eating makes me fat.'

It was an age-old tradition. Each time a harbour pilot boarded, he was not only in command, he was also an honoured guest. Oreste crossed into another room. 'We sleep there on night duty, and we eat together here, and that is why we get along, the great brotherhood of *piloti*.' He opened a cupboard. 'Saffron, pickled fish, one curry, another curry, and another and another curry, from Pakistan, from India, from Indonesia, and herbs and chocolates and spices …' He pointed at the jars and packages. 'Always a gift of food. *La Superba* will feed me *sfogliatelle* pastries and cappuccino. With the Thais this afternoon, it will be steaming rice and spicy cuttlefish, and later, the Japanese, I foresee sushi with seaweed, and before I leave this evening, a Moroccan tagine, perhaps of lamb.'

'It is very dangerous work,' quipped the radar man as we returned to the control room.

Oreste chuckled, checking the roster. He counted aloud the twenty ships due that day. It was surreal poetry. 'The Chinese are a challenge,' he observed. 'When a ship comes in, it must make voice contact, identify itself and get clearance. But the Chinese don't speak Italian or much English. They shout, "Wait, wait," and play a cassette we cannot understand. Then comes rice and shark fin or a century-old egg.' Oreste patted his belly. 'When I was young, I sailed the globe,' he said, sounding Homeric. 'But there's no need now, the globe comes to me.' He checked his watch. 'Let's go.'

Long and sleek, the harbour pilot's craft bobbed at the dock. We slipped on life jackets as the boat tore away, skiing out along the breakwater. Ranged along our route, bright orange tugboats belched out black smoke, blowing their horns. In minutes we were alongside *La Superba*. 'The name,' shouted Oreste over the engine noise, 'is the name of the Republic. La Superba was Genoa before it became part of Italy. It means "the proud one".'

A rope ladder fell between *La Superba* and us. With startling agility, Oreste leapt onto it, scurried up, and disappeared into a hatch on the hull. Before we could think, the speedboat was tearing off again, giving the mammoth ship room to manoeuvre.

Soon the tugs nudged in, and the ship was lashed to the wharf. Oreste reappeared, dangling a paper bag. 'Pastries,' he announced, 'for all of us.'

At the gates awaited Maria-Antonietta. She wore a silk blouse and colourful skirt, and pecked our cheeks in greeting. Oreste walked us through the dry docks, where migrant workers were rebuilding cruise ships under the now merciless sun. 'Italians won't do the dirty work any more,' he explained. From being an exporter of emigrants, Genoa had become an importer of immigrants. 'We're all educated, we disdain the soil, and the boars have taken over our villages.'

After the blinding light of the port, the tangled alleys of medieval Genoa seemed as dark as caves. So narrow were some that the slate roofs on both sides almost touched, eight or nine storeys above. Sails of laundry fluttered between pavement and sky. On a windowsill, weedy basil plants grew. Oreste and Maria-Antonietta pointed them out. We passed hole-in-the-wall shops selling nuts and bolts, candied fruit, shoelaces and buttons, or vegetables preserved in olive oil. Between them, other shops offered ethnic foods, reflecting the influx of African, Asian and South American immigrants. At a produce stand the basil vied for space with plantains.

The shopfront of Da Ugo dated to the 1970s, the kind of façade a visitor walks by without entering. 'They keep it that way on purpose,' Oreste said, holding open the door.

Inside were butcher-paper placemats on wooden tables, and copper pots on white walls. The decibel level flirted with danger. Ugo and his children clearly knew Oreste and Maria-Antonietta. They shook hands, shouting to be heard. The tables were packed. White- and blue-collar workers sat by men Oreste described as 'captains of industry'. Everyone spoke rough-edged Genoese dialect. A few turned to glance as we settled in.

We let Oreste order; it was his territory. Out came plump *tortelli* stuffed with the kind of field greens Oreste grew, dressed with black pepper and herbs. The classic *trenette* pasta with pesto was excellent but not as good as our hosts'. Then came meltingly tender boiled octopus and potato salad, tiny squid in spicy tomato sauce, and golden fried, firm-fleshed anchovies stuffed with herbed parmigiano and breadcrumbs.

Oreste leaned over and cupped his hands. 'Next week the *piloti* are meeting in the hills near Santa Margherita,' he said. 'Do you know what we will eat?' He winked conspiratorially. 'Wild boar. Would you care to join us?'

As we crossed the cool, dark alleys heading towards our train, Oreste and Maria-Antonietta asserted that roughshod Genoa could not and did not want to become like Venice, Florence or Rome. Genoa still belonged to the Genoese, they agreed, though hard-working immigrants and intrepid individual travellers like us were also welcome. 'We no longer fear Barbarians,' he quipped cryptically. 'When the boars come into town, we'll worry.'

'Why?' teased Maria-Antonietta. 'We can raise them. Ugo will put boar on the menu.'

Seasoning Jerusalem

ELISABETH EAVES

Elisabeth Eaves is the author of two nonfiction books, *Bare* and *Wanderlust*. Her travel writing has been anthologised in *The Best American Travel Writing 2009* and *The Best Women's Travel Writing 2010*. She has worked for the *Wall Street Journal* and *Forbes* magazine, and her writing has appeared in numerous publications, including *Harper's*, the *New York Times*, *Slate* and *WorldHum*. Elisabeth was born in Vancouver, lives in New York City, and is still not entirely sure if she wants to settle down.

Khan al-Zeit, the street of the oil merchants, was where I stayed the first time I went to Jerusalem, in 1992. It was a souq, a covered passageway lined with small stores, open to the street. I could tell when the owners put out their wares in the morning because the fragrances rose up to my third-storey room. The vats of olives gave off a salty tang, and every bag of spice had its own scent. I smelled turmeric, cumin, cardamom, and more flavours I didn't recognise. Among the food stores there were

37

shops selling cheap sneakers, bras and polyester Leonardo DiCaprio carpets.

Later that year, I went back to Jerusalem and got a job in a hostel on the same street. The building was of ancient stone and I shared a room with whatever guests came along. In exchange for room and board, and a few shekels a week, I cleaned the hostel and fetched guests from the bus station. I led them down the stone steps in front of Damascus Gate, through the long portal, around the donkey carts, and back into the Old City. Damascus Gate was the commercial heart of the Muslim quarter, and the plaza just inside the gate was thronged with vendors and shoppers. My charges were always from the most neutral places: Switzerland, Canada, New Zealand. I led them up Khan al-Zeit and inhaled as we passed the spices.

In 1998 I went to Jerusalem again, now with a summer job as an intern for a wire service. During my first two visits I had rarely ventured into Jewish West Jerusalem; now I would live there. The Muslim quarter of the Old City had always felt like a tidier extension of the Arab world, so this was my first real introduction to Israel. It was the first time I was surrounded by Hebrew and Jewish Israelis. In West Jerusalem the white stone buildings seemed to glow at night, and outside of the Orthodox neighbourhoods the girls wore tank tops.

On my first day at work my boss introduced me to another intern, Sarah, an ambitious photographer.

'You from the States?' she asked.

'Yeah. No. I mean –'

'Where'd ya go to college?' she asked, cracking gum.

'University of Washington,' I said.

'Jews-U?'

I stared.

'Jews-U? Wash-U?'

I still couldn't make out what she was talking about.

'Washington University?'

'University *of* Washington. In Seattle. U-dub.'

'Ohhhhhh. I thought you meant Washington University in St Louis. Never mind. That's what people call it. Are you Jewish?'

'No.'

'Right, see, I assumed you were Jewish. Anyway. I went to Penn. We should get a drink.'

I agreed.

Sarah and I rented a breezy ground-floor apartment in the neighbourhood of Rechavia. Together, we took the bus every day to the well-fortified JMC, the Jerusalem Media Centre, where nearly every foreign news organisation had its offices. Almost everyone else in my bureau was either Jewish or Arab. Some were from Jerusalem, while others had come from elsewhere to work – Jordan, Egypt, England, the United States. Underlying their nonpartisan professionalism, they all had a visceral reason for being here that I lacked. I felt a slight envy.

My first reporting assignment was on Jerusalem Day, which celebrated Israel's capture of East Jerusalem in the 1967 Six Day War. My editor asked me to do a man-in-the-street story, and I thought immediately of Damascus Gate. When I got there the steps were strangely deserted. So was the plaza just inside. On Khan al-Zeit, men were heaving their bags of spices and buckets of olives back into their stores, rolling up their polyester carpets and stowing them away. They were padlocking the metal grates across their storefronts and retreating into nearby doorways. Plastic bags skittered along in the dry breeze.

I approached an old man who was standing on the lopsided stone steps leading up to his door. 'It's a tragedy,' he said; *il-nakba,* the disaster. He was locking up and lying low. 'Go in peace,' he said, before his grate clanged shut. When I made it back up to the western part of the city, an old man told me proudly how he had fought in the war, how he had helped take Jerusalem. 'The first thing we did was pray at the wall,' he said.

----◼

In a way, every story was like that first one. A quote from one side and a quote from the other. There was nothing, it seemed, that could be covered without reference to the conflict – not a film festival, a crime story or the gay pride parade in Tel Aviv. The conflict sold the stories to the outside world. At first I thought my understanding would grow, and that by the end of the summer I would have gained some key insight. Like the many outsiders who had tried to broker peace, I thought that something other than a permanent state of war would eventually make sense. I thought it was just a question of missing knowledge, and now I was acquiring knowledge every day.

And yet things did not start to make sense. Every fact was countered by another fact. I drilled back through time, as though penetrating layers of sediment. There was yesterday, when an Israeli bulldozer demolished an Arab home; then last year, when the Arab family had squatted on the property; then 1967, when the Israelis had taken the property in a defensive war; and on back to 1948, when the Arabs had fled their Jerusalem homes. Then there were the British and the French, who everyone said had messed things up in the first place. And on and on it went, to the Bible, to millennia ago, when God had granted the land to the Israelites. If you had a stake in things, maybe one narrative or the other eventually started to make sense. If you came in with an equivocal view, things remained irresolute.

We travel in the hope of bonding with new places. To get that feeling of belonging, we side with the locals. We pay attention to their hopes and dreams. We try to imagine ourselves in their place. We listen to their music, try on their clothes, eat their food. In return for our sympathy and respect, we ask them to love us back. This longing for connection is the traveller's neediness. Connection, though, requires bias. I had come without one, and the way I spent my time made it difficult to get one. I pinged back and forth every day between enemy lines. They didn't look like enemy lines; there were no check points, and I could walk between the two sides, but as I did, the language and dress changed, the things people thought and said changed, and suddenly I found myself in a new country.

The one thing that didn't change was the food. Falafel sandwiches with hummus were served in both halves of the city. Oranges, eggplants and olive oil were consumed. Mint and tomatoes were chopped into salads, and meat was slaughtered as specified in the holy books.

———————————

I befriended Ben, a television producer who worked across the hall from my bureau. He was short and black-haired, the son of Moroccan Jews, Israeli-born and US-raised. He had grown up in the Northwest and, like me, had attended the University of Washington. We talked about professors we had in common, and I felt a connection to him through our shared background. He was an American who knew my grey-green home turf. He was an Arab. He was a Jew. The first time we went out he ordered me lemonade with mint.

Ben called at midday and said he wanted to show me the *shuk*, the Jewish market. He led me into the Mahane Yehuda, a sprawling web of tightly packed alleys and stalls. I had poked around its edges but had never been into its heart. Now he took my hand and guided me in, past hawkers shouting, '*B'shekel, b'shekel, b'shekel,*' over mounds of vegetables.

Leading me from a wide alley into a maze of narrower lanes roofed with tarpaulins, we entered an unsigned restaurant, ducking under a low door into a cramped, white-tiled room that was packed with men. Some wore Orthodox black-and-whites; others were brown-skinned and rough like tradesmen, with stubble and dirty clothes. The heat, the close quarters and the absence of women made it feel Arab to me, recognisably Middle Eastern. We sat next to a wall, facing each other across a long table that quickly filled with diners. They trapped us into place. Ben ordered for both of us, and a man with a dish towel over his shoulder delivered bowls of hot savoury soup filled with vegetables and balls of dough. I asked what we were eating. '*Matzo kleis*,' Ben said. I felt like I had penetrated an unknown place, and was grateful to him for taking me there.

A few weeks later Ben invited me to a dinner party at his home. It was a Friday, and I had seen Israelis buying and giving flowers on the evening before their Sabbath. On my way I stopped at the *shuk* and bought a bouquet, thinking I would emulate the custom. Ben's apartment was in Nachlaot, an older part of the city where the white rock buildings had aged to shiny yellow. The homes there were divided by footpaths, stairs and the occasional bridge, like a drawing by MC Escher. When I handed Ben the flowers, he blushed. I suddenly felt insecure about my attempt at cultural assimilation, and wondered if I had committed a gaffe.

Ben had also invited an Australian who worked for the United Jewish Congress and an Irishwoman who was doing her PhD in Bible studies. Lily spent her days poring over fragile texts. She knew more about ancient history than any of us, more than anyone she was likely to meet. That was how she had made a place for herself here in Jerusalem. Journalists are voyeurs; Lily had a real reason for being here.

Ben served hearts of palm, eggplant and lamb with rice. After dinner his other guests left and I stayed. He poured glasses of arak and we sat on his balcony. The strong liquorice liquid was overwhelming at first, then tasted smoother with every sip. A scratchy old tape of Oum Kalsoum, the beloved Egyptian singer, was playing.

Ben asked me if I was involved with someone, and I said I had a boyfriend in New York. I asked him the same question back.

Ben said he had had a girlfriend until recently, but that she had moved back to the States and they had broken up. 'Long distance is tough,' I said, but he said that wasn't it.

'What was?'

'We had …' he paused, 'religious differences.'

'She's not Jewish?'

'No, she is.'

I felt my comprehension beginning to drift.

'Rebecca is studying music,' he said. 'She has a beautiful singing voice. In our religion there's a person who sings liturgical passages in synagogue, called a cantor. Rebecca is in training to become a cantor.'

'So?'

'So in the Orthodox faith, which is mine, women can't be cantors. Rebecca was raised in what is known as Reform Judaism.' He bit off the last two words with distaste. 'She would probably make a very good cantor.'

'So – you broke up with her because she's not Jewish enough?'

'That's not the right way to put it,' he said kindly. 'Orthodox is not more Jewish than Reform. But if you mean did I break up with her because she's not Orthodox, that's more or less true.' He sighed. 'I guess I decided that I couldn't marry her. And if she changed her faith to mine, she wouldn't be able to become a cantor. Men and women don't even sit together in my synagogue.'

Ben no longer seemed comfortingly familiar to me. But I coveted his sureness about his place in the world.

I took Hebrew classes at the YMCA, and noticed the cognates with Arabic. The two languages share *mish-mish* for apricot. *Tamar* and *tamara,* for date. *Shuk* and *souk,* for market. *Shalom* and *salaam,* for peace.

Reem, a photographer in my bureau, offered me her mother as an Arabic tutor and I started going to Mrs Kayyali's house one or two evenings a week. It was in a part of the city I hadn't visited before, a modern part of Arab East Jerusalem. West Jerusalem taxis wouldn't go there, so I walked down to the taxi depot outside Damascus Gate. The house was on a steep road, and built of the same white Jerusalem stone as the rest of the city. Reem, who was in her late twenties and always wore jeans and a T-shirt, still lived there with her parents. Her sister and nieces lived next door. On the wall in Reem's bedroom there was an enormous reproduction of a travel poster from the time of the British Mandate. It had a picture of a ship, with the words in big letters 'Visit Palestine'.

I brought my Arabic textbooks and Mrs Kayyali sat with me on the couch, reading and talking, gently correcting me whenever I made a mistake. Every now and then she excused herself to pray. She often offered to feed me, and one night she served a dish called *maqluba.* The word meant upside-down. After cooking all the ingredients in a pot, you turned it over onto a plate. The dish was made of lamb, eggplant and rice, and she served it with yoghurt. The lamb was so soft it fell off the bone, the rice was velvety, the spices both familiar and strange. I took another helping, and Mrs Kayyali looked pleased.

'How do you make it?' I asked. She said she would show me, so I would be able to make it at home. We made a date.

Reem, who had no interest in cooking, brought me a note from her mother with all the ingredients. I needed eggplants, onions, lamb, butter and a list of spices: cinnamon, cardamom, turmeric and something called *baharat.* I looked forward to shopping, a comprehensible task with a comprehensible goal. Reem wrote down the names in English as well as Arabic, except for *baharat,* which was untranslatable.

'What is it?' I asked.

'It's *baharat,*' she said.

'Where should I go?'

She raised an eyebrow at me.

'Go to the spice market.'

I thought immediately of Damascus Gate. I took a bus from the office along Jaffa road, got out when the Old City was in sight, and walked down the hill, paralleling the city wall, to the familiar portal. It was crowded. I wove my way across the plaza and into the souk Khan al-Zeit, the market on the street of the oil merchants. For all the times I had walked by the spices, I had never bought any. I picked the store with the biggest rainbow, deep red and orange and green, and approached the vendor. He was skinny, smooth-skinned, and moustachioed. I began to go through my list.

'What are you making?' he asked, as though I were not a tourist, as though it were the most natural thing in the world that I should be cooking in my home. '*Maqluba,*' I said. He gave an approving nod, and I felt like I had a reason to be there. He tied up each spice in a clear plastic bag. I sniffed the *baharat;* it was a mongrel mix. I thought I smelled nutmeg and black pepper.

I took my ingredients over to Mrs Kayyali's on a Saturday afternoon and we began to cook. She spoke to me in Arabic seasoned with English, and I tried to take notes. We sliced the eggplant and sprinkled it with salt. We cut the lamb into cubes and sautéed it with onions. Her tidy, tiled kitchen filled with the rich carnivore smell of sizzling meat. We added the spices, and I watched the colours melt into liquid.

Now we heated olive oil in a pot and began to build our layers. First tomatoes, then a sprinkling of rice. Then the meat, the eggplant and more rice. We pressed down on every layer with a spatula, and each one mingled with its neighbours without giving up its essence. We added the lid to trap the heat, then retreated to the couch for an Arabic lesson. Family members drifted in and out, and we passed the late afternoon. When the dish was ready, and it had cooled, Mrs Kayyali took a platter and heaved the pot upside down. The layers were intact, with bright tomato on top.

I took my spices home with me to Rechavia and at the end of a long week, I invited Ben and my roommate Sarah to eat with me. I began cooking in the afternoon in my tiled kitchen, windows open to the rustling trees. I'd always enjoyed the chemical logic of cooking, and thought of cookbooks as sorcerer's manuals. I followed their instructions, and every time the trick more or less worked.

On this night, however, my layers collapsed – like the way, in Jerusalem, the Ottoman years had fallen in on the Crusader years, which had caved onto the Roman ruins below. Sarah and Ben assured me that the *maqluba* was delicious nonetheless, and I began to feel at home.

Couscous and Camaraderie

ANITA BRELAND

Anita Breland has lived and worked in several countries in Europe and Asia. A Mississippi native, she grew up in Texas and began her culinary adventures in Mexico. She has been a Fulbright lecturer in Romania, restored a 400-year-old house in Morocco and travelled solo in India, where she explored the cooking traditions of Kerala. She currently writes from Basel, Switzerland. An ardent believer in cultural immersion through food, Anita joins local cooks in their kitchens at every opportunity. Her writing was recognised by the 2009 Solas Awards, and she blogs about food and culture at http://anitasfeast.blogspot.com.

Seated cross-legged on a worn kilim pillow, Tante Tamou licked her right hand, first wrist to palm, then knuckle to fingertips. Afternoon sun slanted through the doorway behind her. She swept the platter with a practised move, and in self-absorbed satisfaction tongued her forearm almost to the elbow. Only when virtually every grain of couscous was gone did she allow Fouziya to pour water from a battered copper kettle to wash her hands.

'It was a good couscous, eh!' Tamou exclaimed to us through great-nephew Rachid. Accepting a towel, I nodded happily. Couscous steamed and tossed by hand before receiving a blessing of sauce was the centrepiece of the meal. For me, though, Tamou's company was the feast.

Couscous is traditional Friday fare in Morocco, shared with family and friends after prayers at the mosque. The meal is one part couscous, with its meat and vegetables, and the rest, love – of family, food and companionship. Seeing Tamou exuberant in her pleasure with the meal she had orchestrated out of a gift basket from strangers was as heart-warming as it was unexpected.

———————⊨

It was week two of my home-kitchen travels in Morocco with Canadian caterer and cookbook author, Chef Deb. We'd seen women in Fez put in long hours to produce the many dishes with complex flavours that feature in Fassi cooking. Today's visit to a home kitchen in the foothills of the Atlas Mountains contrasted sharply with our previous experiences.

We were introduced to Rachid in Agadir, and three days later he brought us to his ancestral home, a farm between Essaouira and Marrakesh. Fortified with café lattes and sugary pastries, we left Essaouira just after breakfast, a little worried about intruding upon Rachid's relatives. We implored him to let his aunt know we were coming to see her. 'I take care,' he assured us.

We stopped in a dusty village to pick up supplies: two chickens killed and cleaned as we waited; and couscous, chosen by Rachid from the several types arrayed in sacks fronting a street-side stall. We bought November vegetables: potatoes, carrots, parsnips and onions; pallid tomatoes; and for dessert, clementines from a truck parked beside the highway. Vibrantly orange, they were just coming into season.

In Fez, we'd been treated to prized family recipes and lavish spreads. We'd accompanied housewives and chefs into bustling souqs to select fish, lamb and seasonal vegetables. Rachid's request that we bring all the food for the meal had been a hint that this cooking encounter might be something more elemental. The landscape we'd driven through provided another: arid plateaus, pocked with gullies, dotted with gnarled argan trees and little else. We saw no power poles, no other traffic along the rock-strewn track that ended at a squat mosque.

We parked beside the mosque and three women emerged from a walled compound on the far side of a field and ran towards us, dogs yapping about their heels. Rachid hurried to embrace his stick-wielding great-aunt and her teenaged granddaughters, and to calm the dogs. The women smiled and grasped our hands. '*A salaam alaikum*. Peace be upon you.' '*Wa 'alaikum as-salaam,*' we answered. 'And to you, peace.'

They had no idea we were coming. Every Moroccan man proclaims his wife or mother as the maker of the best couscous in the country, and brings visitors home on short notice to prove the point. Women in the household readily accommodate unexpected guests. In any case, Rachid could not have contacted his great-aunt, as neither the farm nor the hamlet half an hour's walk below the mosque had a telephone service.

Tamou looked much older than her probable sixty-some years, but set a brisk pace and brandished her stick as she hustled us through the gate and into a courtyard to a small building of whitewashed stone. We ducked through a low doorway into the single room that was the family's living and sleeping quarters. Tamou and eldest granddaughter Fouziya went to prepare the food that is always offered to guests entering a Moroccan home.

Nadia pinned the curtain back from the doorway and sunlight streamed into the windowless room. The rough stone floor was scattered with faded kilims and a few cushions. Thin mattresses lined a stone platform at one end. A brass tray wrapped in plastic sheeting hung from a hook on one wall, a verse from the Koran in calligraphy just opposite. Nadia removed the plastic, positioned the tray on short accordion legs and draped the table with a cloth. A tray brought down from its perch for the sole purpose of sharing food was the only furniture in Tamou's home.

Fouziya soon appeared with a platter of creamy rice, drizzled with argan oil glistening in amber swirls. We sat on cushions and dipped into the rice with pieces of flatbread. Served at room temperature, this was Moroccan rice pudding, slightly sweet, the nutty argan oil deeply flavoured. We shared a glass of tangy buttermilk. I hate buttermilk, but I downed it with a smile.

'Rachid, please tell your aunt we've brought food,' we urged. 'Ask her if we can help prepare it.' Tamou's grin of assent revealed she was missing a front tooth. Rachid struggled to help us relay our enthusiasm for Moroccan food, and our quest to learn from home cooks. Moments later, he announced that he was leaving to visit an uncle who lived nearby, but would be back for couscous. I was surprised but not alarmed that cooking with Tamou would be in pantomime. The language of food is transcendent.

We'd arrived tramping through Tamou's field, fallow in late autumn. Now, Tamou took us on a tour of her property and pointed out her root cellar, the well and the quern, a Flintstone-sized basin and wheel of granite used to grind argan nuts into oil. Tamou opened barnyard doors concealing farm implements and animal fodder. Life here was an unadorned existence: everything in its place, everything with a use, everything well used.

Chickens scratched at the feet of other animals in their enclosure: a donkey, a dairy cow and her calf, two sheep, their lambs. The little barnyard was well kept and the animals looked healthy, especially the little donkey, unlike the pack animals so often abused by their owners in the alleyways of Fez. Youngest granddaughter Zoubida was out with her herd of eight goats. With a flourish, Tamou presented her camel, secure in its own stall. Farmers here plough fields with camels, but we never learned if this one was 'tractor', transportation, or both.

The clean little farm was a study in self-sufficiency. I was impressed by the orderliness here, so different from poorer homes I'd seen in the Fez *medina,* where some families and their animals live in the same rooms. In a few weeks, a sheep and a goat would be killed for Eid al-Adha. Tamou's family would not have to buy an animal for Islam's Feast of the Sacrifice, a saving of at least 3600 dirham, an enormous amount for people living just above subsistence.

We returned to the living room, and Nadia opened a sack of argan nuts. Each summer, she and her sisters gathered the almond-shaped fruit that littered the ground under the thorny argan trees nearby. Native to south-western Morocco, the trees are plentiful here. The women husk the wrinkly nuts, roast them over an open flame and extract the oil for home use. When they need cash, they sell nuts from their silo to a women's cooperative near Essaouira.

Nadia settled onto the floor, a squared-off stone between her feet. She bashed each nut with a smaller stone to break the vise-like grip of the husk. I tried it, clubbing thumb and forefinger with every painful stroke. Nadia giggled and demonstrated again, shells flying. I could see why argan oil is called 'Moroccan gold'. It is cussedly labour-intensive to produce.

My fingers rejoiced when Fouziya interrupted us, the aroma of mint and absinthe wafting in with her. It was chilly in the unheated room, even in my fleece and boots with woolly socks, and hot mint tea was a welcome prospect. Tamou followed a now familiar ritual, pouring the first glass back into the teapot, then raising the teapot high to stream tea that frothed into each glass.

We sipped our tea with pieces of bread dipped into argan oil and melted butter.

When it was time to prepare the couscous, Fouziya and Nadia bustled to fetch water and kindling. Tamou led us to a free-standing room, a kitchen without running water or electricity. There was no gas bottle, the engine that powers Morocco's urban kitchens. A lone rack held pots, platters, trays and a few glasses. The cooktop was a low stone shelf in one corner, a small space for building a fire underneath, the wall above streaked sooty black. Tamou's was the most primitive of the kitchens we'd seen, practically empty. How does she cook with nothing? Where were the big jars of cumin and *ras el hanout*, the piles of coriander and parsley, the little dishes for serving salads?

Fouziya put one of the birds we'd brought into a pot with slices of lemon and covered it with water. Tamou handed Deb and me the ubiquitous paring knives that constitute the full kitchen kit for many Moroccan cooks, and I thought guiltily of the gadgets and conveniences in my home. We were put to veggie duty before a basin of water set on the stone floor. It was cold, and my fingers cramped as I washed and cored carrots. It was impossible to stay crouched and I constantly shifted position. After ten minutes of this, my knees and ankles screamed for relief. I was thrilled when Nadia fetched me a cushion. I wondered how they could prepare every meal squatting on the floor.

Tamou scooped a tea glass through the couscous Fouziya had dumped into a wide crockery bowl, filling it half full of the grains, then to the brim with water, before draining the water out. She did this three times, muttering her disapproval. We could tell Rachid had not chosen the right couscous, but it was frustrating to not understand Tamou's explanation. When Rachid returned, we insisted he translate for us: 'Good couscous needs just one washing!' Ah, now we knew.

Still on their haunches, Tamou massaged oil into the couscous and Nadia seeded tomatoes through a grater into a bowl on the floor. Fouziya broke branches into small pieces for the fire. Deb and I peeled and sliced vegetables over our basin, as Tamou gestured and kept up a running commentary on the proceedings. Her crackling laugh rivalled the snap of kindling as the fire caught. Stinging smoke filled the room until the flue began to draw it outside. Tamou covered her nose with the end of her headscarf. I coughed as I observed the medieval tableau through smoke-induced tears.

Tamou added argan husks to the fire to raise the heat, and swabbed the chicken with synthetic yellow colorant from a packet. I was dismayed that the lamentable chemical, which contributes nothing in the way of taste or aroma, was used by every home cook we met in Morocco, to supplement or replace turmeric. When the chicken came to a boil with onions and tomatoes, Tamou added the root vegetables and simple seasonings: coarse salt, black pepper and a sprinkle of powdered ginger. No cumin, coriander or parsley here, ingredients used in such quantity in city kitchens. I wondered how this meal would taste without these flavourings.

Fouziya trowelled the couscous into an aluminium pot with holes punched in the bottom, and twisted a plastic bag around it. She set it atop the chicken and turbaned the two pots with a towel. *Voilà*, an instant *couscousière*. Ingenious! The stacked ensemble went back on the fire to simmer until Tamou pronounced the chicken done.

Steam roiled above Fouziya's head as she turned the couscous onto a round platter and shook it vigorously to toss the grains. She mounded the couscous and arranged chicken and vegetables on top. Meanwhile, Tamou had returned the cooking pot to the fire, and reduced its liquid until thickened to her liking. Tamou ladled sauce over the platter and summoned us to the table. The platter was only slightly smaller than the table top. There were no individual plates.

Nor was there cutlery, just a circle of right hands tearing meat from bone and scooping up couscous. Here, as elsewhere, the Moroccans pulled meat from the hot carcass with asbestos fingers, something I found impossible to do. I was grateful when Tamou placed bits of chicken on my side of the platter. The yellow-tinged chicken was tender, the vegetables and sauce more flavourful than I had expected.

Chuckling, Tamou flipped a small handful of couscous back and forth in her palm to form a ball, and popped it into her mouth. She motioned for me to try it. My attempts to imitate the trick were in vain, but I cadged my share of couscous and vegetables with pieces of bread.

———————

The sun was setting as the women walked us to the car. We clasped hands again, and Deb and I were effusive in our thanks for the day. Tamou and her granddaughters had never met an American or Canadian before, but the warm efficiency with which they had welcomed us into their home had made it seem like drop-in visits such as ours happen all the time. When Tamou gave me a fierce hug, I was saddened to know we'd not meet again. Long shadows followed our tumble down the mountain to the highway.

In city kitchens, Deb and I had experienced a richly spiced cuisine of complex flavours and elaborate meals elegantly presented. We had been introduced to exotic and intriguing food combinations. There was none of that with Tamou. She provided us with a glimpse into her rural food culture, its modest flavours and unpretentious hospitality. As our day together unfolded, Tamou's fun-loving nature and generosity of spirit shone through the mantle of her discipline.

I admired this resourceful woman who had prepared a meal for unannounced strangers, transforming the ingredients they brought into a Friday feast – and making it look effortless. She and her granddaughters cooked food in the way they knew, and served it with pride.

Minor discomforts were trumped by wonder as I watched Team Tamou in action. The day opened my heart to that part of a culture's cuisine that lies beyond the taste and presentation of food. I had entered Moroccan home kitchens in search of culinary secrets and insider cooking tips. In Tamou's company, these taste-centric expectations were replaced by a broadened appreciation of homely hospitality.

Women in Morocco inspired me to cook with greater confidence, to put away my measuring cups and trust my intuition. Tamou's example taught me something more substantial. I began to worry less about perfecting a dish, or setting my own table with picture-book elegance. I started to pay more attention to meal-time camaraderie and to feel more generosity towards strangers. Even now, when I pull a paring knife from the drawer, my heart warms at the memory of a remarkable woman celebrating the day we shared with a well-placed lick of her hand and forearm.

Cooking with Donna

WILLIAM SERTL

William Sertl was the travel editor of *Gourmet* for ten years, having started at the magazine the same year that Ruth Reichl took over, in 1999. The position combined his two great passions – food and travel – and he worked with a team of editors that, he says, 'ended up being more like family than colleagues. We certainly agreed on one thing: the first order of business after getting off a plane was figuring out where to eat.' Prior to *Gourmet*, Bill was one of the founding editors of *Saveur* (as well as the travel editor of *Garden Design*), and worked for that magazine from its inception in 1993. From 1986 until 1993, he was articles editor of *Travel & Leisure*. Bill was born and raised in St Louis.

It took me thirty years as a travel editor – best job in the world, everyone said – to realise how much distaste I had for vacations. Not travel. Vacations. So I might not have been the best person to write a magazine article about Mustique, a private Caribbean island in the chain of St Vincent and the Grenadines. Luxury villas for rent on Mustique came staffed with enough servants to ensure that you, the master of the house for a week or two, had absolutely nothing to do except loaf on the beach or sip cocktails made by someone else while waiting until dinner was ready.

I have never cared much about landing at JFK with a tan. I like to come home smarter than I was before I left. Speaking a little better Spanish. Understanding a little more clearly how Parisians manage to look so chic, even when taking out the trash. Bearing a new recipe – always a recipe, for food is the key to culture, the easiest way into a relationship with folks you've yet to meet.

But Mustique, where everyone speaks English and where having servants is the very idea of the place, happened to be the assignment at hand. I had to make the best of it, so I came up with a plan. Among the staff at Sapphire, my five-room manse overlooking the sea, which so far I had seen only in a brochure, would be a cook. I would befriend that cook and break down the barrier that put her in a white uniform and me in shorts and a T-shirt. I would hang out with her. She would teach me to cook, to cook Caribbean.

———————————◀

The dinner bell told a different story.

I arrived at Sapphire in one of the ubiquitous Kawasaki Mules – a motorised vehicle that's bigger than a golf cart but not as sturdy as a Jeep – that every renter on the island is given after landing at the airport. My 'staff' were dutifully lined up, waiting to greet me as I drove past the gates: two gardeners, with whom I would have very little to do during my week's stay, busy as they were puttering around the lavish grounds; two maids – Pearl and Pat – both of whom would become pals, at least for a week; and Donna Jacobs, who ended up a friend.

It's hard to settle into a villa meant for parties of six, seven, eight or more when you're only one person. It's difficult to relax.

I broke the ice with the worst kind of small talk, mentioning to Pearl, the matriarch of the group, that it had been raining on Barbados when we changed planes. 'Did it rain here?' I asked.

'Oh, yes,' she said, 'the rain, it came down.' Ah, that lovely, lilting Caribbean way of phrasing. Islanders always seem to add a dash of sunshine to their speech, making English sound almost musical – no mean feat for what is not the most melodious language on the planet. I was starting to melt. Could the ice be far behind?

I took my seat in the formal dining room, so beautiful and shimmering in candlelight but also open to the breezes swirling through the house. The room was off a central courtyard filled with exotic plants and trees, where birds and butterflies swooped and soared with no regard for manmade boundaries. The warm moist air turned the rambling house sultry, a tropical Wuthering Heights above the sea, open to nature's seduction.

'Here is the bell, to ring when you want your next course,' Pat told me, attempting to hand over a dainty little glass ornament that would have looked more at home in a Park Avenue dining room than on a sunny Caribbean estate. At first, I laughed, without meaning to. Then I baulked, and stood up, pushed my chair under the table and marched directly into the uncharted territory of the kitchen.

Donna was stirring the contents of a pot on the stove. I approached, picked up the lid, and said, 'What's for dinner?'

———————◗◖———————

Donna was a good cook – no question about that. It might be more accurate to say she was a good chef, for the menu of vege-table ravioli in a roux with herbs, followed by seared tuna with wasabi mayo, topped off with a blue cheese and cheddar soufflé – so exquisitely executed and full of flavour it could have been served at the finest French restaurant – gave few insights into any-body's local cuisine. This was high-end vacation fare, something you'd expect at a fancy dining room in just about any big city on earth. I suddenly wanted to know: where did you learn to cook like that? When did you realise you liked to cook? When can I come into your world and step out of the role I am supposed to play?

The answers came quickly. The owner of this villa, Brian Alexander, had only recently retired after thirty years as the managing director of the Mustique Company, the association of owners that rents all the 110-plus villas on the island. Mementos, hanging on walls and casually propped up on tables in hidden corners of the house, spoke of Sapphire's noble history. Nothing was more revealing than a small, faded photo of Alexander greeting a young Princess Margaret dockside upon her arrival on the island, with her sister the Queen and brother-in-law Prince Phillip.

In his managerial position, Alexander entertained a lot. He wanted a good cook and was willing to sponsor Donna for training with New York's French Culinary Institute when it came to Mustique to run a special program. He needed sophisticated cuisine to reflect the worldly crowd he catered to. He needed a dinner bell.

Mustique made even more sense to me when I discovered that the island had been purchased in the late 1950s by a Scottish aristocrat as a private playpen for himself and privileged friends like Margaret.

Donna immediately got that I wanted to hang with her in the kitchen. I was curious about every menu she had mapped out for the week, especially one dish – sushi – that was coming up in a few days. (Sushi? Why not, I thought, with fish this fresh?) Donna wasn't shy about filling me in on her culinary prowess, and I was more than happy to hear how she had always wanted to learn to cook.

There aren't a lot of options for work on a small Caribbean island, where most employees come from the mother island of St

Vincent – larger, yes, but not exactly brimming with opportunities itself. I began to notice the men sweeping the roads and beaches all over the island. So many of them stood and stared as they slowly brushed yet another leaf or scrap of paper out of the way, as if even the tiniest piece of litter might make someone recoil in horror. They were fully employed and yet not doing much of anything at all. Donna, as well as Pearl and Pat, lived on the grounds of my tidy beach castle and might have found a better way. Donna, especially, had a job that was creative and clearly satisfying to her.

As the week went on, lifting pot lids became the major activity in the afternoon, when preparing the evening meal got under way at around five. Donna didn't hesitate to ask for my help. Once I had crossed that threshold into her culinary domain, I became her new sous chef, or maybe just a heaven-sent helper to do the slicing and dicing. 'You cut these, please,' Donna would say, handing over a few red capsicums for a Chinese concoction she was planning that evening. Fair enough, I thought; it's a small price to pay for the privilege of being able to lift pot lids at will. Pearl and Pat looked vaguely shocked as Donna and I became increasingly more familiar. But maybe they also knew that Donna took no prisoners, for I was beginning to feel more and more like an appliance.

I had my own way of paying back. Teasing Donna was easy for me, especially since I had a reliable two-woman audience to count on for applause. A simple question, thrown out in jest but laced with mock gravitas – 'Are you sure you want so many onions in the stir-fry? It might overwhelm the dish' – was guaranteed to get a rise. Donna's you're-a-dead-man expression as she whipped her head around from the stove was as predictable as a Swiss clock.

But I craved more than just an afternoon play date. I wanted to find out where all the fabulous food came from.

'Will you take me to the market with you? And to the fish store before you make sushi?' I asked on that first day. 'We'll see,' Donna said.

After breakfast on the second morning, without a word of warning, Donna appeared on the deck and announced, 'We go now.'

'Go where?' I asked

'To the fish market,' she said. So off we went to the little green 'shack' at the water's edge on the other side of the island. Donna had promised lobster that night, and already the boats, in all shades of Crayola colours, were pulling up on the beach. I marvelled as men held up great clawed creatures, just pulled from the Caribbean. Donna talked with them in a dialect so fast, furious and foreign that I couldn't find an English word to save me, although I knew they were hidden in the conversation. Would I have walked up to these guys and struck up a conversation had she not been with me? Not on your life; I would have felt like a number one fool. Donna was my key into their world, giving me a kind of VIP status that money alone couldn't buy.

The guy who owned the fish market, really more of a store that acted as a clearing house, had 'proud' written all over his handsome, youthful face. His small green hut was a bit deceptive, for inside it was all spit and polish, with trays of whole fish on ice fronting a long sink used for cutting each one up to a customer's specifications. The storage refrigerator was top of the line. On the wall to one side was an Obama sticker. It was mid-January, and our president was about to be inaugurated. I felt a swell of pride that he was being honoured on this small volcanic chunk of land closer to South America than to the United States.

A few European tourists had ventured in to inspect the catch of the day. I felt infinitely superior to them as they poked and sniffed around before settling on a few fillets that were quickly wrapped before they scooted out the door. I was still chatting with the store's owner, still oohing and aahing as more fish came in. After Donna and I picked out our lobster, she took a picture of me next to the man who had caught it, holding it high as we both beamed while trying to say 'cheese', as Donna had commanded.

We were 'downtown' now, which meant that we had to pay a visit to the two other great establishments across from the fish store: the fruit man and the grocery store. The fruit man sat next to his stand on a chair that was slightly tilted for maximum comfort. His hat was halfway down his head. Except for the fact that his table was crammed with exotic specimens in a riot of colours, he struck me as the Universal Fruit Man, for his counterpart was everywhere in New York – indeed, throughout the world. It made me think that all sidewalk vendors must attend a school somewhere to learn how to sit at just the right angle, with their hats perfectly cocked, while mastering the art of the blank expression.

Across the street, something even more familiar loomed: the grocery store. While it had its Caribbean touches, I felt as if I'd been to this place many times in the course of my life. How different can a store be when its shelves are stacked with mostly familiar items? And here I was for the first time surrounded by fellow whites, who were speaking English, yes, but also German, French and Italian. My cultural focus had shifted, but all it did was make me feel cooler than I had before. 'I'm with Donna, folks,' I was thinking, 'so best not to get in our way.'

On a return trip to Mustique – 21 January, to be exact – I bought a local St Vincent newspaper with 'OBAMA' splashed across the front page. I also took a photo of an adorable little blond boy who was sitting on the checkout counter in a sea of his mother's groceries. Suddenly, I was being reprimanded. His mother suggested, in a staccato accent, that perhaps this wasn't a good idea. 'People are on Mustique for privacy,' she said. 'There are many celebrities.'

I immediately realised my error and apologised profusely, even holding up the camera to let her see me deleting the photo. But I couldn't help thinking back to dinners at the villa, where I would take photos with total abandon, mostly of Pearl or Pat carrying out new plates from Donna's stove, to document what would become a treasured book of recipes. Pat pleaded that she was too shy for all of this, but Pearl at least knew how to fight back: 'You do not know how to relax. Why don't you sit down for five minutes and do nothing?' Never, I thought, when I'm having this much fun.

Joyriding all over the island, back and forth to the store and fish market, with the occasional detour for a little sightseeing, became the pre-chopping highlight of the day. The going could be slow on the narrow roads, and Donna never hesitated to tell me to stop if we were passing one of her chums with whom she wanted to catch up – a cart-to-cart conversation, in blazing sun or afternoon downpour – before moving on.

———————

For an entire week, the day began each morning after breakfast with, 'Come on, we go now.' Donna's all-aboard call always felt like a whim, as nothing had ever been discussed prior to departure. On the last day, though, I was prepared but also confused, for Donna wouldn't say where we were headed. She just kept giggling as we drove to the mystery destination and I continued begging for information.

When we reached the beachfront villa I knew something was up, for this place had 'special' written all over it, from the location, smack on the sand, to the long gated entryway that spoke of wealth and seclusion. 'My sister is Mick Jagger's cook,' Donna said. 'This is his place.'

For a child of the 1960s, entering Mick Jagger's home might equal the thrill a modern teen would feel if invited to visit all the vampires on the set of the *Twilight* movies. Denise greeted us at the door for a guided tour. There was Mick's pink pool table. Denise and Donna cheerfully posed behind it for a snap. On a bureau was a picture of his mother, smiling and waving furiously. I laughed. Donna and Denise laughed, because I was laughing.

We all ended up in the kitchen, where I inspected the drop-dead appliances. They made the ones at Sapphire, which looked liked they might have belonged to June Cleaver from 'Leave it to Beaver' at one time, seem horribly out of date. I even wondered if Donna might be a tad envious. I would have been. We finished the tour with coffee and cake, as I learned that the two sister-cooks had six other siblings – five girls, whose names all started with 'D', and a brother, Oral. Suddenly, that was funny too.

On my last night at Sapphire, I drank the juice from my ceviche straight from the bowl, just after Pearl left the room so she wouldn't see my exhibition of bad manners. After dinner, I helped clear plates, as I'd done most nights, and stopped worrying if pitching in might actually be insulting. After all, Donna, Pearl and Pat were professionals, with jobs to do, but weren't they now also my friends? They were both, I decided, and friends don't let friends clear plates by themselves. I rang the dinner bell, and we had a final laugh.

I email Donna now and then to let her know of my progress with her soufflés (the one with marmalade is as killer as her cheese creation). I tell her what worked and what went wrong. She always writes back, with advice for fixing my mistakes. At New Year's, she surprised me with a note of cheer and well wishes.

I wonder sometimes if Donna, Pat and Pearl were sorry to see me go. Or relieved. Maybe they were happy to get back to the dinner bell, with guests who followed the rules, guests who never got in the way of their duties by lifting pot lids and clearing tables. I think about them often and ask myself what I got out of my week on Mustique. The answer is always the same: I met a terrific cook, who shared her recipes with me and took me to the edge of the sea to find lobster. Donna is one of many friends I know who are good cooks, but she is the only one who lives in the Caribbean. We are twenty-first century pen pals. And that's something pretty wonderful to bring home.

Salad Days in Burma

KAREN J. COATES

Karen Coates has spent a dozen years covering food, environment and social issues across Asia for publications around the world. A correspondent for *Archaeology* magazine, she writes a regular Food Culture column for the *Faster Times*. She was *Gourmet's* Asia correspondent until the magazine closed in 2009. Karen is the author of *Cambodia Now: Life in the Wake of War* and co-author of *Pacific Lady: The First Woman to Sail Solo Across the World's Largest Ocean*. She is a 2010–11 Ted Scripps Fellow in Environmental Journalism at the University of Colorado at Boulder. You can get another taste of her writing on her food blog, Rambling Spoon.

It's November in northern Thailand, right on the brink of seasonal change from sultry to sublime. The rains have ended and the evening brings a wintry nip. We crowd around wooden tables with chipped red paint, sipping strong Shan tea from little blue-and-white cups. I grab my notebook and the feast begins.

Salad Days in Burma

For the past three weeks I've been teaching basic journalism to Southeast Asians, and tonight I've invited my Burmese students to dinner. I'd like to repay them for a slew of small kindnesses – for carrying my bag, buying my rice, bringing my tea during classroom breaks. But I'm also hoping for a favour. I'd like them to teach me everything they can about Burmese cooking. I lead them behind a boisterous local market to a small, quiet alley with a little Burmese restaurant tucked inside a garden of leafy trees.

Shredded ginger salad, *gin thote,* arrives with peanut, tomato and onion in a waft of pungent, nasal-clearing goodness. The salad – the *thote* – is the welcome mat of any Burmese meal. This I learned on my first trip to Burma several years before. My students tell me that almost every *thote* begins with shallots fried in peanut oil, garlic mixed with onion, fish paste, salt and something sour, such as tamarind or lime. Chickpea powder, I'm told, is key; it adds a hefty graininess to the salad that I have always loved.

The students order a plate of pork in soybean paste, *wat pone yae gyi.* Sauce is paramount to this dish, I learn. 'The main thing is the juice. It's better than the meat,' says one of the students, who counts eating his wife's cooking among his favourite hobbies.

We try the pork curry, *wat hmyit chin,* with a sweet pickled bamboo that takes months to prepare. 'We have two kinds of bamboo – sour and sweet,' another student explains. This, he says, is like 'infant bamboo, infant of the big bamboo tree.'

A heady dish of fish paste, *nga pi,* comes in a ring of raw vegetables. 'This is essential food,' says the only female in the crowd. 'In Burmese villages some people cannot eat a meal, so they eat this with rice and vegetables, and that's all. Because they are poor.' As a single woman from a family with little money, she rises each morning before the sun to cook for parents and siblings, then goes to work to earn money for the family coffers.

Most of these students are men, and they don't cook at home. But they learn everything by watching the women in their lives. They know as much, in fact, about cooking as their female colleague. Towards evening's end, the eldest in the group leans to my ear, and he says: 'Karen, I want to tell you something because I think it is useful for your story. We all know how to cook our curry because it is in our culture.' Every woman cooks, and she talks to her friends about food. Every man eavesdrops, and he learns the secrets of the Burmese plate.

I ask his opinion of this restaurant. 'Is it the *real* Burmese food?'

'Nearly, *nearly!*' he answers with a big, toothy grin. Translation: it's as good as it gets away from his wife's kitchen.

We're all stuffed and happy, chatting over little cups of tea, nibbling on sweet cubes of jaggery, customarily served gratis. I duck downstairs and open my wallet, but the waitress shakes her head. The bill has been paid, and I never even see it. My students don't have cash to spare. Yet their kindness never runs out, and it's always a few steps ahead of my own.

It's early January. My husband, Jerry, and I are on a plane to Burma, our first return to the country in six years. It's a short flight from Bangkok to Yangon, barely an hour, but it feels like a journey between worlds. Time lags half an hour on touchdown: 10am in Bangkok is 9.30am in Burma, which sets a pace thirty minutes askew to the rest of the region. Author Chris Offutt once wrote that time doesn't move forward; it stays put, and people move through it instead. Humanity has its comings and goings, but time stands still around the commotion.

It's that way in Burma. Little has visibly changed in six years. A few new buildings and billboards, a few cell phones and internet shops. But little else seems different for the people. It looks eerily similar to what I remember. But the Burmese people move – constantly, swiftly, with necessity. And the moving is never easy: rusty old Toyota taxis with broken windows and missing knobs; buses crammed with bodies, bumping over potholed streets; rickshaws with wobbly wheels pedalled by drivers with cracked and callused feet.

Jerry and I spend eighteen hours on an overnight ferry through the Irrawaddy Delta, to the city of Pathein. We sleep in the open, on the hard metal floor above rumbling engines one deck down. Each passenger is given a rectangle of space, approximately two and a half feet wide and five feet long, on which to keep body and luggage. I count 130 people squeezed together, head to head, toe to toe, all of them crammed into a space the size of a three-car garage. Everyone is kind and polite, taking careful steps so as not to tread upon another passenger's mat while moving between the deck and the fetid bathrooms.

Vendors pass through, shouting offers of fish and rice, fried fritters and fruit, and a spectacularly spicy and bitter tea-leaf salad known as *laphet thote*. It's a national snack made from pickled leaves, crispy dried yellow peas and beans, sharp raw garlic, potent red capsicum, a drizzle of oil, a hint of sour. It's a pleasantly bitter sensation, sour but savoury, with a unique crunchy, oily, moist consistency that ends in dragon-fire breath born of so much garlic and chilli. Jerry brings me a flimsy plastic plate with a dollop of salad, and I lap up one luscious green bite after another.

We sleep that night to the constant chug of the engine beneath us and wake to a saffron sun, lifting over the mangroves of a vast delta.

It's three months later, and we're back in Burma. Yangon is a sauna in April, its pavement like hot coals, its air like blistering steam. It's the season of waiting – for rain, for relief, for release.

I'm teaching creative nonfiction writing to a small group of journalists. For days, we hash out the differences between fiction and nonfiction – blatant distinctions to me, but not to my students. Is a how-to manual fiction or nonfiction? A movie review? If a reporter writes a truthful article but makes up the main character, do I call it fiction? (I call it verboten.)

The students hurl questions at me for hours. So seldom is the truth allowed in print that Burma's best writers tell it through imagined stories – this I learned on my previous trip. Forty years of that, and readers' minds are blurred. People know the difference between truth and lies, but they no longer distinguish between fact and fiction. So we discuss Dexter Filkins, John McPhee, Peter Hessler, Susan Orlean. We read Chris Jones' prize-winning story 'The Things that Carried Him', and I email him a list of students' questions about method and story structure (to which he replies at great length).

At lunch break, we take our conversations to the corner canteen. We sit at tiny tables with little stools beneath leafy trees eating homemade curries, soups and *thotes.*

Right around this time, I pitch pickled tea as an article for a new travel magazine, and the editor jumps. When I tell the class interpreter that I've been assigned to do a story on *laphet thote,* his eyes begin to dance. He teaches me a term, *shoo-shee,* which is onomatopoeia for the sound one makes when fanning the lips after eating a piquant plate of the salad. The Burmese don't just *like* this dish. They feel it in their teeth. They gobble it up, then swipe a finger through the juices and lick that finger clean. That last taste, a young reporter tells me, is better than the salad. It is the concentrated essence of every ingredient combined.

I set off with one of my students on an afternoon mission to find the best of the city's *laphet thote*. We trudge through scalding heat and black puffs of smog belched from old buses as we angle towards Sule Pagoda. There we find a long-time shop that serves excellent salads made to order – each customer can select the number of chillies, the amount of oil and the desired amount of pickled tea.

But this is not the way most Burmese eat *laphet thote,* my student tells me. A small plate of *laphet* typically costs 500 kyat (50 cents) at the corner shop. 'This is expensive,' he says. So people of few means – as in, mostly everyone – buy the ingredients in their local market and take them home to prepare. Every market has a *laphet thote* aisle with sacks and bins of pickled tea, dried beans, seeds and peas. 'Many Myanmar people eat *laphet* salad and rice for their dinner,' my friend says. 'They are very busy and they have not much money.'

A week later, I'm in Mandalay to teach a three-day workshop. Early one morning before class, Jerry and I visit a well-known family-run factory that has packaged and sold *laphet thote* ingredients for more than a century. 'The business has been handed down for six generations,' the owner tells me. That history hangs in photos across the family's mint-green living room walls.

He's excited to have foreigners here, beneath dusty old whirring fans, around an elaborate lacquered tray with partitions separating all the ingredients for a proper handful of salad. We're given small silver spoons to dip into the moist pickled leaves, crispy dried garlic, crunchy peanuts, roasted sesame seeds, dried yellow beans, dried green beans, pumpkin seeds, prawn powder and dried insects (which live in local spirulina ponds).

'My favourite is pickled tea leaf with tomato and all the ingredients,' says the man's 76-year-old mother. 'We mix and enjoy very much. We also add sliced cabbage.'

Our host is also an architect, and he tells us about a market he designed, a boisterous place where traders buy and sell the dried ingredients – beans, peas, seeds – eaten in *laphet thote*. We must see it! he insists. He invites us on a tour, and makes plans to pick us up at our hotel later in the week, after my workshop has finished.

———————◀

We never make it to the market. My teaching ends the evening before our scheduled visit. That night, Jerry and I catch a quick dinner of rice, curry and dhal at a Nepali restaurant around the corner from our hotel. When we return, men in green uniforms clog the hotel lobby. They have orders from Naypyidaw, the new political capital, to put us on a train to Yangon that night. No questions, no answers. No phone calls allowed. We must pack and go – the train leaves in less than two hours.

Two officers escort us to the station, and the four of us cram into one small cabin with a wheezing fan for sixteen hours of aching heat. The train rumbles along. Sooty grime cakes our skin. Exhaust spews through the windows. We rumble through the blackest night, through a countryside with no lights.

The officers offer us water. They don't want to be here, but they have no choice. They begin to peel off their uniforms, removing layers in the cloying heat. They never touch us, never search us. They sleep, while my mind races with questions. I pull out my journal and write against the shaky vibrations of the moving train. In the morning, our captors buy us coffee.

When we arrive in Yangon, we are shuttled across the city, back and forth, first to the airport, then to Immigration headquarters forty-five minutes away downtown, then back to the airport, where we're given room to wash and eat in the air-conditioned airport lounge. The authorities take our passports and book us on the next flight to Bangkok. Then, finally, when we are sitting in our Thai Airways seats, in the very last row of the plane, our passports are returned to us with little black stamps across our Burmese visas, one small word written in faded capital letters: 'Deportee'.

We never learn why. Rumours abound; most are ludicrous. The most plausible of all: our plans to meet the *laphet thote* man at his market, which might have been run by someone in the ruling junta – about which we knew nothing at all.

These things happen in Burma – our friends all have stories. We knew a man in Yangon who referred to his colleagues by the number of years they will spend in prison – *currently serving two years, currently serving ten years, currently serving twelve years.* That man's passport was confiscated the last time he returned from an overseas journey. Jerry and I were sentenced to leave – the Burmese are sentenced to stay.

It's summer. That perfect time of year when the temperature of air and skin agree, when the hot desert sun gives way to a blue-black sky with nighthawks making their rounds.

Plink.

My computer sounds, and up pops a little orange Gmail window. Halfway around the world, the Burmese are just waking for the day, and one of my students has come online.

'Good morning Karen … how are you today?'

It's a young woman from Yangon, who tells me she would like to become a better journalist for her readers. If she has time, she says, she will translate some of her articles into English and send them to me.

This is how I keep abreast of my students' lives. The government can brand my passport and put me on a blacklist but it hasn't – yet – been able to impede the miracles of Facebook and Gmail chat. So, early in the morning and late at night, my Burmese colleagues and I tap our way through conversations about story structure, censorship, imprisonment, human rights – and the pleasures of home-cooked meals.

'*I miss & love you,*' my student writes.

She invites me to a traditional Burmese dinner. Someday. '*If we can meet again.*'

Note: I have not identified the Burmese in this story. Several of them asked me not to use their names, for their protection.

Just What
the Doctor Ordered

ALEXANDER LOBRANO

Alexander Lobrano grew up in Connecticut, and lived in Boston, New York and London before moving to Paris, his home today, in 1986. He was European Correspondent for *Gourmet* magazine from 1999 until its closing in 2009, and now contributes regularly to the *New York Times*. He has written about food and travel for *Bon Appétit, Food & Wine, Travel & Leisure, Departures, Condé Nast Traveler,* and many other publications in the United States and the United Kingdom. His website is www.hungryforparis.com.

The removalists had gone, and besides the two of us, as far as I knew, there were only three things left in our flat on Castletown Road in West London – two suitcases and a cold bottle of Strongbow cider in the fridge. Roger and I had sold our place, but caught a week short between when we had to leave the flat and when we could move into our new house, we'd decided on a cheap package trip to Portugal's Algarve coast. What we wanted was lots of sun, wine and, hopefully, good food.

It wasn't just because I'd never been to Portugal that I knew absolutely nothing about Portuguese food. Unlike Italian, Mexican or Chinese cuisine, Portuguese cooking had never entered the culinary canon of ethnic foods known and accepted in American suburbia, where I'd grown up in the 1960s and '70s. So, in my ignorance, I assumed it would be similar to Spanish cooking. When I'd suggested Portugal to Roger, a vegetarian, he'd fretted, 'All I care about is if they have lots of salads.' With no evidence whatsoever to support the claim, I assured him they would.

On that sunny Saturday in early June, the wistful perfume of the lilacs in deep purple bloom in the back garden took the edge off the sharp smell of dust in the empty flat, but also heightened the melancholia inherent in any major personal migration. I decided it was time for some cider. The bottle had a cap, so I had to go upstairs to dig the bottle opener out of my shaving kit. When I opened the bedroom door, I saw a single suitcase sitting there. Mine. I looked in the other bedroom, dashed downstairs, and went from empty room to empty room. 'Roger, where's your suitcase? You did put it in the upstairs bedroom like I told you to, didn't you?'

Twenty-four hours later, driving north to Lisbon to meet Roger's plane, I sourly replayed this scene in my head again and again as I fought with the stiff U-shaped dashboard-mounted gear shift in the tinny little Renault station wagon that had come as part of our holiday. The removalists had locked Roger's bag in a warehouse until Monday morning, so I'd gone ahead to Portugal and Roger was arriving on a later London–Lisbon flight.

It had looked like an easy drive on the car-rental-company map of Portugal, but in my first hour on the road, following old blue-and-oyster-grey enamelled signs to Lisboa, I'd travelled through several groves of alarmingly scarred cork oak trees and arrived at the very same crossroads twice. And now it was getting hot, so hot that my skin was damp under the fat foam liners on my Walkman's earphones. I noticed it was already noon. I hoped this meant that I was at least halfway to Lisbon, but since my map was so worthless, I decided to stop at the next gas station, buy a proper one, and find out exactly where I was.

To my surprise, there was something oddly pleasant, even a little exhilarating, about travelling in a geographical void. To be sure, I knew I was heading north, but that was about it, and if I was late for Roger's arrival at 6pm, well, he'd just have to wait.

At this time, 1986, Portugal had only just joined the European Union (then known as the Common Market), so the imminent flood of adhesion money from Brussels had not yet arrived to modernise, standardise and ultimately ruin everything. Instead, Portugal looked just the way I imagined it always had. Here there was a field of heavy-headed yellow-petalled sunflowers with weak green necks; there, a woman with a black scarf, black dress and white apron vigorously hoeing her vegetable garden – cabbages, kale and potatoes, all of which I smelled on the hot air coming in the windows. I got stuck behind a tractor towing a cart of newly mown alfalfa for a while, then had to jam on the brakes when I came around a bend and nearly made ham of several short-legged black pigs whose bellies barely cleared the melting macadam road.

After another hour at the wheel, I still hadn't come across a gas station, but I was hungry and thirsty and needed to stretch my legs, so I pulled up in front of a low whitewashed house with a few cars parked out the front. When I stepped through the screen door, I saw a group of men in dark suits sitting around a large table. At once they stopped talking and turned to stare at me, a tall blond foreigner wearing shorts, a T-shirt and flip-flops like some idiot who'd taken a wrong turn on his way to the beach.

Drying glasses behind the bar, the stout grey-haired man I guessed was the owner of the tavern didn't budge. For several excruciating seconds I thought of fleeing, then one of the dark-suited men got up, took a rush-bottomed chair from another table, added it to theirs and motioned for me to sit down. I was so caught off guard that I did. *'Bom dia,'* they said collectively, and then offered their names – Rui, Fernao, Jao, Antonio and so on.

'Alec,' I said, gesturing at myself and blushing.

The tavern-keeper brought me a napkin, silverware and a glass, which the man to my right filled with cold fizzy greenish wine from a stoneware pitcher. *'Obrigado,'* I said, using up all of my Portuguese and accepting some bread, which had a deliciously blistered crust and a chewy tart sourdough crumb. Next the owner shuffled over with a plate containing a bit of salad – sliced tomato and onion on a lettuce leaf, plus a scoop of sticky white rice and some potatoes that had been freshly fried in olive oil.

'Frango,' said the man on my left as he edged a stainless-steel platter of roast chicken in my direction, and another handed me a slender bottle of scarlet sauce. *'Piri-piri. Caldo!'* I shook a few squirts of the sauce onto the chicken and tucked in.

I looked up when I realised the conversation had stopped, and with a sinking feeling I understood that they were politely waiting for me to catch up to their own empty plates. The chicken was the best I'd ever had, juicy, wild-tasting fowl full of flavour with crispy skin. The *piri-piri,* which I correctly guessed as being made from small hot red chillies, garlic, salt and vinegar, was so addictively good that I shook a few shots on my fried potatoes and rice. When I glanced up, the man across from me looked amused and gave me a thumbs-up.

I ate quickly, partly because I was very hungry and partly because I wanted to catch up with them. But when I finished, the tavern owner came back and changed my plate. I tried to signal that I'd had my fill, especially of that surprisingly potent wine, but he and my tablemates were having none of it. Seconds later he returned with a heavy ceramic casserole. *'Porco a Alentejana,'* he said, smiling now, and I dug in, serving myself a modest portion of chunks of pork and baby clams in a light tomato sauce.

It was superb. The pork had been marinated, probably in vinegar, before being fried, and the brine-filled little clams had added their salty iodine-rich juices to the tomato sauce when they'd steamed opened. It had been ages since I'd eaten anything so good – aside from several great Indian restaurants, the food in London in 1986 was still more miss than hit – and this dish made me so happy that I willingly made a fool of myself by trying to pantomime my pleasure, a performance that caused two of the sextet to laugh and all of them to smile. As a grand finale, I ate a second portion out of sheer animal gluttony.

Finally, as the owner cleared the table, one of the men turned on a black-and-white television on a rickety table with a lace-edged doily and said, 'Football. You like?' I nodded. '*Tu* – America?' I nodded again. 'Portugal. You like?' I nodded enthusiastically, and the man next to me clapped me on the back. For the first time, I felt comfortable enough to wonder who they were and why they were having lunch together, but of course I couldn't ask and in the end it didn't matter.

Stuffed and in a fuzzy good mood from the wine, I had a shock when I glanced at my watch and saw that this feast had run for two hours. I had to go, but when I stood up, the guy next to me pulled me back into my seat by my belt and said, '*Queijo, frutas, bicas.*' And so we ate delicious soft, creamy breast-shaped cheeses wrapped in gauze, then emptied a tray of fresh peaches, strawberries and small sweet bananas from Madeira, and finally concluded with strong shots of black coffee.

When a gentle-looking older woman with wavy silver hair and an indigo dress arrived with a bottle of port and small glasses on a tray, I stood and walked briskly over to the owner. I took out two escudo notes and put them on the counter. He pushed them back at me and shook his head. I left them there and went to the toilet. To my relief, the money was gone when I emerged, so I walked over to the men with whom I'd just shared lunch, and said, '*Muy, muy, muy, muy obrigado.*'

'*De nada,*' '*Bom viagem,*' '*Salud,*' they muttered. Then one of them said, 'Stop!' He motioned me over, dug into his scuffed-up black leather bag, pulled out a stethoscope, fitted it into his ears, and placed the cold bud of shiny steel on my chest while pressing down on my pulse point with a strong hairy thumb. We all waited, then he shouted, '*Okay! Bom viagem!*' and the gang, a bunch of tipsy doctors – they all had the same heavy, well-worn briefcases – had a good laugh.

During the long hot drive to Lisbon that followed lunch, I got almost teary a couple of times as I mused on this magical meal. Why had those men been so kind? And why was that food so good? Was all Portuguese food this good? I found no answers to any of these questions. Instead, my only certainty was that I would be marked forever by a craving for good simple Portuguese country food – and that I would never forget the spontaneous hospitality offered by unknown doctors to an awkward foreign boy during a nearly wordless meal.

Later, when Roger and I were driving south, he asked me why on earth I had rolled up two escudo notes and put them in the ashtray of the car. I told him it was a private joke, which indeed it was. It took more than a few years, however, before I realised that this lunch with the Portuguese doctors had also become a precious point on the personal compass I use whenever I travel.

The Hair of the Cow

LAURENCE MITCHELL

Laurence Mitchell is a freelance travel writer and photographer with a penchant for places that are firmly off the beaten track, particularly countries in transition like the new republics of the former Soviet Union. Nothing makes him happier than a lumpy bed, an utter lack of tourist infrastructure and an indecipherable menu, although he is also pretty content with a decent *shashlyk* and a beer. As well as writing for magazines, he is the author of travel guides to Serbia, Belgrade and Kyrgyzstan. Laurence is also responsible for *Slow Norfolk and Suffolk,* a book that takes a personal, 'Slow' look at his home patch of East Anglia in the United Kingdom. His website may be viewed at www.laurencemitchell.com.

Georgia's reputation as a place of great hospitality, wonderful food and dynamic people was well known to us prior to our arrival in the country, but it would be Kazbegi, high in the Caucasus mountains, about as far as you could go along the Georgian Military Highway without ending up in Ingushetia or Chechnya, where it would be put to the test.

We spent our first afternoon climbing up to the Tsminda Sameba church perched on a peak high above the town, the sort of location that was so impossibly picturesque it ought to figure on the cover of a guidebook – and in fact, it did. We had been in Georgia only three days, yet already we had a strong impression as to the character of the country – it was a place of strong opinions, uncompromising geography and almost unbearable beauty. Everything was a bit larger than life, especially here in the mountains, something akin to a scruffy yet extroverted Switzerland on acid.

We were hungry after our walk but an electricity breakdown meant that the evening meal promised by our village hosts would be delayed for some time. We waited as patiently as we could and eventually the solitary light bulb in our room flickered back into life. An hour or so later, tantalising savoury smells started to spike the air, already mountain-cold now that the sun had slunk behind the white cone of Mount Kazbegi. A further hour of stomach rumblings went by before we were finally called through to the dining room.

We were to eat with Giorgi, our guide, along with his friend from the village, also confusingly called Giorgi ('Giorgi 2'), and Jimaal, the homestay owner. Following tradition, the women of the house would remain out of sight in the kitchen, preparing food and generally keeping out of the way of the serious men's business of eating and drinking.

Entering the dining room, we found the rough wooden table in the middle of the room was groaning under the weight of numerous bowls, dishes and plates of food. I could not help but notice a prodigious amount of booze at the ready too – wine, vodka, beer. Was this to be some sort of village party? 'No,' said Giorgi with some bemusement, 'just the five of us.'

Giorgi explained, 'In Georgia, we think it is good to have too much food like this. Our hosts would be ashamed if they did not provide you with enough to eat and drink. There should always be too much food.' Quantity aside, the variety on offer was quite staggering, even more so considering that much of it had been home-produced in one way or another. There were green beans in garlic and butter, a heap of freshly baked bread, a rich stew of meat and vegetables, fried potatoes, plates of tomatoes and cucumbers, and slices of salty homemade cheese. Naturally, any such spread would be unthinkable without *khinkhali* – Georgia's signature steamed meat dumplings – and a large plate of these sat steaming away centre stage. Even more tempting were those dishes that allowed for Georgia's flair for improvisation: boiled nettles with garlic and pomegranate seeds, and the almost unpronounceable *pkhali* – young beet leaves mixed with crushed walnuts and garlic. And on top of all this there was that serious quantity of drink to consider.

Georgian feasting tradition dictates that you should drink only after a formal toast has been made by the toastmaster, and that you should never make a toast with beer as that would be highly disrespectful. In practice, this meant that you could drink as much beer as you liked but you would still be required to sink an unfeasibly large amount of alcohol in the form of wine and spirits as well. Giorgi was appointed *tamada* – toastmaster – for the evening and he started off with a couple of meandering, fairly run-of-the mill speeches in Georgian and English. Many more were to follow: toasts to us, to our Kazbegi hosts, to Georgia, to Great Britain and so on. Initially, we responded as we thought was expected of us, draining our glasses to the bottom, but we soon changed this to reducing our draughts by half a glass at a time when we realised we could get away with it.

Hardly surprisingly, the conversation around the table became quite animated after a while; at the same time, none of the Georgians showed any obvious signs of drunkenness – that would be unforgivable in this booze-soaked yet proud land where you were meant to able to take your drink like a man. As is often the case in Georgia, the conversation inevitably turned to the subject of one Josif Dzhugashvili – better known to the world as Stalin – the country's most (in)famous son. Giorgi fielded our questions about the man, undoubtedly the world's best known Georgian, with skilled diplomacy and not a little patriotism. 'Some people in Georgia still admire him as a strong man. We all know that Stalin was a mean *sonofabitch* but at least he was *our sonofabitch.*' Actually, he didn't say *'sonofabitch'* but instead used a rather ruder pejorative that suggested even unhealthier family relationships.

Another Georgian tradition states that once present at the *supra* – the feast table – you should not leave it under any circumstances until the proceedings have run their full course. However, with a large volume of beer, wine and spirits swimming around inside me, I hoped that an exception would be made. I offered my excuses, mostly because I badly needed to pee but also because I wanted to see if my legs still worked; they did … just.

The outhouse was at the end of the garden across a small lawn. With no moon, the night was molasses dark and from the house I headed blindly in the appropriate direction with my arms outstretched in case of unexpected obstacles. Halfway across the garden I actually did come across something quite unexpected when my hands made contact with what felt like a warm hairy wall. Unable to see what it was even at this close range, I ran my hand along it to explore, and discovered the unmistakable furry notches of an animal's backbone. Luckily I had enough drink inside me to remain quite cool and concluded that this was either a really large dog or a rather small cow. I skilfully circumvented the animal – the latter of the two possibilities as it turned out – and went on my way in search of the outhouse.

I related this little adventure to my table companions when I returned. Giorgi found the whole incident highly amusing and translated for his friend. This caused great hilarity and Giorgi 2 responded in Georgian in-between guffaws. Giorgi translated in turn: 'My friend said that you should have known it was a cow. If it had been a Georgian dog, it would have killed you.' I am sure he was right, although I wasn't particularly impressed with the way he seemed to delight in the viciousness of Georgian dogs. Thankfully, the cow in question was anything but aggressive and was no doubt quite used to drunks bumping into her in the dark.

More food and drink followed and I soon found myself looking forward to the time when the two, now almost empty, half-litre vodka bottles would be polished off and we could all head to bed. But this was not to be, as Jimaal quietly slipped away for ten minutes before returning with two more bottles he had bought at the kiosk near the bus turnaround. More toasts and further immoderate drinking was necessary before we could finally stagger off to our room.

Next morning, I woke up severely dehydrated and with a poisonous headache. By the time I emerged to join the others, breakfast had been neatly laid out in the kitchen. There was herb tea and some of last night's leftovers as well as freshly baked *khachapuris* – the Georgian snack staple, a deliciously rich variety of cheese bread. Little pots of molten butter were placed at the side to enrich the bread further – the product of my friend, the family cow, as was the cheese for the *khachapuris*. Standing beside these offerings were some ready-poured glasses of vodka and the bottles with the dregs from last night's session. This time I felt able to refuse with impunity. Even in Georgia, they would not wilfully set out on a drinking session first thing in the morning. Would they? They might, however, be tempted by just a little 'hair of the dog' – or in this case, perhaps, the hair of the cow.

Siberian Chicken

ANTHONY SATTIN

Anthony Sattin is a journalist, broadcaster and the author of a number of acclaimed books of history and travel, including *The Pharaoh's Shadow* and *The Gates of Africa*. Anthony has spent much of the past couple of decades travelling around and writing about North Africa and the Middle East. He was described by one British newspaper as 'like a cross between Indiana Jones and a John Buchan hero', and was voted one of the ten greatest influences on travel writing by *Condé Nast Traveller*. His most recent book, *A Winter on the Nile: Florence Nightingale, Gustave Flaubert and the Temptations of Egypt,* has been called 'a triumph of the historical imagination'. You can find out more at www .anthonysattin.com.

I have eaten chicken in many places around the world: served on a stick at the Satay Club in Singapore, around a fire on a starry night in the African savannah, curried in an Indian palace, straight off an Argentinean grill, wrapped in a Shanghai dumpling. Yet whenever I think of chicken, I think of a place I have never been, Siberia, and of a long train ride with a pair of lively women.

I suppose I have the international railway bureaucrats to thank for the women. In 1995, I set out from London to travel to Moscow by train on the aptly named *Ost–West Express*. I was hoping to travel through to Moscow on the Russian car but, for a reason I could never fathom, it was impossible to reserve the eastern leg of the journey in advance. When I reached Warsaw, I found the train was full. Instead, there was space on a later train, the *Polonez,* a Polish service that followed the same route.

The train was almost empty when it pulled out of Warsaw central station. Alone in the carriage, I stretched out on one of the benches, worked out how to flip it over into a bed, pulled down the window to watch the city slide behind us, and saw the River Vistula sparkle in the afternoon sun. A few minutes later, we reached the east side of town. The platform of Wschodnia Station was heaving and even before the train stopped, a large bag was pushed up to my window. When I stood up, I saw two young women shouting at me in Russian and gesticulating that I should take it. Five more packages followed. Another four were dragged in by hand.

The women filled the luggage racks with their bags and then covered the floor. They even managed to raise the level of what had been, until then, my bed. My bed? Nothing was mine now.

As we pulled out of Wschodnia Station, the women introduced themselves. This one was Katya, short, dark-haired, plump, with a melon face. The other was Svetla, who was pretty, fair-haired and big-hipped. She was obviously proud of her flatter stomach, for she wore a T-shirt that was both too short and too tight. She was also halfway to filling her mouth with gold. They were both in their mid-twenties, lively and in good humour. We shook hands and there was a moment of laughter at this gesture. With the formalities over, they took off their coats and checked that their bags were properly stowed – this was a business trip, after all. Then they set up a table on one of their bags, spread out some paper on it, and unpacked a bag of food. They ripped apart a roast chicken, while we ran the gauntlet of international conversation: Charles'n'Di (still!), Gorbachev and Putin, Chechnya, children, the goods they were travelling with ('clothes', they insisted, which they would sell back home). That, and the weather back home in Irkutsk.

From Poland we were heading towards Belarus. The Belarus Embassy in London had assured me that I could cross their country if I had a Russian visa, which I did. But I had been woken in the night on entering Poland, had had a torch shone in my face, and had been questioned about the Middle East stamps in my passport, my name, and my origins. So as we approached the border between Poland and Belarus, I became quiet. But while I was a little tense, Katya and Svetla were unmistakably nervous.

The frontier between Poland and Belarus follows the River Bug. I traced its movement across my map: it was one of the fault lines between East and West, a crossing place, as slender and sensitive as an exposed nerve. We came up to it across open countryside and slowed as we approached the border: two rows of fences and rolled wire. I assumed the space between them was mined.

Guards in towers watched over the stillness as we clanked onto an iron bridge over the river. The train was moving slowly enough for someone to have jumped off without getting hurt, and for guards to have shot them before they hit the ground. Across in Belarus, beyond the electric fences, a phalanx of officials in great coats and high, peaked caps waited for us. Katya looked at them and crossed herself.

Unlike the Polish police, the Belarus immigration official spoke excellent English. He asked for our passports and returned them duly stamped. Then a customs officer came on board to check the luggage. I held up my British passport and he smiled, so when we started moving again I assumed, in my innocence, that we were in the clear and that whatever followed would be a brief formality. I was wrong.

It didn't take the officer long to spot the bags under my bed, and to guess that they weren't mine. He demanded my neighbours' passports, and when the train came to a halt a few hundred metres further east in the imposing station of Brest, he put the documents in his pocket and signalled for Svetla to follow him over to the customs shed. Katya sat with her head in her hands. *Problemi!* Meanwhile, babushkas, old farm women in heavy dark clothes and flowery headscarves, appeared at our window offering bread and milk, *shampanski* and *wódka*.

Soviet-built tracks are wider than those in the rest of Europe, apparently to stop armies invading by train, although as Hitler followed this route, it doesn't seem to have worked as a deterrent. What it did now was delay us for several hours while the *Polonez* was shunted into sidings to have its bogies replaced. The shadowy, cavernous shed, the team of oil-blackened men winching up each carriage in turn, all that banging and clanging was like something out of a Soviet propaganda film.

After the shed, we were shunted onto the station platform. Katya remained sombre, playing with her calculator and flicking away the unwanted attentions of bag ladies. I went over to eat something at the unexpectedly grand station restaurant. Unable to read the menu or to understand the waitress's explanation, I ordered the only thing I could: chicken and vodka.

An hour or so later, the light faded and disappeared, the waitress handed me a bill, guards marched up and down the platform, and the driver sounded the train whistle. Katya said nothing, but looked even whiter than before and as brittle as a doll. Then, just as the last whistle blew, Svetla jumped on, breathless, triumphant.

Dollari and wits had got her through. The friends hugged, cried and giggled in relief. *'Shampanski?'* asked the last, desperate babushka. 'No,' Katya insisted, already worrying about the *problemi* ahead, of getting their bags onto an internal flight from Moscow, of getting out of the airport in Siberia. 'Yes,' I said, thinking we would need some cheering, and bought several bottles and a bottle of vodka to chase the bubbly down.

The *Polonez* finally lived up to its express status: we shot through the Belarus and then the Russian night. While Svetla remained quiet and Katya was tense and terse, the rest of the carriage was in celebratory mood. Someone unpacked a new tape machine and the corridor was transformed into a casino, cluttered with small gambling tables and already opaque with smoke. The *shampanski* and vodka flowed faster than the River Bug. The attendant, who knew what was coming, locked himself into his compartment.

When my neighbours finally caught up with the mood on the train, Katya pulled out another plastic bag: while I had been in the station restaurant, she had found another chicken. We squatted around the offering, greasy hands dismembering the bird and passing around the first of the bottles I had bought.

'Mmmm, chicken!' Katya cooed, to which I couldn't resist asking, 'Don't you have chicken in Siberia?'

The women laughed at my simplicity. Of course they had chicken in Siberia. Was there anywhere that didn't have chicken? Chicken was one of the world's great levellers, something we all have in common.

'But it tastes different in different places,' Katya explained. 'I bought this one in Brest from a woman who raised and cooked it herself. See how much flesh it has! In Siberia' – and she said that word with such emotion that even I had to sigh, 'in Si-bare-ia, it is cold. Very cold. Our chickens have to stay inside. They don't get fresh air, they don't exercise, they are not meaty, they have no fat.'

'It's not just the taste she likes,' Svetla said, teasingly, slightly drunk, patting her firm, flatter stomach and flashing her gold teeth. 'She thinks that if she sticks to chicken then she won't get fat.'

'No, no. It's not that. I eat them for this,' and she pulled off the wishbone. 'Come, Englishman, let us pull and see if you will be lucky. If not, we will drink your other bottle.' From the outcome, it was clear she had pulled that trick before.

By the time we reached the third bottle, the Siberians were swinging between glee at having got into Belarus and gloom about how much it was going to cost to get home. By the end of it, chicken bones had been thrown around the compartment and we were all out in the corridor, laughing, wise enough to stay off the gambling tables and drunk enough to try dancing to the rhythm of Russo-Balkan dance anthems.

The bunk was short and the celebrations long, but I was eventually lulled to sleep by the rocking of the train on the Russian track. I woke to silence (earplugs), to the sight of snow, and to the sweet, smoky smell of cold roast chicken. But Katya was not eating again. She was not even in the compartment. Instead it was sweet, slender Svetla. Thinking I was asleep, she had the chicken out of the bag and her hand inside its cavity, extracting a small plastic wad. I couldn't see clearly what it was, but it was definitely not giblets or other innards. She wiped it quickly, divided it into two smaller wads and used them to pad out her bra.

The small-town factories and villages of wood-clad houses looked derelict after all I had seen further west, in Belgium and Germany. At each country railway station, there was only one sign, a red arrow pointing to Moscwa.

Moscow came up fast and suddenly we were out of the empty snow-white countryside and into the city. The roads alongside the track were jammed. When Katya tried to open the compartment door, it was already too late; the corridor was full. 'Ah, Moscwa,' she said, excited. 'Ah, Bolshoi,' I added. 'Kremlin,' said Svetla. 'Pushkin,' I said. 'McDonald's,' said Katya. 'Chicken burger,' said Svetla. We all laughed.

At Moscow's Belarus Station, a porter forced his way in and tried to grab the nearest, lightest bag – mine – but we chased him out again. Cases went flying through compartment windows. On the platform, people carried clothes, electronic keyboards and other Western, capitalist produce past statues of Marx and Lenin.

This was the end of my journey, but not of Katya and Svetla's: Siberia was still far, far away. The formality that had hung over our first meeting was now forgotten and when we parted, we kissed and hugged. I watched them disappear into the crowd with their many bags and their two wads of – what? Cash? Drugs? Forged papers?

That night, unpacking my bag in my hotel, I found a chicken bone among my clothes, a reminder of the party. The bone was soon discarded, but the memory remains.

The Scent of Love

STANLEY STEWART

Stanley Stewart has written three award-winning travel books: *Old Serpent Nile, Frontiers of Heaven* and *In the Empire of Genghis Khan,* the last about his journey by horse across Mongolia. He is also the recipient of numerous awards for his magazine and newspaper articles. Stanley was born in Ireland, grew up in Canada, and now divides his time between Rome and Dorset.

The smell was the first thing I noticed about Outer Mongolia. It is a smoky aroma; a sweet, slightly rancid scent with strong milky base notes. Woods with campfires and tepees and drying reindeer meat might have smelled like this. An Irish dairy with jugs of cream and a peat fire burning in the next room might have smelled like this. In the end, love smelled like this.

I was on the *Trans-Siberian Express.* Not long after crossing into Mongolia from Russia, the train stopped at a deserted country station in the grey pre-dawn. When I stepped down to stretch my legs, the air was freighted with that haunting aroma.

The day brightened and the train clattered southward. I sat by the window and gazed out on the vast emptiness of Mongolia. After the claustrophobic forests of Siberia, this landscape was a revelation. It was as if God had gathered all the world's leftover space and dumped it here on these grassy steppes. Mongolia was a vast vacant lot, overgrown and empty, on the edge of the world.

For hours there seemed to be no sign of habitation – no roads, no towns, no fields, no people. Then suddenly a cluster of tents – the round white tents of Central Asia known as *gers* in Mongolia – sprouted like mushrooms in a valley. Horsemen appeared, three of them, silhouetted against the sky on a ridge above the tracks.

This is Asia's secret, I thought; a vast medieval world of nomads, slumbering in the heart of the continent, criss-crossed by winds and clouds and caravans of camels, its air scented with smoke and milk and meat.

———⚟

Some years later I came back to Mongolia. I wanted to cross the country by horse, to ride through those unhindered landscapes. I discovered it is possible to ride a thousand miles in Mongolia without finding or needing a restaurant. From Bayan Ölgii in the lap of the Altay to the Sacred Mountain of Burkhan Khaldun, I was warmed, welcomed and fed in countless *gers*. All were marinated in that special Mongolian fragrance, that bittersweet aroma. Filtered by limpid air, carried on freshening winds, it was a smell that emanated from the extraordinary Mongolian diet, a diet central to Mongolian life.

In the rich grasslands of Arhangay, the world was unfolding long languorous limbs. I rode through a succession of valleys, their grassy curves open to acres of sky. Each was an echo of the one that had gone before, vast, treeless, uncomplicated. They might have been sculpted by winds, smoothed to elemental simplicities. Detail and elaboration had been blown away, leaving only the essentials of shape and colour: the sensuous slopes, the yellow of the grasses, the hot troubled blue of the sky.

All morning pillars of rain menaced the horizons. At midday a storm engulfed me. The sky darkened suddenly, the winds rose to gale force and a moment later freezing sleet lashed across the slopes. I dismounted and turned my horse, so its rump faced this sudden violence.

The temperature plummeted, and for half an hour the world was reduced to a maelstrom of hailstones. It was like a Biblical visitation, a moment of God's wrath. Then the storm vanished as mysteriously as it had appeared, leaving only curling snakes of mist on the baking grasslands. The valleys stretched out again as the sun spread across their flanks. It was as if nothing had happened. I mounted and rode on through the innocent afternoon.

At day's end I arrived in a wide valley where tents and flocks were spread across the spring grass. It could have been a tableau of the American plains before the arrival of Europeans: white tents, tethered horses, pillars of camp smoke.

I pitched my own tent close to a quick stream, and within an hour a dinner invitation arrived. A gangly youth on a gangly horse bore a brusque message from his father – come and eat. He motioned to a *ger* in the middle distance where flocks of sheep were converging in the twilight.

I had long since given up trying to issue invitations myself. Mongolians were wary of foreigners' strange foods. Besides, the nomads were clear about our relationship. This was Mongolia. They were the hosts; I was the guest.

When I arrived at the *ger* I found two young girls milking a herd of shaggy ginger-haired yaks. Yak milking is a tough job requiring nerves of steel, a domineering manner and a weight-lifter's build. The consensus in Mongolia is that it is best left to the womenfolk. The girls were bullying the big beasts with resounding slaps on their hindquarters while their three older brothers, weedy boys conspiring in adolescent silence, were inside the *ger,* where their mother was serving them bowls of warm yak milk.

My host was something of a yak himself – a huge grizzly fellow with a long obstinate face and mournful eyes beneath a shaggy wool cap. When Tuvud came through the door of the *ger* bearing a saddle and a horsewhip, his sons scattered to the refuge of their grandmother's *ger* next door. Taking his place without speaking, he accepted a bowl of tea from his silent wife.

Then we settled down to dinner. A young ram had just been slaughtered and as a special treat a large plastic bowl of sheep parts was laid before us. I was handed a twelve-inch hunting knife and told to dig in.

Mongolians don't believe in wasting any of their beloved sheep. Everything was in the bowl, floating in a sort of primeval ooze: lungs, stomach, bladder, brain, intestines, eyeballs, teeth, genitals. It was a lucky sheep dip; you were never sure what you were going to pull out. I fished carefully, not too keen on finding myself with the testicles. My first go produced an object that resembled an old purse dredged up from the bottom of a stagnant canal. I think it might have been an ear. I had better luck with the intestines, which were delicious, and once brought to the surface, went on for quite a while.

Sated with sheep guts, our lips glistening with fat, Tuvud and I settled back for an after-dinner chat. Farting thunderously, my host asked what we ate in my country.

'Less meat, more fruit and vegetables.'

'What kind?' he asked.

'Oranges, lemons, melons, zucchini, eggplant, salads, lots of things.'

Unimpressed with this litany of unknown foods, he asked for a description. Unwisely perhaps, I began with the salad. He recoiled in horror when I explained the attraction of raw leaves.

'Like an animal,' he said, shaking his head sadly. 'You will be eating grass next. Raw leaves are food for animals, not for men. It is no wonder you are such feeble people.'

In a very literal sense Mongolians are what they eat. They are nomads; their lives are intimately connected to their herds and flocks, and they eat what their animals provide – meat, milk, cheese, curds. Even their alcoholic drinks are made from milk – fermented mare's milk, which becomes a sour frothy beer known as *airag,* and a distilled spirit, a kind of milk vodka called *arkhi,* an unpredictable tipple like a liquid landmine.

Far from being anxious about its limitations, Mongolians view endless meals of mutton with great pride. Parents in Ulaanbaatar, where fruit and vegetables are now freely available, send their children to their grandparents in the countryside for a couple of months, as a farmer puts calves out to pasture. They believe a summer of curds and lamb and fresh yak's milk will fatten them up, will make them strong, will make them Mongolian. If you ask a Mongolian about the nomad's ability to survive hardship, they will talk about the food, the meat, the fermented mare's milk. It is who they are, and it is what allows them to live the life they do.

It is the food that scents the air of Mongolia so pervasively, a subtle mixture of mutton fat, milk and curds, and of the animal dung fires on which it is all cooked. It seems inescapable. It is the aroma of every *ger,* but I have smelled it too in distant valleys apparently empty of habitation, in the stairwell of apartment blocks in Ulaanbaatar, even at the airport amidst the tang of jet fuel.

I stayed four days in Tuvud's valley while I looked for fresh horses and a guide to accompany me on the next stage of my journey. My immediate neighbours, whose *ger* lay a quarter of a mile away, were a very poor couple with four children. Though their resources were limited, their hospitality was boundless. The women came to call every morning, bearing pails of yak's milk and yoghurt, chatting incessantly, delighted to have someone new to talk to.

One evening, when I was ensconced in their *ger,* happily trading bowls of fermented mare's milk, conversation turned to the strange habits of the capital, Ulaanbaatar, Mongolia's only city, where people lived suspect lives of houses and salaries. My neighbour had met a man recently who had been there. Much about the place was extraordinary – the streets, the cars, the buildings – but what stuck in his mind was a stall in the main square where a man sold cups of tea.

Silence fell over my fellow diners. They had never heard of such a thing. Tea is the opening gambit in the ritual of hospitality that is central to the world of the nomad. It is the first thing to be offered freely to any visitor to a *ger,* whether an old friend or a complete stranger. They shook their heads at the idea of a world so barbarous that people went about selling tea to one another. This is what comes of cities, they muttered.

I too tried to look suitably shocked. It was a moment of cowardice. I was unwilling to let on that the sale of tea was commonplace in my own uncivilised country. I wasn't sure I could offer any reasonable explanation.

———————◀

A year after my ride across Mongolia I was waiting in Hong Kong airport for my Mongolian girlfriend. I hadn't seen her in six months and when she appeared beyond the glass, all suddenly seemed right with the world. She looked wonderful in a beret and a leather jacket. And then she came out through the arrivals hall bearing the scent of her homeland. The moment we embraced, I was assailed by that nostalgic smoky aroma. It was the smell of a thousand miles of Mongolia, of countless invitations to countless meals, and of the open hospitality of the steppes. Now a world away, in a city that was the antithesis of the empty steppes, it was the scent of love.

The 'Cue Quest

DOUG MACK

Doug Mack is a freelance writer based in Minneapolis, with a digital home at www.douglasmack.net. His articles and essays have appeared in the *San Francisco Chronicle*, WorldHum.com and many other publications. He is currently working on a book about his attempt to tour Europe guided only by a 1963 copy of *Europe on Five Dollars a Day*.

I don't suppose my father would want me to classify him as a barbecue nut, at least not at the outset. He'd want you to know, first, that he is an architect and a professor, that he is not a 'nut' in any form but a studious scholar. He is a historic masonry expert. Fittingly, his own façade is stoic and proud – but there is one sure-fire way of coaxing cracks, of making his eyes glimmer with schoolboy mischievousness and his thick white moustache flex with glee.

Barbecued ribs. Specifically, pork ribs in the Kansas City style, slathered in a robust, tangy, tomato-based sauce. Not any ribs will do, mind you. Only the good stuff, please, or else you'll *really* see Mr Unflappable come to life, all flustered scowls and dark mutterings unbefitting of a scholar.

Dad indoctrinated me into the cult of the 'cue long ago. Some of my earliest restaurant memories are of visiting rib joints around Minneapolis, and I've known good sauce from bad since long before I could spell 'insipid'.

The core of this indoctrination, however, occurred away from the table during my childhood bedtime stories, when the marquee attraction was often an essay from Calvin Trillin's trio of food books, *American Fried, Second Helpings* and *Alice, Let's Eat.* Oh, sure, we went through all the classics of the children's lit canon too, with their talking animals and their oh-so-plucky young protagonists and their Very Important Lessons to be learned. But those always felt like half-hearted side dishes in comparison: nutrient-rich and ostensibly good for me, but utterly unsatisfying and borderline nauseating, like cauliflower or beets.

My favourite of Mr Trillin's essays, the ones I most savoured and went back to for second helpings, were the ones about the restaurant he called the best in the world, Arthur Bryant's Barbeque, in his hometown of Kansas City.

It has always shocked me that Dad has never been there, never fact-checked Mr Trillin or even set foot in that barbecue-mad town. We've talked about it for years: *A barbecue road trip! We should do that sometime!* And then, inevitably, one thing after another gets in the way: school, work, health, *life.*

But now, somehow, here we are: on the road. Mom's off on a church trip to Paraguay, so Dad and I have decided, finally, to make a pilgrimage of our own. We're somewhere just south of Des Moines, nowhere near Kansas City, but we're already sniffing the air, hoping for a telltale wisp of smoke. We think we can make it out, just a hint, somewhere in the distance. Our mouths are already watering, our stomachs grumbling a timpani rhythm.

In the manner of fathers and sons everywhere, we don't really talk much, by which I mean, essentially, at all. But I've tossed a certain book on the back seat and when I take over driving, Dad pulls it out, unprompted, and begins reading out loud. We're a good fifteen or twenty years removed from the last bedtime story, but his inflection hasn't changed a bit: steady, professorial tone, becoming distinctly more reverential when he comes to the hallowed words 'Arthur Bryant's'.

Forget almost smelling it: we can almost taste it. Hearing the words again provokes a rush of nostalgia and memories, like Proust's madeleine – but trust me, Marcel: barbecue is better.

———————◄

We have a few other stops before we can get to Bryant's – we want to check out the full range of goods on offer in Kansas City. I've tried to figure out exactly how many options we have – that is, how many barbecue places there are here, total, from sidewalk vendors to fancy restaurants with tablecloths and, we've heard rumours, even proper porcelain plates with parsley or some such highfalutin' garnish – but I can't find a firm number. Most sources simply say 'over a hundred' and leave it at that, but somehow, that seems low. Looking through the online directories leads me in the opposite direction, overestimation, since every bar in town, plus a few random consulting firms, seem to have added themselves to the 'barbecue' keyword search, in hopes of jumping on the bandwagon.

Dad and I have a long list of contenders to sample, and we hope we're up for the challenge. I've stashed a bottle of Pepto-Bismol in the glove compartment. We'll end with Bryant's. And we'll start, right now, with one of the hoity-toity places, Fiorella's Jack Stack.

Our server doesn't blink when we mention that we're on a barbecue road trip. She quickly points us to the menu section titled 'Ribs, ribs & more ribs', her hand pausing along the way to discreetly gesture to the text: 'Highest-rated barbecue in the country – Zagat Survey of America's Best Restaurants'.

But something's amiss. The menus are professionally designed and printed; the art on the walls is tasteful; the whole place is clean to the point of bland. Our napkins are cloth. The display of sauce bottles by the entry appears to have been carefully arranged by an interior designer. And when my food arrives, it is served on, God help me, a silver platter. With a dainty bowl of sauce and a twee little serving spoon.

This is just wrong. As Mr Trillin and my father have taught me, and my own relentless research has confirmed, barbecued ribs are best when the setting is decidedly inelegant. They should be served on butcher paper or a paper plate; porcelain is sometimes acceptable, though pushing it. But nothing fancier. It takes patience and a single-minded fanaticism to cook ribs properly, so any frippery is, I always fear, a signal that the proprietor has something on his or her mind other than the meat, and has quite possibly resorted to the microwave and Liquid Smoke.

I take my first bite, wincing, calculating how much Coke I'll need to wash away the … Oh. Never mind. These are some good ribs: a rich flavour; a subtle, buttery edge; an agreeably robust sauce. I sample the various meats on my silver platter and think, well, maybe the people in this city really do know what they're doing.

I look over to Dad for validation, but he volunteers no opinion. When I pry, he offers a shrug that the casual observer might mistake for carefree indifference. But from years of experience in deciphering the precise posture and rhythm of this gesture, I understand the true meaning: disappointment.

Out of courtesy, or perhaps pity, he waits until we're back in the car to explain, with a sigh: 'They just weren't that tender.'

'Would you throw rocks at it?' I ask, channelling Mr Trillin.

'Well …' he pauses, then chuckles. 'I suppose I would not throw rocks at that barbecue.'

The next morning, a haze hangs in the air everywhere we turn, taunting us, tempting us. Outside a gas station on a forlorn stretch of State Line Road, we see a man – at least, we guess it's a man, though his face is obscured by a thick grey cloud – stoking the fire inside a homemade smoker built from half a rusted fifty-gallon drum. We make a mental note to come back later.

The haze follows us to Country Club Plaza, where there's an outlet of Gates Bar-B-Q. But we're not ready to eat yet – the architect wants to take a stroll around this historic shopping district, see the buildings. It's a discordant place, part mall, part Seville-on-the-Plains, full of Spanish-influenced buildings and an overabundance of courtyards, fountains and statues. We spot an aggressively hip Italian restaurant, of the variety that Mr Trillin mockingly calls 'La Maison de la Casa House', full of pretty people eating pretty food – and not seeming to be enjoying themselves one bit.

Our stomachs grumble out of pity for them and we head back to the car, then west out on Merriam Lane, a highway with a distinctly desolate, backwoods feel, to Kansas City. Just when we're starting to wonder if we're lost, we spot the haze again and follow it to our destination. The setting here is much more along the lines of what we've dreamed of all these years: an endearingly deteriorated house with a brick patio out front and, standing sentinel on the side, a massive brick smoker, its doors held shut by a hatchet jammed between the two handles.

Woodyard Bar-B-Que is just that: a wood yard selling oak, hickory, apple and other types of wood for those who want to do their own cooking. In the 1950s, the father and grandfather of the current proprietor, Frank Schloegel IV, would grill lunch for customers who came to buy wood; eventually, due to popular demand, the barbecue business became official.

Mr Schloegel IV is standing behind the counter when we arrive, amiably chatting with the customers. When we mention where we're from, he points towards a group of motorcyclists pulling out of the parking lot. 'Those guys came down from Owatonna' – a town in southern Minnesota – 'just for lunch.' Dad and I exchange arched eyebrows, impressed.

As we settle in, we realise we might never leave. There's a subdued conviviality among the employees and our fellow eaters, and as we sit on the shaded, almost overgrown brick patio, we feel for all the world like we're at the best backyard cookout ever, just chatting with friends, enjoying the summer day. The food makes it all the more idyllic. The meat has a complexity I've never experienced before, a seductive, subtle fruitiness that initially catches me off-guard but quickly wins me over. That telltale gleam of delight creeps into Dad's eyes as he eats, and within an embarrassingly short period of time our paper-lined plastic baskets go from overflowing with meat – ribs, burnt ends, pulled pork and chicken – to being merely abstract art of sauce and grease splotches. Dad still isn't ready to crown a new rib champ, but he has no quibbles.

We nurse the last drops of our house-made lemonade, looking for every excuse to linger, inhaling the heady smell of the smoker, bantering with Mr Schloegel, and comparing notes and napkin-counts with the barbecue aficionados at the other tables. When we eventually depart, it is with a series of sauce-stained waves.

In the parking lot at Woodyard, Dad re-teaches me one of the great things about the barbecue: it is, perhaps, the most egalitarian of foods, beloved by people from all walks of life. Drool is a great equaliser. See those cars next to each other, the shiny convertible and the broken-down jalopy? That's a sure sign of good food.

———◖═

We're pleased, then, to see the same thing outside our dinner destination, B.B.'s Lawnside BBQ, where there are an equal number of beaters and Beamers.

We're hoping for some music to go with our meal. Kansas City is, after all, one of the birthplaces of jazz, Dad's favourite music to go with his favourite food, and B.B.'s has a reputation for its live acts. But we arrive just after one show has ended and the next band, scheduled to start hours later, is just setting up. No matter: we'll settle in for what we hope will be a long, glorious night.

Our server is – yet again – all too eager to give us a tutorial on her restaurant's offerings. 'You'll want the ribs, of course,' she says. She looks us over for a moment, sizing up these two skinny, dorky, out-of-their-element-looking guys. 'You should probably just split a full rack, and *maaaybe* a couple of sides.'

We're not sure whether to be offended by this judgement, but when the platter arrives, we're grateful. The slab is roughly the size of a surfboard. But we make room. For this, we will always have room. The ribs are surprisingly light and perfectly charred, and tender, Dad notes, nice and tender, though he's still – *still!* – not entirely won over. (I am, but who am I to question the master?)

Midway through the meal, the meat hits an unfamiliar note on my palate, one that I want to characterise, somehow, as wistful. After a few moments of thought and a gulp of my local Boulevard beer, I realise it's not the taste that's getting to me, it's the whole experience. I'm having, as I did in the car, a neo-Proustian moment, except it's more bittersweet than comforting or delightful.

We're here, finally, doing the trip that we've always planned. And somehow this fulfilment of my childhood dream seems like final, uncomfortable closure on my childhood. I'm the one drinking beer and Dad, recently diagnosed as being gluten intolerant, is the one who cannot imbibe. I'm arguing with him about who will pay for the meals (though he won't let me). I'm noticing, for the first time, his slyly sarcastic side – and the slight hobbling, with age, of his proud runner's gait.

The band begins its sound check, rousing me from my melancholy musings. A blues harmonica player named Rockin' Jake wanders through the restaurant, wailing away. Dad smiles, and I gesture to him that he has a piece of meat stuck in his teeth.

It's awfully tempting to stay. Here we have the perfect roadhouse atmosphere (slightly rundown but cheery, walls covered with concert posters and beer signs, floor packed with tables), and even a couple of ribs left. As I eye them, wondering if I have room for just one more bite, Dad utters words that I never thought would pass his lips: 'We might be overdoing this. I hope we're not tired of barbecued ribs by the time we get to Arthur Bryant's.'

This is a problem. Years of anticipation, and now we're wimping out? What about all the contenders we're going to have to skip?

But Dad's right. We're stuffed. I'm desperate for some of the Pepto-Bismol stashed in the car. And we absolutely have to save room for Bryant's.

So we're sorry, Gates Bar-B-Q. Apologies, Oklahoma Joe's. Mea culpa, Danny Edwards and Hayward's and Rosedale and LC's and that guy with the sidewalk stand on State Line Road. It breaks my heart, but we won't be stopping by, at least not this time around.

Sunday morning starts with the weirdest thing, although maybe it shouldn't be surprising after last night: Dad and I talk. Not just about barbecued ribs but about life, everything. We stroll around the grounds of the Nelson Atkins Museum of Art. We sit in a public garden and chat for a good hour, enjoying the tranquil stillness of our surroundings and the ease of our far-ranging discourse. There are no earth-shattering epiphanies, just good, adult conversation of the variety that we haven't had since I became, well, an adult.

Eventually, though, the subject returns to food. We talk about the joys and disappointments of the places we've been in the last two days – Dad's still not sure he's tasted anything better than his favourite barbecue joint in Minneapolis. This only makes me more eager to get to Arthur Bryant's. Dad is patient, savouring the anticipation, but I'm willing time forward, like a student waiting for recess: *hurry up, clock!*

After a torturously long time, Dad decrees that he's ready, and we head to Arthur Bryant's. I'm disappointed there's no trumpet fanfare or chorus of cherubs as we walk in, but the scent of the place makes up for this omission. It's intoxicating.

At the front of the line, the counterman asks what I'm having. It's the cue I've been waiting for all my life, and I know my lines. 'Pork ribs, beef ribs and burnt ends.' It's this last part that I'm most eager to sample, the food about which Mr Trillin waxes most rhapsodic.

'We're out of burnt ends,' the counterman says. I'm crushed. It's like going to Paris and learning that the Eiffel Tower has been dismantled. I'm terrified that this is an omen.

We find a table and, unsure how to mark this long-planned occasion, do a weird little toast with our ribs, clanking the bones together. And then, the moment of truth.

Well … we needn't have worried – these ribs would have brought even the most tired, jaded palate to life. They have a flavour that is at once vivacious and grounded, delightfully unexpected, yet elementally familiar, like a bass drum and a snare combining to make the most boogie-inducing jazz riff. Even better is the velvety pulled pork, which was my substitute for the burnt ends – it's like the greatest, meatiest pudding ever made. Within a bite or two, I have, at last, a new standard of excellence for barbecued meat.

Dad agrees.

Looking at the newspaper clippings on the walls, it's clear we're in good company, given the lengths to which people will go to get their Arthur Bryant's fix – one guy, apparently, flew here from Los Angeles, picked up 140 pounds of ribs, and flew back to serve them at a party.

It's the sauce that seals the reputation – tangy, gritty, slightly spicy, unlike any others we'd sampled. When the restaurant's namesake died in 1982, the (now-defunct) *Kansas City Times* ran a cartoon of Mr Bryant arriving at the gates of heaven, where St Peter asks, with a hopeful look in his eyes, 'Did you bring sauce?' By the time we're done, utterly sated, our hands have started to turn orange. I want to put that sauce on everything, scoop it up with my fries, my bread, my spoon, my bare hand. I'm surprised there are no signs reading 'Please do not squirt sauce directly into mouth'.

As we leave, Dad's spirits are buoyant as he extols the wonders of the sauce and cracks jokes about the carloads full of frat boys that have just pulled up. I can almost hear him thinking, 'See, those stories I read to you were true, not fairy tales.' He's beaming, big-time, and his gait isn't hobbled at all – in fact, there's a spring to it.

Propane and Hot Sauce

LIZ MacDONALD

Liz MacDonald lives on the Central Coast of California. She is pursuing an MFA in creative nonfiction at San José State University, and is working on a book about the nature of beekeeping and the American workplace. Her work has appeared in *Reed Magazine*, where she served as managing editor for the 2009 issue.

I parked the car, feeling sceptical of Laurie's assurance that the world's best hot sauce would be found here. The yard functioned as a parking lot, appliance showroom and propane dispensing station. In the centre, a tanker trailer gleamed in the sunlight, a silver monolith standing its ground warily against the yellow Caterpillar tractor parked across the street. Around the tanker, like worshippers on a pilgrimage, stood several high-end stainless-steel stoves nestled in weeds and tall, scraggly grass. If it weren't for the ohia trees and trade winds, I'd think I was back in southern Ohio. A vinyl sign hung from the roof of the squat white building, corroborating Laurie's claim and announcing both the name and the wares of the store: Propane and Hot Sauce.

Laurie and I made our way across the lot, over gravel and packed earth, weaving around stoves and haphazard piles of lumber. Around the side of the storefront, an ageing yellow Labrador retriever lay in front of a corrugated-tin smokehouse. The dog remained still, except for her eyes, which followed us, and a slight tremble in her upper lip.

Laurie had sent me my first bottle of Paradise Pepper Sauce eight years ago when she had spent some time on the Big Island while taking a break from college. A spice-lover marooned in the Midwest blandlands, I was instantly hooked. The well-balanced flamer hit your tongue with just enough heat to raise sweat beads on your forehead, but not so much that your eyes turned bloodshot and bulged in their sockets. The capsaicin burn was tempered with just a hint of sweetness, the faintest breath of vinegar, and a garlicky aftershock. It improved any cuisine: eggs, burritos, pizza, steamed kale. Paradise Pepper Sauce became my constant culinary companion, my condiment of choice.

Laurie's stay on the island lasted less than a year and soon enough she was back in Cincinnati to finish college. My hot sauce hook-up had run dry, and like any junkie, I went through a difficult withdrawal. Tabasco, Tapatio, Cholula, Sriracha and a number of boutique brands cluttered the shelf in my refrigerator door, but none delivered the perfect blend of flavours that Paradise had seared across my palate.

When Laurie returned to Honolulu for grad school, I was quick to plan a visit and insisted we hop a flight to the Big Island for a little grocery shopping.

We stepped through the open sliding glass door into the store. Instead of shelves neatly lined with products and an attentive clerk, the room looked like an abandoned garage sale. It contained antiques, bric-a-brac and more stoves – brand-new stainless-steel numbers and '50s Magic Chefs in Easter egg colours. In the centre, a wicker chair was draped in mosquito netting. Both the netting and the chair had scraps of paper taped to them, with prices handwritten in black ballpoint pen. On the walls, flyers advertised pit-bull-mix puppies and used pick-up trucks for sale.

We moved into the second room, which contained more antiques and a tall thin refrigerator bearing two computer print-out signs: 'Smoked Ahi Tuna Jerky for Sale, $21 Per Pound' and 'World's Most Energy Efficient Refrigerator, Popular in Japan, $1200'. I zeroed in on the row of red bottles in a white wicker spice rack in front of the cash register. The object of my desire: Paradise Pepper Sauce.

I rushed over to inspect and was met with disappointment. The rack contained only three tiny bottles of the superior original flavour sauce, and several larger bottles of the lesser mango- and papaya-flavoured recipes.

'Let's see if they have some more,' Laurie said. We milled around, waiting for someone to appear.

Several minutes later, a man wandered in through another sliding glass door leading to what looked like the back lot.

'How can I help you, ladies?' he asked. His thick Boston accent contrasted with his island appearance – tie-dyed shirt, knee-length denim shorts, flip-flops.

'Is Dave around? I'm an old friend,' Laurie said.

'Ye-ah,' said Boston. 'Dave,' he shouted in no particular direction, 'some girls here to see you.' No response, but Boston nodded anyway. 'You can go on back.' Apparently our gender gave us a free pass.

Laurie led the way through the second sliding glass door, around a corner and out to a wooden deck overlooking a hillside of wild green that fell away to the glittering ocean below. Banana trees laden with ripening and rotting fruit loomed over the deck.

Sitting beneath the fronds enjoying a 24-ounce Miller Lite was Dave. He reminded me of a Tom Robbins wise man with his bright, curious eyes, deep tan, strong brow and wild grey hair. He wore his faded Hawaiian shirt open and was shoeless, revealing his toenails, which were painted red and black on alternating toes.

'Laur!' he shouted.

'Hey, Dave,' Laurie said.

'Where have you been? What have you been doing?'

'I'm living on Oahu now, going to grad school, studying communication.'

'Well, that's good, because you suck at it,' Dave said.

They caught up a bit. During her island stint eight years ago, Laurie had lived and worked on the farm Dave owned down in Waipio Valley.

As Laurie and Dave talked, I looked around. The storefront was just the façade of a much larger compound made from a series of rooms, seemingly joined at random – a shanty town constructed of rattan and bamboo with no clear division between indoors and out. Creeping vines climbed up the lattice walls, and mango and papaya trees crowded up in any open spaces. A curdling bucket of what once was mayonnaise sat on the deck rail. Empty beer cans and overflowing ashtrays were balanced on ledges and nooks.

'You've done a lot with the place,' Laurie remarked.

At that moment a diminutive man in frayed denim short shorts appeared. He had the thickest layer of grey body hair I have ever seen, and brandished a plate of chocolate truffles.

'Would you ladies like a truffle? They're lavender. I made them myself.' He peered at me expectantly with bloodshot blue eyes. Creeped out, I wondered when Laurie would bring up the hot sauce so we could be on our way.

'That's Harlan,' Dave said.

As is the island custom, Harlan greeted Laurie with a hug. I knew I'd be next and regretted choosing the skimpiest of the tank tops I'd packed when getting dressed that morning. I steeled myself to come into direct skin contact with his hirsute embrace.

After the hug, Laurie accepted one of Harlan's truffles and I reluctantly followed suit. After nonchalantly inspecting it for stray hairs, I put it in my mouth. The chocolate melted on my tongue, rich and sweet, followed by a wave of lavender so floral and airy I felt light-headed. I would have hugged him again for another. Harlan put the plate aside and, grinning, asked, 'You ladies want some pot?'

'You gotta have some pot,' Dave said. 'We've been smoking all day out of this papaya shoot, like a one-hitter.'

Harlan brandished said papaya shoot, inserted a bit of marijuana into the tip, and offered it to me. I waved it off – I'm an uptight mainlander and pot makes me too paranoid. Besides, I had to drive the rental car from Honoka'a to Kilauea once we got the hot sauce.

Laurie accepted, took a toke, and passed the papaya pipe to Dave.

As the pot made its way around the group, Dave explained the work he'd done with the place. He, Harlan, Boston and some other dudes had built the additions to the store over the course of a few weekends. They intended to rent out the flimsy rooms to tourists to supplement their propane, propane-powered appliance, truffle, tuna and hot sauce revenue streams. Just as soon as they got around to putting up a website.

'You gotta see the opium beds,' Dave said. 'I got some Thai opium beds for the rooms.'

'What?' Laurie mumbled, eyes glazed.

'Come on, I want to show you the beds.'

We followed Dave through the maze of thatch rooms, each outfitted with the finest stainless-steel propane-powered appliances, until we came upon one of the beds – a low platform with a teak canopy hand-carved into an intricate, interlocking pattern.

'I got three of these cheap on my last trip to Thailand,' Dave explained. 'They had them in the opium bars. You'd just smoke some opium and lie back on the bed and stay there for an hour or a week or whatever.'

I regretted not hitting the weed when offered. I could imagine passing a pleasant afternoon stoned and sprawled out, gazing at the intertwining design of the bed posts, listening to the distant surf and the wind rustling in the palm fronds, and snacking alternately on tuna jerky with hot sauce and lavender truffles.

Dave led us back to the deck ('Want some mayonnaise?' he asked as we passed the putrefying bucket), where we settled down on the sun-beaten patio furniture. Harlan fired up the papaya pipe again, Dave cracked open another Miller Lite, Boston wandered over, and everyone settled down for a good bullshit session.

'We were just saying we needed some new women to look at – we're sick of all the same old gals around here,' Dave said. 'Then you two dropped in.'

It was clear a hot sauce purchase would not happen for a while.

Laurie and I listened as the men put on a good show. Dave's painted toenails were mocked, the result of a lost bet having to do with his beloved Washington Redskins. We also learned that the Redskins were the organisational model for Dave's rental propane tanks – each tank was numbered to match one of the player's jerseys, which is how he kept track of them. At one point a lighter was dropped, and when Harlan bent to pick it up, Dave delivered a playful kick in his ass. A chorus of hooting went up; this too was one of the compound's running gags – trying to get someone to bend over so you could boot them in the behind.

'For a week straight, there was a $10 bill on the living room floor, but nobody would bend over to pick it up,' Dave howled. 'Finally Harlan needed some beer, so he went for it. We got him good.'

We sat for over an hour as dappled sunlight filtered down through the banana fronds and snatches of Velvet Underground drifted out from an unseen radio. The conversation floated from one topic to another – the conquest of a vacationing red-headed real estate agent who turned out to be clingy and nuts, a good dog that had died the year before, Dave's upcoming trip to Thailand for hernia surgery.

At one point my eyes drifted over and met Harlan's bloodshot gaze.

'Swee-eet Jane,' he sang softly, closing his eyes and tilting his head to the side.

Finally Laurie gathered up her bag.

'Hey, Dave, Liz wanted to buy some pepper sauce. Do you guys have any more big bottles of the original recipe?'

'I don't think so, Laur,' Dave replied.

My heart fell.

Seeing my reaction, Dave added, 'You could ask Ed. He's in the smokehouse.'

The guys stayed seated on the deck as Laurie and I walked back through the maze of rooms to the smokehouse. As we approached, the old yellow Lab stood and started barking furiously.

'Quiet, quiet,' Ed ordered, coming out of the corrugated-tin smokehouse. The dog settled, the hairs on her scruff still rankled. Clean-cut, tall and sweating, Ed looked to be the industrious straight man compared to the pack of clowns on the deck. He wiped his hands on his barbecue-sauce-stained apron.

'Hey, Ed,' Laurie said, 'do you have any more big bottles of the original Paradise Pepper Sauce?'

'No, hon. I haven't made any in a while so there's just the bottles on the rack.' He turned back towards the smokehouse, nodding over his shoulder as we thanked him. The Lab watched warily as we retreated back to the deck.

'He says no more big bottles,' Laurie announced. 'So I guess we'll just take what's up front.'

On that note, Dave and Harlan stood to be hugged goodbye. We obliged, and Laurie promised to stay in better touch. I said I'd hold her to it – those little bottles wouldn't last long and I'd need to be resupplied in the near future. We made our way to the front of the shop, trailed by Boston. I grabbed the three remaining small bottles of original Paradise Pepper Sauce, and a big bottle of mango-flavour for good measure. Laurie reached into the world's most energy-efficient fridge for a package of tuna jerky, and Boston rang us up.

Thirty bucks lighter, I cradled my treasures in my folded arms as we walked back across the front yard to the rental car, dodging lumber and stoves. We made it to Kilauea by nightfall, just in time to see the glowing lava slide off the land and send plumes of steam hissing up from the sea.

Later, back on the mainland, I got a call from Laurie. She told me the guys' supplier had stopped making the pepper base. We'd gotten the last few bottles of Paradise.

Perhaps they'll change the name of the store to Propane and Truffles.

A Pilgrimage to El Bulli

MATT PRESTON

Matt Preston is a food journalist, restaurant critic and television personality, best known as a judge on *MasterChef Australia*. Matt's food column appears in newspapers across Australia, and he writes for *Vogue Entertaining + Travel* and *delicious*. Matt has won several Food Media Club of Australia awards for his articles, and in 2008 he won the Food Journalist of the Year Award at the Le Cordon Bleu World Food Media Awards. Previous positions include five years as the National Chief Judge for Restaurant and Catering's National Awards for Excellence. Matt was the Creative Director of the Melbourne Food and Wine Festival for five years from 2005 to 2009.

I have wanted to eat at El Bulli ever since I started writing about food and restaurants, ten years ago. So much so that when I was offered the role of a *MasterChef* mentor judge on the same day as my booking at El Bulli was confirmed, it was the table for four that I rang friends and colleagues to boast about. It is one of the great contemporary culinary legends that in the three days in

October that El Bulli accepts bookings, it receives more than a million emails chasing just 8000 seats for dinner. Getting a table here is harder than any other restaurant in the world, and prized accordingly.

El Bulli dominates the top position in most lists of the world's best restaurants, and has held top spot in *Restaurant* magazine's influential list (compiled from the votes of hundreds of leading foodies, critics and chefs) for the last four years, beginning in 2006.

Even in the strangely self-obsessed world of top chefs, this ranking is seldom railed against by chef Ferran Adrià's peers, a tacit agreement that he is that rare thing – a culinary maestro who has inspired a paradigm shift in fine dining, a sort of Mozart of the kitchen. Of the other establishments in the *Restaurant* top five, two are run by disciples who cite time cooking at El Bulli as the ignition for their careers and ideas, and the other two share Adrià's principles of innovation: using food as an invocation of memory to create a connection between chef and diner at a far deeper and more fundamental level than mere nourishment. The woman I love snorts at this as pretension and good marketing, but I liken it to when we eat our grandmother's food: suddenly we taste not just the ingredients but our history, our heritage, our relationship with her, and everything that happened every other time we ate it. This analogy only lessens the wifely eye-rolling a little.

Ferran Adrià's cooking is built around the chef's desire to present familiar flavours in new and unfamiliar ways. To achieve this, the restaurant is shut for the months of the European winter while Adrià retires to his workshop-cum-laboratory to imagine new ideas and techniques to achieve a menu that alters radically each season. The question underlying my pilgrimage is whether the result of this process is actually dinner or just culinary high-wire antics aimed at impressing through their very newness and innovation. Or to put it another way: is El Bulli yummy?

I'm about to find out.

———————◀▬

Adrià's restaurant is a nondescript three-hour drive east along the coast from Barcelona. There is a strange 'butterflies in hobnail boots' sense of anticipation clattering round my gut as we drive into Roses, the seaside town closest to El Bulli. Roses is a most unlikely neighbour for the world's most out-there restaurant. The crescent of coarse yellow sand is crusted with layer upon layer of fading five-storey family hotels, and the beach is packed with kiddies, solid-calved old ladies paddling in black and elderly blokes preening in budgie smugglers. It all looks like a scene from one of those lurid Technicolor travelogues of some long-lost era. The esplanade is lined with cheap cafés that smell of frying and stale beer.

Our hotel is pure Roses too – a one-star at the wrong end of the beach with matchstick furniture and faded prints of fishing boats. It is the only place in town with rooms left, though. Note to self: next time you get a booking at El Bulli in December, book the hotel right then too!

It is seven hours before dinner, so we potter on the beach, try to siesta, and generally mope around until it's time to get ready. I suppose this is how football players must feel before a Grand Final. As our appointed hour approaches, my wife and I sit in the rickety hotel bar waiting for my friend and *Sydney Good Food Guide* editor Joanna Saville and her sister to arrive. I'm nervous like before a first date – and appropriately a pimple pops up on my forehead.

After a search for spot cream – how do you say 'Clearasil' in Catalan? – and a check for aftershave levels, the four of us cram into a little local taxi to wend twenty minutes up and away over the headlands towards a far sleepier tourist cove that was once best known as a scuba-diving location. There, clinging to one side, is the low-rise adobe home that houses El Bulli. That busy but goat-track-narrow road of precipitous drops and views over a shimmering crystalline Mediterranean helps distance the tat of Roses, building the anticipation with every hairpin turn. It was to this coast that Dalí fled the world and it's fitting that it now provides a home to chef with a similarly twisted bent to his thoroughly modern mien.

A strange thrill shimmers across all of us as we turn into the drive past a long scree of artfully piled stones, but the welcome overwhelms any initial trepidation. When I met Adrià in Australia at the culmination of his world book tour, he was tired and quite distracted. Here he is animated and relaxed, and his tanned face wrinkles into a smile as we walk into his kitchen. In white chef's jacket, apron and blue jeans, he is nuggetty.

We stand in front of the giant bronze bull's head that has fooled some – yes, that's my hand sneaking up embarrassedly – into thinking that the restaurant is named after it rather than the previous owner's obsession with bulldogs. Adrià demands pictures. He crosses his arms over his belly and laughs as I do the same. 'It's a good way to hide the stomach,' he observes in a mix of Catalan and pigeon English.

His modern kitchen, with the sleek lines of an art gallery, is filled with an army of forty-five young chefs. Adrià's fame and Spain's culinary training regime, which includes mandatory work experience, means the place is full of chefs earning little more than knowledge and the honour of working in the best restaurant in the world. This system of apprenticeship allows top Spanish restaurants like El Bulli to run ratios of chefs to customers that bubble around one to one.

A meal at El Bulli starts with snacks on the small terrace that overlooks the rough bay of Cala Montjoi and the path that leads around it. Every so often families in bikinis, boardies and sarongs traipse past on their way back from the beach and look in. This parade, plus the wood-beamed, country pub-style dining rooms full of bulldog figurines and what could pass as the dodgiest paintings from a Rotary Art Show, makes El Bulli seem like a surprisingly un-elitist spot. It is a world away from the gilt, snootiness and champagne-chariots of many French three-star places.

'Snacks' is such a prosaic term for the creations that arrive: glassy wafers flavoured with vanilla or sweet tart pineapple studded with unlikely success by the salt-bitter contrast of black olive pieces. Then there are crazy salty candy shells that crack sweetly and send shivers down the spine as a filling of intense buttery liquid peanut splashes across my palate. After these faux peanuts, more oral fireworks come with Adrià's famous olives. These virtual olives are prima facie evidence of his love of deconstructing food to re-engineer the flavour in different ways. Here a smooth pliable dusky-green jelly-skin holds the olive-flavoured juice. I bite and it explodes, splattering intense olive liquor across my mouth.

We drink a bottle of elite Kripta cava, Spanish wine made in the champagne manner. It is so fine – elusive and bright at first, more mellow and toasty as it sits in the glass – that it could make a Reims widow nervous, and we 'snack-on'. Odd delicate crackers of Japanese intent; sticks of sugar cane soaked with the flavours of mojito and caipirinha cocktails that you suck; fat half cherries coated in the flavour of salty sour Japanese plum. These ooze a combination of cherry juice and plum wine, so much so that after my second one it looks like I've been hit with a spray of bullets – spreading bright red splotches across my cream jacket.

It's a disaster spotted across the terrace by maître d' Luis Garcia. When a similar thing happened at a very glitzy three-star in Paris – yes, it's amazing that I ever put on weight, judging by how little food actually makes it to my mouth – a flock of waiters in tails descended and fussed over me in that 'look at the gauche Australian' sort of way that they must be taught in waiter school, probably on the same day they learn 'putting down Americans the de Gaulle way'. At El Bulli, however, Garcia sidles up and diffuses any embarrassment with a matter of fact demand for the jacket. This response breaks any remaining tension at being here.

Now we move into one of the two beamed dining rooms for the dinner proper. Thanks to the absence of music, the atmosphere is akin to a library reading room. The only sounds are people going, 'Mmmmmmm,' people going, 'Hmmmmmm?' and waiters issuing instructions on how each course should be approached. For each one of the ensuing edible tableaux comes with terse bullet points on how to eat it, perhaps as an insurance against diners breaking teeth on the fluid-lined sculptures that act as plates here: 'Eat this in one bite,' 'Suck the flower but don't eat it,' 'Eat this leaf,' 'Two bites but don't eat the leaf.'

For chapter after chapter, this epic goes on with the sort of breathless enthusiasm of a small child showing off all his new Christmas presents. It's a relentless assault. As the meal progresses, Adrià's current culinary obsession with Japan, with the soy bean, sesame seeds and pine, become increasingly clear. There's a plate containing over a dozen different expressions of the soy bean, from sprouts and slimy fermented Japanese *natto* to miso, soy and what tastes like milky beancurd skin. While young pine needles come candied, pine milk is partnered with gin in a cocktail, and we reacquaint ourselves with pine nuts in little gel packets that we dip in a sort of sweet pine resin tea and then pop into our mouths. The packets dissolve on the tongue to deliver a pine nut praline, a pine nut butter and a pine nut oil. Wow!

These obsessions make for a slightly unbalanced meal. Some dishes are wonderful, bursting with flavour and turning my tongue inside out with unexpected textures and combinations, like the little parmesan gel ravioli with coffee grains, a fat scampi that's raw at one end and golden-fried at the other, and a plate of 'mimetic almonds': here a wedge of black-olive-dusted apricot sits amongst young green almond kernels, toasted almonds and various other similarly shaped 'expressions of almondiness' with different textures such as the almond jellies, and even what the waiter confirms are the occasional apricot kernels.

Other jaw-dropping moments revolve as much around the produce sourced as the techniques. A strange raw little leaf, Dutch-grown and dotted with dew drops of vinegar, tastes uncannily like oysters; petals from a rose imported from Ecuador fool us into thinking they are artichoke leaves, thanks to an artichoke vinaigrette. 'Here, nothing is as it seems,' says the waiter, who clears the plates as if quoting an El Bulli motto.

More perplexing is a giant hollow egg of frozen coconut cream where the sweet shell is eaten sprinkled with curry powder. It's one of many examples of how Adrià likes people to eat with their fingers rather than cutlery; it's also an example of how modern Spanish restaurants, like the French, struggle with the use of unfamiliar spices. The curry powder has a raw spice taste.

Overall, the menu of thirty-nine courses, or tastes, starts sweet and ends exploring iodine-like flavours in dishes such as almost-raw tasting sliced kidney and a mix of green tea, caviar and rather wibbly-wobbly heat-wilted tendrils of sea anemones that look like some phaser-blasted alien from *Star Trek*. These are interesting maybe, but both are distinctly un-yummy. And they are not alone. There are other dishes that don't ring any bells for our party, like raw cockles with fennel and the flavour of Japanese citrus yuzu, slabs of cooked *jamón* fat with abalone, poppy and little sprigs of what we take to be seaweed, and that plate of soy which seems far less exotic when viewed from an Australian rather than Spanish perspective.

This is El Bulli's first season after the departure of Ferran's brother and muse, Albert, from the long-held role of pastry chef. Compared to the rest of the menu, for me the desserts lack the lunacy, cohesion and same breathless over-excitement. The most spectacular-looking dessert – called 'roots' because it resembles bonsai-sized tree roots in soil – is a jumble of chocolate and yuzu that never quite gels for me.

As we come to the end of our meal, I pause and reflect: was my pilgrimage worth the wait – and the effort?

El Bulli, it seems to me, is like the culinary equivalent of the Paris catwalks, with a new collection of dishes each year. While you might appreciate the cutting-edge nature of what you see, nothing is going to be turning up on your high street any time soon. For example, three years after their debut at El Bulli it is only now that Adrià inventions like foam-gun-aerated sponge have started creeping onto Aussie fine-dining menus.

This reckless desire to reinvent his menu every year is really what makes El Bulli special – but it also ensures that it will reflect Adrià's sometimes outlandish current culinary obsessions. You could argue that his menu of thirty-nine tastes would be improved with some serious culling, but in a way this would be self-defeating because you learn as much about Adrià's approach to food from the missteps as from the winning dishes.

In the end, restaurants are like cravats – your favourite depends on your mood and your needs at that particular time rather than which has the prettiest pattern. But thinking back on all the wonderful meals I have enjoyed in my life, for me, thanks to its reckless pursuit of the new, El Bulli has to be considered the leader of the pack. As this long-anticipated pilgrimage comes to its end, I am convinced more fervently than ever that a meal here should be the aspiration of any serious foodie, even if, or perhaps because, you will career from dishes that plunge you into paroxysms of pleasure to those that may confound or even disgust you – undercooked kidney anyone? A meal here will never be boring and will always leave you asking why, how and is this is the future of food?

As I finish these thoughts, the irrepressible maître d' returns with my now-spotless jacket. It's the sartorial equivalent of Adrià's culinary magic. At El Bulli, I think, nothing is as it seems.

Postscript: In the year after my June 2009 visit, a couple of significant changes occurred. In April of 2010, the Danish restaurant Noma displaced El Bulli in the top spot on *Restaurant* magazine's list. Much more shockingly, and sadly, in February of that year, Ferran Adrià announced that he would be closing El Bulli in 2012 and would concentrate instead on setting up a university of gastronomy. In retrospect, I'm enormously grateful that I was able to make my pilgrimage when I could. But now I'm wondering: perhaps his university will be pilgrimage-worthy as well …

Ode to Old Manhattan

ANTHONY BOURDAIN

Anthony Bourdain is the author of the bestsellers *Kitchen Confidential, A Cook's Tour* and *Medium Raw*. His work has appeared in the *New York Times* and the *New Yorker,* and he is a contributing authority for *Food Arts* magazine. He is the host of the popular television show *No Reservations*.

I love old school, hometown places. When it comes to Manhattan, this means places like Katz's Deli, and Keen's, and Russ & Daughters, uniquely New York institutions that have survived the brutal caprices of style and changing tastes – and are still worth going out of your way to patronise. Let me make this clear: 'old' does not necessarily mean 'good'. Just because it's a 'New York institution' doesn't mean you want to eat there. If it did, New Yorkers might have actually eaten at Tavern on the Green – and Luchows would still be open.

Peter Luger? You can have it. Grand Central Oyster Bar? Good luck. The places I'm thinking of just happen to be institutions. They just happen to be old. Newer, more … pragmatic enterprises couldn't or wouldn't do what they're doing. Most – if not all – of these places are dinosaurs, among the last of mostly extinct herds that once, long ago, ruled New York's concrete jungle. But these remaining eateries, though perhaps no longer 'culturally relevant', and certainly not 'hip' – and about as far from 'trendy' or 'hot' as anything could be – are in fact what make New York special. All are still great after all these years.

I contend they deserve love and respect from anyone serious about food or about having a good time. Good food is always 'relevant'. Manganaro's Grosseria and that awesome time warp of a French restaurant, Le Veau d'Or, are businesses that would very likely be more profitable selling sneakers or tube socks or designer cupcakes. They hang on – in a particularly unfriendly economic climate – for the simple reason that they're owned by magnificently stubborn people who happen to own their buildings.

Manganaro's is a bit of vintage Italian-America that people raised on a more al dente, post-Batali, northern-inflected, lightly sauced, meatball-free Italian cuisine might not appreciate. But it's a vital step back in time, another world, and an essential one to remember and to cherish. If you don't like the spaghetti with red sauce and meatballs in the back dining area at Manganaro's? If you don't 'get it'? You're just not drinking enough red wine.

There is better French food in New York these days than that they're serving at Le Veau d'Or. But if you can't have one of the kooky-great times of your life at this absolutely untouched-by-time frog pond – with its delightfully irony-free, sixty-year-old menu? Then you really have no true love for French food – and certainly nothing resembling a heart. It's the bistro that time forgot – a last link to a golden age of tableside carving, curly parsley as state of the art garnish and desserts last seen in the pages of the *Larousse Gastronomique.*

Snobs will no doubt carp that Katz's has been covered to death on TV and in films – and they will groan (accurately enough) that every damn lazy-ass food writer from elsewhere looking to cover the 'real' New York (in an afternoon) will write about their few bites of pastrami at this downtown institution, make a few oblique and obligatory 'When Harry Met Sally' references and move on. But there's a reason Marco Pierre White, for instance, loves the place – and why so many people keep going back: not *just* because they 'don't make 'em like that any more' – but because it's damn good pastrami. Period.

The herring and smoked and cured fish they sell at Russ & Daughters would be just as desirable if the store were a spanking new gourmet shop – instead of a century-old institution that grew up from a street cart. The product speaks for itself. Russ & Daughters occupies that rare and tiny place on the mountaintop reserved for those who are not just the oldest and the last – but also the best.

I do make allowances for personal history, for the sentimental attachments and wilful blindness that come with growing up with a particular kind of food. On a recent return to Hop Kee in Chinatown, I was – before moving on to the more delicious and authentic delights of the 'phantom menu' (supposedly reserved for Chinese patrons) – unable to resist the charms of the clunky, corn-starchy *kwailo* classics I'd first encountered as a kid. It had been a long, long time since I'd had an egg roll, or wonton soup, or a scary-bright sweet and sour pork – and by this time, after having eaten all over China, Hong Kong, Singapore and Taiwan – that old-style 'not really Chinese' stuff had become genuinely exotic again. For those of you less inclined to nostalgia, I highly recommend the whole flounder and the crabs.

My point? Patronise these places and you not only honour Manhattan's rich culinary and cultural tradition – you give yourself permission to relax and have a helluva good time.

$\mathcal{D}orego's$

MATTHEW FORT

Matthew Fort's food writing career began in 1986 when he started a column about food in the *Financial Times Saturday Review*. In 1989 he became Food and Drink Editor of the *Guardian,* a position he still holds. Since then he has written for a wide variety of British, American and French publications. He was Glenfiddich Food Writer of the Year and Restaurateurs' Writer of the Year in 1991, Glenfiddich Restaurant Writer of the Year in 1992 and Glenfiddich Cookery Writer of the Year in 2005. In 1998 he published *Rhubarb and Black Pudding,* a book about the Michelin-starred chef Paul Heathcote. His second book, *Eating Up Italy,* was the Guild of Food Writers' Book of the Year in 2005. His new book, *Sweet Honey, Bitter Lemons,* a food portrait of Sicily, won the Premio Sicilia Madre Mediterranea in 2009. Currently Matthew is a judge on *The Great British Menu,* and he co-presents *Market Kitchen* with Tom Parker Bowles.

Dorego's, there's nowhere quite like it. Never has been, I dare say. One of a kind, it's a sort of a bar, a sort of a restaurant; seedy, louche, easy-paced, open-hearted, democratic, with the beauty of the truly idiosyncratic *sui generis* – although that's not a phrase you're likely to hear in Dorego's. It looks out over the point where the Keiskamma River meets the Indian Ocean, one of the world's great views. It's a place out of time, of dreams, memories, reflections – and a solitary pelican.

There's a sign on the left-hand side of the main road, about an hour out of East London in South Africa's Eastern Cape province, as you head north towards Port Alfred. The sign is chipped and faded, a bit battered by time, weather and human usage. It reads 'Hamburg'. Usually there are a few goats tugging at the scrub with absent-minded madness on the verge, and one or two people waiting patiently for a somewhat unpredictable local taxi.

Follow the sign and turn off onto the dirt track that lollops in a leisurely fashion across land undulating in voluptuous curves on either side; bare grass, smooth, stitched from time to time by fences of wire or scrub, pocked here and there by squares of tilled earth. You pass clusters of huts, some thatched, some topped with corrugated iron, all painted in the vivid pastel blues, yellows, pinks and greens and bold geometrical patterns favoured by the local Xhosas.

Go slowly, with a certain amount of trepidation, partly out of respect for the uncertain surface of the road, and partly because from time to time rangy cattle move with elegant nonchalance across your path, taking no heed of your impatience. Or there are goats to scatter, or groups of people to edge around. A *buckie* – a pick-up truck – passes at speed in the other direction. The dust thrown up by its wheels hangs like a plume of smoke in the hot air; the brilliant sun shines through it in a golden haze.

Presently, down to your left, a kilometre or so away, a river, *the* river, comes into sight. Keiskamma means 'puff adder' in Xhosa, the language they speak hereabouts, because the sinuous curves of the river mimic those of the snake. You can see how the river uncoils across the flat base of the valley, the land on either side green and fertile, squared up into fields, before rising quite sharply to escarpments on either side, along one of which you are driving. The river is broad, half a kilometre across perhaps, as brown as the tilled earth in the fields, glossy and smooth.

And then, up ahead, suddenly the rough track disappears beneath tarmac and you can see houses on the near riverbank, a bit retro, suburban, painted white for the most part, a warning that Hamburg is just around the next bend.

Not that there's much to the town, really. This part of South Africa was part of the Siskei, one of the 'independent' homelands set up at the height of the apartheid years following the doctrine of separate development established by Dr Hendrik Verwoerd, president from 1958 to 1966. Except the Siskei never developed in the way the rest of South Africa did, and Hamburg was never developed at all, unlike the more famous, white, seaside towns – Knysna, Plettenberg Bay, Cape St Francis.

This is a fact about which I, for one, am supremely happy. It has kept the place unspoiled by crass commercialisation and contemporary vulgarities. Hamburg is a time capsule of white vernacular architecture of sixty years ago, modest, kindly, unshowy by today's standards, a bit tight-arsed if truth be told. In recent years, though, one or two brave souls have built more modern houses and painted them in myriad hues, picking up the colour sense of the huts speckling the surrounding land, respecting the spirit of the place.

Pass the straggling town, past Mrs May's Hole in the Wall for Fresh general store, and the ramshackle hotel, the town's only one, and suddenly the road, having hugged the riverbank, swoops up to your right and away from the river. On your left is a dirt track that continues to keep faith with the river, broad and flat. Bounce along this and it leads you out towards the estuary proper, past a sparsely occupied camping site spread out below a line of thick, dark green coastal scrub, to Dorego's.

In a sense, Dorego's is more impressive at a distance than it is close to. It's a large, solid, square, single-storey wooden building on stilts as massive as a rugby prop-forward's thighs, beneath a classic thatched roof. A *stoep* – verandah – runs around the front and sides, with wooden steps leading up to it.

Assuming it's open – not always a safe assumption with Dorego's, as opening hours tend to follow a whim of particular individuality – you enter through the door into a broad open space, dark after the brilliant glare of the outside. In front of you there's a pool table, in a remarkable state of preservation, given the battering it gets nightly from Dorego's well-oiled if not well-heeled clientele – although you do need to lift one end of it if you want the balls back at the end of your allotted time. To your right is a small bar manned by Leslie.

Leslie, in some ways, is the heart and soul of Dorego's. The place is owned by Dorego – I never learned his Christian name – a Portuguese refugee from Mozambique. Or rather it was owned by him until last year, when too many years of sitting in his sweat-sodden singlet and grubby shorts, his massive paunch resting on his thighs, guzzling Castle beers throughout the day and sharing news, views and tales of the old days with his oddly assorted customers, finally caught up with him and laid him in his coffin, leaving the diminutive Mrs Dorego and Leslie to look after the place as best they could.

Leslie is a large man with a moon face, which is sometimes hard to make out in the crepuscular gloom. He always moves at his own pace, deliberate in the most deliberate sense of the word. I have never seen Leslie hurry, even when the customers are five deep and clamouring for their first, or one hundred and first, drink of the day. Beer is the preferred tipple, cans of Castle mostly, kept chilled in an antiquated ice-cream freezer behind the bar. There's a small supply of Amstels for the better class of toper, a curious range of spirits to mix with Coke, and wine, in place of which you would be advised to drink aftershave. And these Leslie dispenses with placid benediction, never hurried, never flustered, never quicker, never slower.

There are a few ramshackle tables with ramshackle chairs ranged around the single space that serves as bar, pool hall, talking shop and, when the occasion demands, restaurant. Or you can take your drink out onto the *stoep,* and lean against the railings and look out over the river.

It's late afternoon, mid-tide. The wide sand flats look like unrefined caster sugar, pale amber-gold. The blue-brown-slate water wanders, apparently as leisurely as Leslie, scrolling this way and that in a series of generous curves between the sandbanks. Black stick figures punctuate different points of the riverscape, fishermen out after cob and grunter. There are a couple of business-like boats moored mid-stream. More fishermen. Away to the right, the river speeds through a narrow channel and then spreads out into a broad front, a quiet insistence confronting the booming, bullish, cream-capped rollers of the Indian Ocean, creating a great churning mass of conflicting currents.

And somewhere, on one of the sandbanks, is the solitary pelican. Now, pelicans are gregarious birds. Normally, they move in twos or more, formations of pelicans skimming just above the waves like squadrons of avian Pegasus flying boats. But not this one. Oddly, he's never been given a name. He turned up on his tod years ago, and has remained here ever since. There have been the occasional rumours that he had found a mate at last, but these have always proved chimerical. I don't think Hamburg's solitary pelican is gay. Like some humans, he just prefers his own company. He is what used to be described as a confirmed bachelor and, as such, has become the mascot of Hamburg. If Hamburg had a crest, a solitary pelican would be on it.

And, suddenly, there he is, gliding effortlessly down onto the river, ruffling the smooth surface briefly, waddling up a sandbank, stretching his wings and shaking his feathers before sinking down onto his tummy and tucking his great bill back along his body and dozing off. He seems to have eaten well.

And so should we. The violent African sunset, with its concatenation of colour, has turned the river to the purest, rippling, liquid gold. In a few minutes it will be dark and the sky will be silvered with stars, the velvety blackness pricked with lights from the houses. The brightness thrown by Dorego's will throw shadows across the grass around.

The menu at Dorego's is even less extensive than the drinks at the bar. There are fresh oysters, from just along the coast. And then there's a choice of *piri-piri* chicken, *piri-piri* fish or steak, the unique feature of which is a fried egg on top, Hamburg's plebeian version of *escalope de veau* Holstein, if you like. And chips and salad and ice cream. That's it, although if you ask ahead, you can get spicy Portuguese sausages and *bacalhau,* salt cod.

But food isn't about frills and fancy gear and plate poetry. Food is about time and place and people and memory, people and memory most of all. That isn't to say that the food at Dorego's isn't top notch – of its kind. Mrs Dorego, diminutive and neat as her husband was the reverse, masterminds the kitchen, and the oysters are silvery, slippery, saline, shot through with iodine. Now try the chicken. It's pert and singing with spice, and as your teeth break the skin with a crisp rustle, you find there's the sweet, earthy harmony of a bird that has lived a brisk, outdoor existence.

Not the chicken? Well, the fish, cob or grunter depending on the day's catch, has the muscular firmness and sparkle of something that, just a few hours before, was finning its way through ocean or river currents. And if the steaks aren't exactly buttery tender, as you chew, the amiable, musky juices pressed from the fibres of the meat make you realise that, when it comes to flavour, you may have to work at it, but you'll take a touch of toughness over tenderness every time.

And so we gather, John and El and Lindsay and Lois and, in no particular order, Sarah, Emma, Lulu and Dana, and John Kincaid and his brother Morkel and anyone else who happens to be staying or shows up, and me. Someone chivvies Leslie about the drinks, and the arguments and laughter and conversations and teasing and all the other hullaballoo of family life start up again, and food arrives, two plates of oysters, gone in a twinkling, the shells stacked up in tottering towers, and tonight someone had the good sense to order up those sausages and *bacalhau*.

You can tell there's a fine sensibility at work in the kitchen, a cook who knows the pleasures of robust flavours and big textures and generous spirit. And for those who can't quite get their minds through the fiery heat of the sausages or the rich, rank, boiled-wool perfume of the salt cod or its macho saltiness, there are the *piri-piri* chicken and the steaks and the fish and chips, characteristically pale and soggy, and the excuse of a salad. But who cares because the warmth is there and the humour and the sense of well-being and affection and love, and I know, just know, that this is a time and place and people I will remember forever, and that one day I will call it all to mind and write it down just as I remember it.

Tijuana Terroir

JIM BENNING

Jim Benning lives in Southern California, where he has little trouble feeding his addiction to Mexican food. He is the co-founder and co-editor of the online travel magazine World Hum. His writing has appeared in *Outside*, *Men's Journal*, the *Washington Post* and the *Los Angeles Times*, as well as in travel anthologies. His virtual home is www.jimbenning.net.

When Tijuana makes headlines north of the border, the news is never good. It was particularly bad in the months leading up to my visit. The war between the drug gangs and the Mexican government was raging. Murders were rampant. Bodies were found hanging from bridges. Even miles north in San Diego, where I was living, you could almost hear that heartbreaking old José Alfredo Jiménez song line wafting from the city's bars at night: *'No vale nada la vida.'* Life is worth nothing.

I hadn't visited Tijuana in a while and I was missing its mad restlessness, its chaotic streets and, to be honest, its food. So despite a newly issued travel warning urging visitors to 'exercise extreme caution', I decided to make a trip down there one afternoon for lunch. Which raises an obvious question: is the food so good it's worth risking your life for?

At the 'Last USA Exit' sign, I pulled off the freeway and parked in a giant lot abutting the border fence. Dark clouds were rolling in off the Pacific, heightening a sense of melancholy I often detect at the crossing, a place of more goodbyes than hellos. I found myself walking towards the turnstile just as several Border Patrol agents who'd nabbed a young man were ushering him back into Mexico. And so he and I walked into the country together, the Mexican and the gringo, one of us by force, the other by choice, both of us hungry, albeit, on this day, for very different things.

A young woman in a polo shirt handed me a flyer. I thought it might be a coupon for a taco or margarita, a friendly 'Welcome to Tijuana' gesture from a restaurateur trying to drum up sales. But times had changed. In fact, it was an advertisement for life insurance, touting, in big, bold letters, 'security for you and your family'. A Mexican soldier with a rifle slung from his shoulder looked on. My heart sank. I watched as the young man I'd walked across with disappeared into Tijuana's streets, then I made a beeline for a string of yellow taxis.

I asked a driver to take me to one of my favourite restaurants, Carnitas Uruapan, a classic, fifty-year-old family spot specialising in live mariachi and *carnitas,* the rich, savoury pork dish originally from the state of Michoacán but popular throughout Mexico.

'Of course,' the driver replied in Spanish. 'You know what they always say: "If you visited Tijuana and didn't go to Carnitas Uruapan, you didn't really visit Tijuana." '

He hit the gas and asked what I did for a living. I told him I was a writer.

'Please don't write about how dangerous Tijuana is,' he said. 'It's all lies. Americans don't even visit any more. They're scared. It's hurting the city. If you're in the drug trade, it's dangerous. But if you just mind your own business, if you're just visiting, Tijuana is not dangerous. Please be sure to write that. It's the truth.'

A few minutes later he dropped me in front of the restaurant, with its weathered red and white façade and fading illustrated sign that got me every time. On it, a smiling pig wearing a chef's hat and apron beamed, holding a platter laden with another pig, this one ready to eat. It's the kind of anthropomorphising of a meal you rarely see in the United States. We Americans are soft. We're uncomfortable seeing such visual, playful representations of the true sources of our delicacies.

I sat down at one of the restaurant's long orange picnic tables just as the mariachis began trickling in for the afternoon, each in an elegant brown suit, clutching a trumpet, guitar or violin. I ordered a Bohemia and a plate of *carnitas,* and soon my lunch was before me: chunks of glistening pork alongside refried beans, sliced onions, tomatoes and coriander, accompanied by a bowl of lime wedges and a stack of steaming, freshly made corn tortillas.

I wasted no time in concocting a taco, piling *carnitas* on a tortilla, then adding sprigs of coriander, slices of onion, a squeeze of lime and a spoonful of salsa. It was a beautiful sight, and the first bite was exquisite. The pork – simmered in a mix of orange juice, lard and a little condensed milk – was rich, crunchy and, best of all, slightly tangy. I savoured the earthy tortilla, the spicy salsa and sweet onions, and washed everything down with a swig of beer. I was in heaven.

The mariachis struck up a tune, and soon a young couple with two small kids at a table near me called the men over to request a few songs. All nine mariachis – lean, jet-haired young men and plump, grey-haired elders – gathered around the table, string-players and singers up front, trumpet players behind.

They launched into a song and the couple ordered tequila shots, and then a round for the mariachis. Soon the woman at the table brushed back her long dark hair, sat up straight as a rail and began belting out the lyrics, so that the mariachis stopped singing altogether and simply played, giving her the spotlight.

I could feel the room heating up. The beer. The tequila. The plaintive violins and soaring trumpets, the deep thumping bass of the *guitarrón*.

Later, the couple would tell me that they were from Guadalajara, near the birthplace of mariachi, and that they had been living in Tijuana for a couple of years. They were in the city for work and they didn't like it. One day they would return to Guadalajara. But for now, they came to Carnitas Uruapan every couple of weeks to eat well, enjoy some tequila and immerse themselves in the music they loved.

The woman requested *'Seis Pies Abajo'*, or 'Six Feet Under', a love song redolent with dark Mexican fatalism. As the mariachis played, she sang, her voice resonant and strong, if not always on key:

May death take us both
It's better to be six feet under
Than to know you were deceiving me

When she finished, several diners burst into applause.

'Brava, señora!' an older woman shouted. *'Brava!'*

And then it hit me why I'd come to Tijuana for lunch. Sure, I could probably find *carnitas* that tasted as good back in San Diego, a city known for its great Mexican cuisine. But we don't eat food in a vacuum, and there is more to a meal than the sum of its ingredients. Much like the *terroir* of winemaking lore – the connection between grapes and the unique soil and climate they grow in – there exists a kind of cultural *terroir* related to our food. To eat ethnic food in the place that gave it life, and to immerse oneself in the history and culture of that place, can transform an otherwise mundane meal into an extraordinary experience.

It's why cappuccino tastes richer and creamier in Italy; why bratwurst is more satisfying in Germany; why you can order salmon *nigiri* all over the world these days, but it will never taste as good as it does in Japan. By my lights, it's reason enough to travel.

After my meal, I left the restaurant and stood out front to hail a cab. A cold wind was blowing. Rain was on the way. The street before me was pockmarked, and many of the nearby buildings were ramshackle and rundown. I had every reason to feel gloomy. And yet, I didn't. Between the *carnitas* and beer, the heart-wrenching mariachi and my fellow diners' love for it all, I felt more grounded than I had in some time. I felt connected to this place. I wasn't six feet under. I was utterly alive.

$\mathcal{L}ike\ \mathcal{F}ather,\ \mathcal{L}ike\ \mathcal{S}on$

ANDREW ZIMMERN

Andrew Zimmern is the host, co-creator and consulting producer of Travel Channel's *Bizarre Foods with Andrew Zimmern*. He is the Author of *The Bizarre Truth*, and the winner of the 2010 James Beard Award for Best TV Personality.

The celebrated French chef Paul Bocuse was born on 12 February 1926, which makes him only a few months older than my father. My dad is the most important person in my life, professionally speaking. He taught me how to travel, how to write, how to tell a joke, how to 'take the room', how to shop for socks, how to tie a tie, how to eat and how to cook. He devours life, literally.

Bocuse is arguably the greatest chef of the last century. Many people judge him in that light, so don't take my suggestion for granted. Since the days of Apicius, everyone has wanted to know who cooks what and how they rate, and while Joël Robuchon has been given the title 'Chef of the Century', it is often thought that without Bocuse, there would be no modern food movement.

Without my dad, there would be no me, and whenever I think of my father, I think of Bocuse, and of one meal in particular, and I think of fathers and their sons, and of my son, and of what is possible thanks to the adventurous tug of the windward spirit and the aphrodisiac of travel that can change lives in the blink of an eye.

Bocuse, the Lion of Lyon, came from a family of millers who traced their love of food back seven generations to the mid-eighteenth century, when the Bocuse family opened a restaurant of sorts in their flour mill. Paul Bocuse was chosen by his ancestors for greatness and he began his career cooking with Claude Maret in a small restaurant in Lyon in 1942. World War II was raging and food was a black market commodity. He went on to apprentice at La Pyramide in Vienne with Fernand Point, a master of classic French cuisine.

Back then, there was only French cuisine – everything else was just great food. The world was different. There was no *Throwdown! with Bobby Flay*. There were no celebrity chefs, no Food Network, no shelf in the corner magazine shop stocked with arcane tabloids devoted to subjects ranging from hot peppers to barbecued ribs. The only place to eat Chinese food in New York City was Chinatown and no-one in America sold fresh rucola. I am only exaggerating a teensy-weensy bit for dramatic effect. The food world as you know it did not exist. And *that* I am understating in the extreme.

Point abandoned the rich heavy sauces of über-classical French cooking back in the early twentieth century. Bocuse always considered Point his master, and while widely and rightfully considered a classicist, he pursued a revolutionary idea to its conclusion: that food must be cooked to allow for the natural and true flavours of the ingredients to shine through, and that quality, technique, improvisation and fantasy all play roles in defining great cuisine. To cut to the chase: Bocuse went on to open his eponymous restaurant in a suburb of Lyon in the late 1950s and earned one Michelin star in 1961, two in 1962, and three in 1965. He opened restaurants around the world before Wolfgang Puck was old enough to carry a spoon; he opened restaurants in Japan before there was a Nobu Matsuhisa and a cooking school in Osaka before there was a Culinary Institute of America. He branded wines and gourmet food lines with his name and opened the first world-class restaurant in Disney World in Orlando, Florida, in the French Pavilion. In the 1960s and '70s he was a god in the food world. He was bestowed with the Meilleur Ouvrier de France in 1961. That's almost fifty years ago. He has received the Légion d'honneur medal and is one of the men credited with developing nouvelle cuisine (Bocuse famously claimed that restaurant critic Henri Gault coined the term as a way to describe the food prepared by Bocuse and other top chefs for the maiden flight of the Concorde in 1969).

But I digress. As a young boy, I travelled a lot with my dad, and it was through him that I learned that going great distances, in the opposite direction of the herd, was the best way to see a country, a culture and its people. Hitting the road and travelling as far as we could in one day just for a great meal was how we rolled. When I was seven, we drove to Massachusetts for a ski weekend and got rained out, so we toddled into Boston on a Saturday afternoon in time for dad to get us to his favourite ice-cream parlour for a Broadway Sundae (coffee ice cream with hot fudge sauce). In Spain one year, he insisted we drive out from Madrid to a 400-year-old restaurant underneath the Roman aqueduct in Valle de los Calledos just for a real taste of roasted baby pigs and lambs, nearly foetal, weaned only on milk. They were awesome. I was ten.

The year before we hauled ass in his buddy's flashy new Ferrari all the way from Milan to the little town of Bergamo simply because a restaurant there served up the best pumpkin gnocchi and grilled quail in northern Italy. As we feasted in that ancient setting, looking down the valley with the twinkling lights of Milan in the distance, I clearly remember deciding that if finding the perfect meal meant going to the last stop on earth, it was worth the trip.

My dad and I spent as much time cruising the food aisles at Harrod's, exploring San Francisco's Chinatown or shopping for socks at Marks & Spencer as we did looking at the British Museum's Elgin Marbles. Dad argued that you can soak in as much Roman culture ordering shirts at Brioni as you can touring the Colosseum, and that when it comes to food, a little leg work – or putting an extra 200 klicks on your rental car – is worth it.

But dad insisted that this traveller's creed didn't mean that you had to leave the country – or even your area code – to practise it. He would often remind me that sometimes it's easy to forget how much there is to explore right outside your own front door. When I grew up in New York City, during the 1960s and '70s, really fresh food just wasn't available the way it is today, but there were still amazing connection points to our food sources, the flip side of today's food world. There wasn't a whole lot of good eatin' fish in the Hudson River in the '70s and the whole urban farming idea wouldn't catch on for a few more decades. So every summer, my dad would drive us out to Montauk, Long Island, from our summer home in East Hampton. It was only about twenty miles from home, but it felt a world away. We'd sit at the dock, watching fishing boats unload crates of fresh seafood pulled right out of the Atlantic. Like paparazzi hot on some young starlet's trail, my dad and I would hound these crates to the clam bars on Montauk's docks just to eat the freshest food we could.

Andrew Zimmern

There was one big family-style tourist restaurant on the docks of Montauk called Gossman's. They had pretty fresh stuff, but their lobsters were kept alive in aerated, commercial tanks, standard ops, then and now, for larger commodity seafood restaurants, but minute by minute, day by day, the meat would break down and become less intense, mealier, softer, benign, less flavourful, less everything the longer they sat in those tanks. Time is the enemy of food, even when that food is still alive.

We skipped places like Gossman's whenever we could, favouring smaller, local clam bars. In those days, Salavar's was the working-class seafood shack – a small joint that started hawking doughnuts and egg sandwiches to commercial fishermen, stevedores and dock crews before the sun came up. It sat about 500 yards down the road from Gossman's, but had a distinctive townie vibe. Real people ate, argued and hung out at Salavar's. So did we. We adored places like Lunch the Lobster Roll and the Quiet Clam; unspoiled and unvarnished South Fork–style seafood was what we sought out. My dad was a savant hunting these places down. Remember, this was the 1960s, before the jet-set crowd had discovered the Hamptons. And these were the unspoiled clam shacks we spent our time eating in.

That was summer. In the winter we lived to ski. In 1976 we took a family ski trip to Val d'Isère in the Rhône-Alpes region of France. The first two days were insane: six inches of fresh powder fell each night, the March sun was warm and bright each day, and we were ecstatic. On our first night we dined in a little pizza place that our breakfast waiter at the hotel insisted we check out and I had my first pizza Bismarck, a tomato and mozzarella pie with double-smoked farmer's ham and a single egg baked in the middle. Ripping off the crust and dunking it in the runny yolk reminded me of sitting in my grandmother's house on weekends eating eggs-in-the-hole. I was in heaven.

On our third ski day, it began to snow, and by afternoon we had been forced off the mountain by white-out conditions that never stopped. It snowed so heavily, for so long, that food delivery to the Alpine ski village ceased after a week. Trucks couldn't get over the pass. Worse than that, there was no skiing. Wet, heavy spring snow can bring about horrific avalanches, and the French Mountain Patrol insisted the snow would have to stop for twenty-four hours for them to dynamite the pistes to ensure the safety of the skiers. By day nine we were eating sardines and crackers in the hotel lobby three meals a day. We all anxiously awaited the first new truck deliveries over the pass. There was no such luck, but after ten days the snow stopped and cars were allowed on the roads. The ski patrol announced that skiing would resume in thirty-six hours, but ten days of no food and no skiing equalled no fun in our book, so dad piled everyone in the van and drove all day across France to Paul Bocuse's restaurant in Collonges-au-Mont-d'Or in Lyon. Looking back, I can tell you that trekking to the absolute last, physical place you can get to, with the goal in mind to seek out a unique food experience, is the best travel advice that I ever learned, and I learned it from my father. He walked the walk.

Now remember, in the 1970s Bocuse's restaurant was universally regarded as the world's finest. Today, the idea that a chef's food is only as good as his ingredients isn't novel. Neither is the concept that simple food can be as good as, if not better than, highly complicated, technique-driven food. However, Bocuse cooked with a reverence for tradition and with a child's curiosity in a time when heavy, highly stylised cooking was still the norm. Instead of elaborate sauces and ornate presentations, Bocuse relied on the fresh ingredients of Lyon and provincial France.

What was even more unusual was to see a vanload of Zimmerns and Vales (we always travelled with my dad's best friend and his family) and one Wakabayashi (my best friend Clark often joined us) pull into the driveway at Bocuse – four of us kids, no less! We had no reservation but got seated anyway, and as I walked through the restaurant, I can clearly remember the images of kitchen help, women in their fifties in traditional long skirts and head coverings, running out into the gardens for the season's first herbs.

The dining room was ornate by any standards, impressive to a young man back then, and I was intimidated. Who wouldn't be? But the aromas were deep and exhilarating, and many dishes were still being served and finished tableside. The action was intense. Everyone ordered a few courses; I think the adults ordered two first courses and a main. I remember the look of shock on my father's face when I spoke, finally, to our captain, choosing my meal last as is still my habit, handing my menu back to the tuxedoed server and confidently ordering the chef's tasting menu. Dad just shook his head in disbelief. He exuberantly supported my food life, but plonking down a few hundred dollars for the fine dining version of a Happy Meal wasn't his idea of a good time.

I began to sweat, literally, as the first course arrived: it was a small pyramid, no bigger than a thumb tip, of mousse de foie gras, silky and unctuous, reeking of sauternes. When the waiter clearing it asked me if I liked the foie, I told him if he had another I would eat it right then and there. Was this guy polite or just a moron? I had licked my plate. Actually licked it! The meal, my meal, proceeded onward. I think I had four courses before the entire table was served a balloon of truffle soup *en croute,* arguably the hottest dish in the world that year. In February of 1975, Bocuse had served his famous *soupe aux truffes* for a presidential luncheon at the Élysée Palace on the day he was awarded the Légion d'honneur; ever since that day, the soup has been served at the restaurant as *Soupe aux truffes noires V.G.E.* –

V.G.E. being the initials of the then French president, Valéry Giscard d'Estaing. The soup came in an enormous white bowl (technically a *gratinée lyonnaise*), crowned with a thin, brittle, buttery dome of puff pastry.

I think I got my first food woody when I tasted that dish. Deep and forested, the soup's truffle intensity came on like a freight train, and in the bottom of the bowl, hidden beneath the consommé, was a *torchon* of foie gras and a fistful of sliced black Périgord truffles. I ate crayfish *au gratin*, and salt cod brandade served bubbling and hot in the style of Nîmes, sea bass and bream, trout and veal, beef and chicken, and of course I ate the chef's famous Bresse chicken with morels and cream cooked inside a pig's bladder, carved tableside and served like an antique, with rice and a small medley of vegetables. It was a revelation. I had never tasted mushrooms like this, seen truffles slid under the chicken's skin before, or seen a pig's bladder at all. The effect it had on me was staggering. I knew then and there that I would work at and live a food-driven life.

I wish I could recall the desserts or cheeses, but I do remember the anger in my dad's face when he got the bill. That subsided when the great one himself, Bocuse, the man who inspired the creation of no less a personage than the great (and fictional) Auguste Gusteau in the movie *Ratatouille,* the chef who has been awarded three Michelin stars every year since 1965, strode through the room to see the fourteen-year-old who was eating his way across the menu. I got a handshake and a menu, signed of course, and an invitation to return. I was sold. I slept all the way back to Val d'Isère and to this day consider it the finest meal I have ever had, not for the quality of food, which was superb, but for the sum total of the parts. My dad was my hero.

At eighty-three, my father is still as tenacious a traveller as anyone I know. About eight years ago, he moved to Portland, Maine – which is the last stop on the subway all on its own. If you hold the state of Maine under a magnifying glass, you'll see that its coastline looks like a thousand little fingers pointing into the Atlantic Ocean. In some areas, these peninsulas are protected from the brunt of the Atlantic storms by islands, creating quiet waters perfect for fishing and lobstering. I don't care how many times you've dined at fancy seafood restaurants in Chicago or New York: until you've had lobster fresh from the cold waters of Maine, you really haven't had *Homarus americanus,* the true lobster.

The very first time I visited Dad in Portland, he insisted we drive up to the Five Islands Lobster Company, a third-generation, family-owned lobster fishery, for what he felt was the best lobster roll in the state. The Five Island's food shack is like Red's in Wiscasset, or Day's in Portland, one of those under-the-radar joints whose address is passed amongst foodies like heroin junkies trade reliable connections or old school New Yorkers use to trade in rent-controlled apartments. I am probably performing an act of culinary self-mutilation by revealing my most precious source, but here it goes.

Five Islands is one of those rare food finds, if you can find it at all. You drive about forty-five minutes north of Portland on the I-295, make a right and head east on the US-1. You begin to head east down the county road 127, onto the paved road, turn left onto a dirt road and drive right up to the eighty-year-old, barn-like wooden structures where you can park and get some fresh air. Just look for the sign saying 'Five Islands Lobster Company'; you can't miss it. The family still goes out every day and lobsters. That's their main business. You can sit and watch their boats coming in with crates and crates of lobsters, some headed off to the world's finest restaurants and fish shops. However, the family keeps the best stuff for themselves. Steamer clams, haddock, hake, clams on the half shell, local shrimp, oysters or their famous lobster: It's fresh, delicious, and they're cooking it on the spot.

Enter the wooden swinging door and you'll notice the requisite mugs, T-shirts and bumper stickers for sale at the counter. Crayon and magic-marker-drawn cardboard menus line the walls of this crazy little room that houses the standing cooler where you fetch your root beer and the counter where you order. Somehow, they've managed to squeeze a kitchen into the back of this teeny space. Everyone orders the same things: Maine lobster rolls or deep-fried belly clams, or in my case, both. These items pair perfectly with their made-from-scratch dill and lemon tartar sauce, homemade coleslaw and hand-cut French fries.

The thing that sets Five Islands apart from the rest of the clam shacks I love is not just that the lobster marches straight from the traps to the kitchen. This family takes their product so seriously that they don't want a giant food service truck unloading on their dock. They could doctor up a decent tartar sauce from a jar, but they don't: they make their own from scratch, and the quality of their lobster rolls and hand-dusted fried clams exceeds well beyond that of their competitors. The Five Islands lobster roll is a singular experience. You don't even notice the mayonnaise coating the meat, even as you put the overstuffed toasted hot dog bun into your gaping maw. I am usually good for two, plus that little side order of clams.

Sure, I am an eater, but mostly I am a traveller. I am definitely not a tourist. Occasionally, I do touristy things (we took our son to Disney World four times last year), but I've spent roughly ten weeks in the People's Republic of China and never seen the Great Wall. That's not to say hitting tourist attractions isn't worthwhile, but at the end of the day, what do you want from your travels? Do you want to see how people lived thousands of years ago with busloads of other foreigners, or do you want to know what it's like to live there today? Do you want to experience the best a culture has to offer? I can assure you authenticity isn't found in a museum, notable church or crumbling old castle. Honesty and authenticity are found at the end of your fork – if you are eating in the right places. Thanks to my dad, I learned to find them.

Oh, and Bocuse has a son too. Jerome Bocuse is a graduate of the Culinary Institute of America (class of 1992), a chef (how could he not be!) and a director of the Bocuse d'Or USA Foundation; since 1996, he has also overseen Les Chefs de France, the French restaurant at the Epcot Center in Orlando, Florida. He listened to his dad, and the rest – as they say in France – 'eez heeestory'.

Dinner with Dionysus

HENRY SHUKMAN

Henry Shukman won the 2003 Jerwood Aldeburgh Prize for his first poetry collection, *In Dr No's Garden,* which was also a Book of the Year in the *Times* and *Guardian,* and was shortlisted for the UK's Forward Prize. He has been Poet in Residence at the Wordsworth Trust, a Royal Literary Fund Poetry Fellow at Oxford Brookes University, and now lives in New Mexico, where he writes for the *New York Times* and teaches at the Institute of American Indian Arts. His poems have appeared in the *New Republic, Iowa Review, Hudson Review, Harvard Review, Times Literary Supplement* and *London Review of Books.* His novel *The Lost City* was *Guardian* Book of the Year in the UK. Most summers he teaches fiction and poetry in Loutro, Crete, at the World Spirit Institute (www.worldspirit.org).

The red copper wine carafe endemic to Cretan tables is a highly unpredictable source. Out of it comes local wine that's sometimes crimson, sometimes pink (not rosé, but truly *pink*) or sometimes yellowish-brown, and that more often than not tastes of blackberry juice mixed with a little vinegar. But just occasionally, you get a real surprise.

The Old Phoenix Hotel stands on its own little bay on the barren, vertiginous shore of southern Crete, a half-hour walk from the village of Loutro – which is itself a sweaty, death-defying two-hour cliff walk from the nearest town, Sfakia. This part of the coastline is so steep and lofty, at a spot where the White Mountains stomp right down to the shore in grey cliffs 2000 feet tall, that no road has yet been built. If you want to visit Loutro (not for the faint-hearted), unless you take the ferry, a hike or a pitching open boat are the only ways to get there. If you do take the ferry, the little steep bay will keep you prisoner until you get back on it.

The Old Phoenix stands all alone on its rocky shore. Some intrepid German hiking families come to stay for a few days, some backpackers pass through, and some of the Loutro visitors will hike or kayak around a headland for the afternoon. But it's just too inaccessible ever to be thronged, even in the middle of summer. Yet it's well worth the journey. The restaurant, which is just a terrace under a trellis of vines overlooking the pebble beach, has some unexpected treats.

The first of them is the wine. This year, it's brown. I don't think I've ever had brown wine before. It's a colour distantly related to the rosé of a Bandol rosé from Provence – a brownish, peachy pink – but darker, dirtier. The white wine that they have here is fine, drinkable, unremarkable, but this stuff, an ancient liquor that has been around since before Homer's day, whose legacy probably reaches back beyond the Minoan past, over 3000 years ago, and for which the epithet 'red' is a euphemism, is another matter. It's a special thing. Trodden (rather than pressed) by the bare feet of local farmers and their wives, from the vines that grow on the steep, south-facing slopes above the tavern, some call it *kerasi,* some call it rough, some call it potent. I'd call it diabolical, both in flavour and effect. Dionysus is alive in it.

It doesn't make you tipsy; it's more psychotropic than that. It makes you slightly mad. True enthusiasm – god-filled-ness – takes over, and you let loose the ties to common consciousness. This, of course, can be dangerous. Bad things can happen. Rows, break-ups, betrayals, perilous risks such as canoeing back around to the next bay across the phosphorescent sea in the dark – under its influence you feel anything could happen. It's a last, lost playground of, if not Dionysus himself, then some other minor Olympian.

This is all assuming you can get it down. It's bitter, it's sour, there are overtones of vinegar, and notes of honey. It's a crazy wine, all over the place. At least, until something out of left field happens.

At first, at the beginning of the meal, I simply couldn't get it down. One sip, and I turned to the white wine instead. But then something happened. A conversion experience overcame me, appropriately enough, with the eating of a goat stew. What we were served was young goat, not kid but teenage, large enough to have chops as big as an average lamb chop, though with finer, sharper ribs. You had to be careful not to cut your lips on them. The meat had been stewing gently all day in olive oil made from trees growing up the dry hill above the restaurant, and in the selfsame brown wine, made from the nearby vines. Thyme and sage, a little salt, some melted onion, and that was it.

It was glorious. The meat had kept its shape and its tender consistency, but softened away to nothing after a few chews in the mouth, releasing a flavour like lamb but without the tang, like fillet steak but without the saltiness, like venison but without the gaminess. It seemed the ultimate meat, the perfect, ideal, meatiest kind of meat. Ur-flesh. And goat is, after all, more or less the West's original meat. When Homer's heroes broke off from battle or sail, it was occasionally to wild venison that they turned, sometimes to lamb, but most often to goat. And when the gods needed honouring and placating with an aromatic sacrifice, it was goat thigh bones wrapped in goat fat that usually sizzled and smoked into the sky.

This goat's long hot bath in the brown *kerasi* wine transforms my palate. I don't know what the chemistry of this experience is, but after a few mouthfuls of the goat stew, when I next sip from my little tumbler of rusty-brown fluid, the hitherto rejected wine has become totally different. All the rough edges have gone. Suddenly the wine is fragrant, focused, sweet in the right places, strong just the way I want a wine to be strong. I can't remember ever having a wine this well suited to a meal.

Under the vine trellis, with the sea lapping fifteen yards away, a stony bare headland reaching out into the night, the water turning a viscid purple around it, and the sky dark as a red grape now, with a new moon like a fingernail paring, and one pinprick of a star beside it – and out the back the silvery ancient olives with trunks as thick as Doric temple columns, and the White Mountains of western Crete dark now, a dull deep grey that seems to be melting, becoming gauzy and porous, in an analogous way to how these goat chops have softened after their day over the fire: it all suits the wine down to the ground. There's nothing on earth I'd rather be drinking than this small glass of brown liquid poured from the copper carafe – still nearly full – that a quarter of an hour ago caused me to wrinkle my nose in disdain. Somehow, it's as if it has become an emissary of the land all around us, and by letting it in, I'm letting the whole landscape in too, am slowly dissolving, as the evening progresses, into the very softness of the Aegean night.

At the back of the hotel and restaurant is a small whitewashed cell where two big plastic vats of the wine stand, the product of these very hills. Next to them are three gleaming steel vats of olive oil, filled from the Phoenix's own trees.

I've never been a big fan of Greek food – over-oreganoed, over-thymed and overcooked. But tonight I've been taught a lesson. There's a culinary wisdom still alive in this ancient island culture. Goat, grape and olive: they've been nourishing humanity for 5000 years, and they still do.

A Feast on Fais

LAWRENCE MILLMAN

Explorer-author Lawrence Millman has written fourteen books, including such titles as *Last Places, An Evening Among Headhunters, Lost in the Arctic* and *Our Like Will Not Be There Again*. His essays and articles have appeared in *Smithsonian, Atlantic Monthly, National Geographic* and *Outside*. Lawrence chooses his travel destinations based on the internet: if a place doesn't have internet access or a website, he packs up his gear and heads there.

So unusual are visitors to Fais, an outlier of Yap and one of Micronesia's most remote outposts, that I felt all eyes gazing at me as I wandered about the island. 'Look,' those eyes seemed to say, 'he walks upright just like us. He must be a human being too.'

To my own eyes, Fais seemed like a happy combination of the old Pacific and Monty Python's Flying Circus. No-one was wearing Western clothes, not even the torn, permanently smudged T-shirts other Pacific islanders seem to consider the height of fashion. In lieu of tackle, shark fishermen would take a coconut and thrust it into the shark's mouth. The only book I saw on the island, a Bible, was being used as cigarette paper.

Not surprisingly, Fais had all sorts of taboos, and as much as I tried to act in accordance with them, I kept making gaffes. For example, one excruciatingly hot day I needed some sort of shelter, so I stumbled into an official-looking structure with low windows and a thatched roof. I stumbled back out again, for the chorus of nervous female giggles told me I'd invaded one of the island's menstrual huts.

If I'd been a local, I would have been fined a year's taro for this not inconsiderable blunder, but I wasn't even reprimanded. For, as one of the island's chiefs told me, 'American menstrual huts probably look very different from the ones here.'

In spite of my gaffes, the island decided to hold a feast for me the evening before I was scheduled to leave. At first I protested, saying I was hardly worthy of such attention. 'But we always give *wassolas* like you a feast,' one of the other chiefs explained. I got the impression that even if I had been (for instance) a visiting child molester *wassola* (outsider), I still would have been given a grand send-off.

If you're having a feast in this part of Micronesia, you don't just sit down and open a hundred cans of Spam, although Spam is considered haute cuisine throughout the Pacific. Nor do you slaughter a pig, a goat or a monitor lizard. Instead, you go out and kill the appropriate number of fruit bats, aka flying foxes. These bats are such an important feast food in Western Micronesia that whole colonies of them have been wiped out, and some species are now close to extinction.

So there we were, my hosts and I, seated on mats in the open-sided village meeting house. Except for a few small children, everyone was chewing betel nut.

As Arctic explorer Knud Rasmussen famously remarked, 'Give me winter, give me dogs, and you can have the rest,' so a denizen of the Western Pacific might remark, 'Give me a mat, give me betel nut, and you can have the rest.' Sitting on a mat confirms a mental state already predisposed towards relaxation, while chewing betel nut – not an actual nut, but the seed of the areca palm – produces a mild euphoria, not to mention a mouth condition that looks like terminal gingivitis.

At last a couple of boys arrived with our recently dispatched rodent meal. The bats had rounded ears and pointed muzzles – hence the name 'flying fox'. It could have been my imagination, but I thought I detected sneers on their faces, as if they were plotting some sort of revenge on anyone who might consider them edible. The *fanihis,* as they're called, were soon placed in an underground oven, then cooked, fur and all. The process took an eternity, since on Fais something isn't cooked unless it's overcooked.

I confess that the longer the bats were cooked, the more relieved I felt. For the fruit bat is the primary host of the notorious Nipah virus, and if a bat isn't cooked long enough, it can pass the virus on to the diner. What happens to someone who gets infected by NiV? A choice array of maladies, including disorientation, encephalitis, convulsions, coma and – in roughly half the cases – death.

While the bats were cooking, I snacked on a jellyfish appetiser, drank palm wine and swatted mosquitoes. At one point, the island's high chief sat down beside me. Through his son, who spoke some English, he asked me how I'd enjoyed my visit to Fais.

Certain idioms inevitably get lost in translation, so when I replied that I'd liked Fais very much, although it had been a bit hard for a *wassola* like me to get used to seeing so many topless women, the chief looked quite appalled.

'But all our women have heads,' he declared.

When I gestured at a couple of topless women seated nearby, he seemed not so much appalled as confused. He must have wondered how I could have managed to find my way around the island, given my inability to see an object so obvious as a human head.

Mercifully, the removal of the bats from the oven put an end to our surreal interaction. There was an expectant hush among my fellow feasters. Soon I had one of the bats in my hands, and then I was making an incision in its furry breast.

The meat didn't have the sweet flavour I would have expected from a creature whose diet is exclusively fruit. It tasted more like what I would have expected from a creature whose diet is exclusively formaldehyde. Indeed, I found myself wondering whether formaldehyde was being used as a bat marinade on the island.

I ate the breast, then pushed aside the rest of the bat, mumbling something about how I preferred the meat even to that of monitor lizard.

But you've hardly begun to eat it, my hosts protested. They pointed to the bat's hairy glandular pouches and large pharyngeal sacs, then made smacking sounds with their lips. They pointed to the bat's wings and elongated external ears, and made even louder smacking sounds. Even the dorsal and pectoral flight muscles inspired them to smack their lips.

Well, at least nothing goes to waste around here, I told myself, and began nibbling on various parts of bat anatomy.

The ears weren't bad. Not bad at all. No, they were downright awful. They tasted like they'd never been irrigated or even cleaned. Also, they left me with a mouthful of fur. As for the wings, they had the texture and perhaps even the flavour of monofilament.

Just when I thought my culinary trials had come to an end, the wizened elder seated next to me pointed to my bat's penis, and with a certain universal gesture, he indicated that it would put lead in my pencil. Yet another gesture indicated that I should eat it.

Now, I've dined on plenty of exotic foods in my travels – smoked kitten in Borneo, seal eye in Nunavik, big-ass ant *(hormigas culonas)* in Colombia, half-digested stomach contents of a walrus in East Greenland and lutefisk in Minnesota – but I'd never eaten bat dick before. I can't say that the prospect of eating it now appealed to me.

The elder repeated the aforementioned universal gesture, flashing me a lascivious grin. Even though I didn't want any more lead in my pencil, I figured I'd be offending my hosts if I refused to eat the bat's penis. Also, every traveller's mantra is (or should be): Eat what your hosts eat, and then you'll understand them a lot better.

So, with a quick flick of my knife, I sliced off the bat's organ of generation, popped it in my mouth, chewed and then swallowed what tasted like a piece of leather soaked in Angostura bitters. No, I'm being overly kind. The organ in question tasted like a concentrate of uric acid wrapped in old tyre tread.

The feast went on, but I didn't feel like approaching any of the scantily clad women seated around me for a postprandial liaison. The bat's pièce de résistance, so to speak, had no more effect on me than if I had eaten a bowl of vanilla yoghurt.

A few hours later, the feast was over. As I was heading back to my tent, a teenage boy with a buzz cut approached me. 'That was gross,' he said.

'What was gross?' I asked him.

'Eating your *fanihi*'s penis,' he observed. His face was contorted into a grimace.

'But I thought it was the custom around here.'

'Maybe long ago, but not any more. Well, a few old guys might still do it, but they'd get better results if they just watched a porn video.'

Only connect, said English novelist E. M. Forster. At least I'd connected with one person, the wizened elder, and validated a time-honoured tradition in his eyes. Unless, of course, that elder had been pulling my leg. Might he have made a bet with his friends that he could convince the gullible American to eat a fruit bat's penis? It didn't seem altogether out of the question ...

That night I hardly slept a wink. There seemed to be something trapped in my stomach. Something that desperately wanted out. Around 3am, I got up, staggered out of my tent, and liberated it, whereupon I imagined a furry creature suddenly rising from the ground and fluttering off into the night on big dark wings.

Long Live the King

JOHN T. NEWMAN

John T. Newman was born in Gary, Indiana, but by the time he was three years old, his family had returned to California, where their roots go back to before the Gold Rush. He grew up in, and around, the San Francisco Bay Area and holds a BA from the University of California at Santa Cruz and an MFA from San José State University. He has travelled all over the world, and spent a period of ten years, when he was working for a scuba diving magazine, travelling exclusively in tropical countries. He is the author of *Scuba Diving and Snorkeling for Dummies*, and dozens of travel stories. He currently lives in Santa Cruz, California, with his wife and seven cats.

There it was again. That insidious undertone beneath the faint scent of nutmeg, cloves and sacred jasmine drifting across the deck. The reek of decomposing flesh. The stench of death.

I couldn't come up with many rational explanations. Some compound of sulphur dioxide drifting across the narrow channel from the chuffing black volcanic cone of Gunung Api? But the cloud belching from the gut of the caldera was drifting *away* from our anchorage. The breeze was coming from Neira island – carrying its mysterious aromas, the warbling cry of the muezzin calling the Muslim faithful to evening prayers, and the harsh squabbling of parrots from the green darkening slopes. Perhaps the flower of some species of *Rafflesia*, a plant that is pollinated by flies and produces a giant blossom that smells like rotting meat? *Rafflesia* are native to Kalimantan, 700 miles to the west, but I'm not sure they even grow here in the Banda Islands.

That these tiny islands in the tepid equatorial waters of the Western Pacific are home to fantastically exotic flora is axiomatic. These are the legendary Spice Islands. It was these mythic, fecund groves that Columbus was seeking when he stumbled onto the New World. It was here that the Portuguese, the Dutch and the English battled for control of the world's only source of mace, cloves and nutmeg in the seventeenth century, staining the soil, and the sea, with blood – each other's and that of the indigenous people. It was on these little islands that the legendary fortune of the Dutch East India Company was built. It was for these islands that the Dutch traded Manhattan to the English.

Today the native spices are no longer so rare. They are grown in tropical countries all over the world and the Bandas are largely forgotten, except for the occasional tourist. Most of these are scuba divers – underwater the Bandas are even more dazzling and exotic than they are topside. We were among them. We'd flown into Ambon from Bali to board the MV *Pindito*, a 124-foot *pinisi*-type schooner converted to a liveaboard dive boat. *Pindito* books most of its clientele from Europe. With the exception of Smiley, the photographer, and myself, our group was entirely Swiss. We'd spent the previous three days working our way down to the Bandas, a dozen small islands surrounded by deep ocean, 160 miles south-east of Ambon, diving some of the most dazzling coral gardens in the tropical Pacific along the way. On the fourth day, we dropped anchor in the harbour of Bandaneira, the capital and largest town. The setting sun washed the towering nimbus that loomed over Gunung Api in shades of pale peach and apricot. The harbour, still as a summer lake, was awash in the drifting enigmatic scents of heaven, and horror.

I went below to join the rest of the passengers in the lounge for a dinner of fresh fish, rice and veggies. For dessert we were presented with a large bowl of what looked like miniature eggplants, and which the Indonesians called, without a trace of equivocation, the Queen of fruits: the mangosteen. The mangosteen tree doesn't grow in places where the temperature dips below four degrees Celsius. It doesn't even do well below fifteen. The fruit doesn't travel well, either, so fresh mangosteens are not well known outside of the tropics. Like the rest of the spectrum of toothsome equatorial produce, it is different enough from its temperate cousins to defy comparison. The rind is purple and leathery. The flesh is segmented like a tangerine, but as white as a lily and not nearly as acidic. The taste is flowery with buttery caramel overtones – in other words, ineffably exquisite and orgasmically delicious. Smiley and I wolfed nearly the whole bowl in a spontaneous gustatory blitz-orgy.

'Wow,' Smiley said, 'if that's the Queen of fruits, I wonder what the King is?'

Peter, our host and dive master, chuckled and scratched his stubbled cheek. 'That's durian,' he informed us. 'Durian is King of fruits.'

'Can we get some?'

'Probably, but durian, it is not like this one. Durian takes some getting used to.'

'King of fruits,' Smiley mumbled. 'Wow.'

———————⋹

At dawn, the eastern sky showed the swollen purple of an ugly bruise, and the day quickly deteriorated into the kind of prodigious downpour that occurs only in that narrow belt of boiling atmosphere within a few degrees of the equator. Fantastic cascades of tepid coffee-coloured water gushed from every gutter, drain and downspout, and ran in muddy rivers through the streets. By afternoon the rain had cleared and the sky was bright blue, and we decided to tour the town of Bandaneira. I wanted to make a phone call home, so Peter gave me directions to the post office, where the island's only public phone could be found. We agreed to meet in an hour at the open-air market near the dock.

I ambled through the narrow streets past tidy homes surrounded by gardens spilling over with nutmeg, clove, orchids and giant flaming crotons. On a sunny afternoon, Bandaneira seemed a peaceful and prosperous place. The post office was at the top of the hill, in a small, prosaic concrete building. The walls inside were painted pale green and hung with the stern portraits of government officials back in Jakarta, in Nehru jackets and those caps that look like an inverted canoe. There was a single counter. A few flies circled endlessly in the middle of the room. A postal official slumped at his desk in the heat. He nodded to me, and when I picked up the phone, he smiled faintly and closed his eyes again.

When I'd finished my call, I headed down the hill for the market. Before I'd gone far, I was being trailed by half a dozen local kids. They trooped along behind me at a safe distance, giggling and clowning, and chattering in their own tongue.

I glanced over my shoulder and waved. 'Good afternoon,' I said.

One little man in a baggy T-shirt and filthy red shorts stepped forward and assumed what looked like a wrestler's crouch.

'Hollywood!' he declared, as if he were challenging me to a match to once-and-for-all redress the cinematic insults my home state had foisted on the world. But it would hardly be fair. I outweighed him by at least 140 pounds. Still, he was a tough-looking little guy.

'Do you speak English?' I asked.

'Hollywood!' he repeated, and they all erupted in gales of shrill laughter.

I started down the hill again and they shadowed me. A man on a beat-up bicycle laboured up the hill with a big basket tied to the fender behind the seat. I passed a yard with a prodigious flamboyant tree ablaze with scarlet blossoms. Scents drifted on the air: jasmine, and damp earth, and something else – the faint stench of putrefaction again.

It didn't seem like my juvenile escort spoke much English, but I thought it worth a try. I stopped and turned to the kids.

'What's that smell?' I said, grimacing and holding my nose. 'What stinks like that?'

The little fellow in the red shorts took a boxer's stance, his fists held low.

'Rambo!' he shouted, and they all collapsed in rollicking hilarity.

I didn't necessarily disagree with his critical opinion, but I didn't remember the film emitting an actual odour. I waved to them and continued down the hill to the market. They followed along for a block or two, but when I ignored them they finally lost interest and scampered off.

The open-air market was two rows of plywood booths under shade cloth, hung with bright banners and coloured flags. The stalls and the alley between them were crowded with shoppers examining baskets of rice, beans and lentils. Stacks of rangy new-butchered meats teemed with green flies. Children offered scruffy parrots and shoddy handicrafts for sale. Skinny forlorn dogs wandered through the crowd. I found Roland and Katarina, two of the Swiss travellers, at a booth haggling over batik sarongs. Smiley was nearby snapping pictures.

We worked our way through the crowd. The stalls ended near the dock, where a produce merchant was doing a brisk trade. His wares were displayed in hanging bunches, heaped in baskets and spread out on sheets of cardboard on the ground. A whole galaxy of succulent tropical exotics appeared: bright yellow star fruit and mangoes, stacks of emerald avocados, half a dozen varieties of unfamiliar citrus, snake fruit, jack fruit, pineapple, sapodillas, pomegranate and great fuzzy bunches of crimson rambutan, a fruit with sweet, pearly flesh and the delicate nose of rose petals – a scent that unfortunately was impossible to appreciate at that moment because the mysterious stench was back, with a vengeance. I was contemplating buying a bag of mangosteens when Smiley elbowed me.

'Check it out,' he said, pointing at a dozen oblate spheroids at the merchant's feet. 'The King of fruits.'

'Doesn't look all that regal, does it?' I said.

They were pale green, about the size and shape of a cantaloupe, and the skin was covered with a dense thicket of silvery thorns, like an overgrown hedgehog.

'I'm going to buy one,' Smiley declared, but Roland, who was already haggling with the merchant for one of the prickly potentates, offered to share his with us. He reached some agreement with the seller, hoisted one of the spiky monarchs and put it in his bag. As we returned to the boat in the lengthening shadows, the stink followed us.

Back on deck, with an hour to dinner, Roland decided that morsels of his princely produce would serve nicely as hors d'oeuvres. He got the durian from his bag, fished out his big clasp knife and split the thing open to reveal a pale custard-like flesh – and the answer to the olfactory mystery that had haunted me since my arrival in the Bandas.

When I was a child I lived in a rural area near the town of Sebastopol, California. The region was mostly farms and apple orchards back then. There were no sewer lines; everybody who had indoor plumbing had a septic tank. Our neighbours up the road were once forced to dig theirs up to make repairs. Naturally, this drew a crowd of kids. We all wanted to know what kind of mysteries might be going on underground in a septic tank. It wasn't very impressive when they first lifted the heavy concrete top, but when the gloved hero in overalls plunged a long pole through the thick brown crust that floated on top, everything changed, and very quickly.

We took to our heels without so much as a gasp. I remember wondering, as I streaked across the farm fields clawing at my face, if a smell could kill you. It was days before the world started to smell ordinary again.

And so it was with the redolence of the King. Roland grimaced and jerked his head away.

The smell of the durian has been compared to rotting onions, stale vomit, skunk spray, pig shit, an infected wound, putrescent corpses boiled in fetid effluvium and strained through the filthy sweat socks of 40,000 sufferers of terminal trench foot – or all of them combined. Even the famed British naturalist Alfred Russel Wallace, a paragon of scientific objectivity (and master of understatement), was forced to admit: 'The smell of the ripe fruit is certainly at first disagreeable.' But Wallace was one of the nineteenth century's most intrepid adventurers. Not only did he steel himself to sample the legendary durian repeatedly, he became, in time, one of its champions. In 1856 he raved:

> The five cells are silky-white within, and are filled with a mass of firm, cream-coloured pulp, containing about three seeds each. This pulp is the edible part, and its consistence and flavour are indescribable. A rich custard highly flavoured with almonds gives the best general idea of it, but there are occasional wafts of flavour that call to mind cream-cheese, onion-sauce, sherry-wine, and other incon-

gruous dishes. Then there is a rich glutinous smoothness in the pulp which nothing else possesses, but which adds to its delicacy. It is neither acid nor sweet nor juicy; yet it wants neither of these qualities, for it is in itself perfect. It produces no nausea or other bad effect, and the more you eat of it the less you feel inclined to stop. In fact, to eat Durians is a new sensation worth a voyage to the East to experience ...

Personally, I have accepted my gastronomic gutlessness. If I want the flavours of cream cheese, or onion sauce, or sherry wine, then I'll damn well *have* cream cheese, or onion sauce, or sherry wine – and without the rank bouquet of an open sewer. Smiley, on the other hand, was determined to show no less grit and cultural broad-mindedness than Wallace. Pinching his nose shut, he popped a slice of durian into his mouth. He rolled his eyes. He seemed to be cautiously searching for something alarming in the basic taste. Apparently finding nothing, he released his nose – and instantly began to gag. He danced around the deck like a lunatic suffering first-degree burns, flapping his arms and twisting his face into a series of hideous, tormented grimaces. By all appearances, the hints of cream cheese, onion sauce and sherry wine were still some way down the road of appreciation. Initially at least, there was nothing subtle about the flavours of durian, and ultimately Smiley proved no match for the King of fruits. He spat it over the side.

The Swiss were unimpressed with Smiley's agonies, in spite of the villainous stench. It is common knowledge that Americans are gustatory sissies. Even our cheeses are bland and innocuous. It was no surprise that Roland and Katarina, after a brief interlude of confident laughter, stepped up to demonstrate the rugged superiority of the European palate.

They each sampled a reeking morsel, and tried, briefly, like a team of talented, perfectly synchronised thespians, to affect insouciance. But the King does not suffer such displays of informality. Roland shuddered, grimaced, and hung his head. He parted his jaws like a yawning mutt and let his mouthful of durian drop to the deck – a pale, half-masticated blob that lay in its slimy envelope of saliva like some ghastly mutant foetal horror. Katarina smiled bravely, but you could tell Roland's swift defeat had shaken her; her eyes looked anxious and uneasy, and they began to water profusely. She tilted her head to the side with a vapid grin frozen on her face, and hovered there for a few seconds, in that delicate moment of breathless equilibrium before the descent of inevitable catastrophe.

She started gagging. Not just gagging – she was suffering the violent wrenching convulsions of a poisoned rat. Her body jerked in syncopated spasms, like the victim of powerful, random jolts of electricity. She staggered to the rail, spat her mouthful of durian into the sea, and fled below deck without another word, searching, I suspect, for something to gargle with – a bottle of mouthwash, or maybe a cup of diesel fuel drained from the engine.

Roland sighed, took the remaining fruit to the rail and was about to consign it to the sea when four of the Indonesian crew besieged him, chattering and waving their arms in protest. With some spirited sign language they got Roland to understand the scope of the tragedy his disposing of this stinking produce represented, and he was happy to hand it over to them. They retreated to the far end of the dive deck, squatted on a locker and divided the thing up. Their rapturous slurping, appreciative nods and grunts of satisfaction seemed to indicate it was a particularly magnificent regent. The King is dead. Long live the King.

I went below to look for some mangosteens. The King demands respect. He is nothing to be trifled with by rank amateurs; but the Queen, I knew, would welcome me in wanton, intemperate gratification.

Mango Madness

AMANDA JONES

Amanda Jones is a travel writer and photographer living in the San Francisco Bay Area. Her work appears in books, magazines and newspapers worldwide, including the *Los Angeles Times*, the *San Francisco Chronicle, Vogue, Travel & Leisure, Town & Country, Islands, Brides, Food & Wine, Condé Nast Traveler* and the *Sunday Times*. She has been published in several travel anthologies, including Salon. com's *Wanderlust: Real-Life Tales of Adventure and Romance*, and Lonely Planet's literary anthologies *The Kindness of Strangers* and *By the Seat of My Pants*. Amanda has done story development for National Geographic's *Explorer* television series and her black-and-white photographs of African tribes were exhibited at the United Nations film festival. Amanda is also an activist for the empowerment of women in the developing world. Prior to becoming an independent writer, she worked for Condé Nast's *Vogue* in Sydney. Her website is amandajonestravel.com.

I suspect every traveller faces an ethical dilemma occasionally. Mine happened to come in the form of a mango.

I was in my third week in southern Ethiopia, during a time when no-one travelled to Ethiopia for pleasure. I was with five other hardened travellers, all of whom were there, like me, to visit the tribes of the Omo Valley, the notoriously inhospitable Mursi being our ultimate goal.

Living as they had for millennia, the Omo tribes were flamboyant, wearing little clothing but for elaborate body paint and the odd skin loincloth. But in place of their former spears the men now sported cast-off Russian AK47s, which the Mursi tribe was reputed to use with disconcerting frequency.

Mursi women were particularly exotic. They wore a lip-plate, slicing their lower lip in their teens and stretching it to carry a spherical disk the size of a skeet-shooting clay; the bigger the disk, the more desirable the woman. They painted their bodies painstakingly and wove items like spent AK47 shells and cow horns into their hair.

Given that we were determined to photograph the Mursi women, we were not going to be dissuaded by the ornery reputation of their men. We'd developed a strategy and were prepared to meet them with a show of insouciance and strength. Despite this bravado, we were all silently apprehensive about an encounter with the Mursi, unsure how they would react to our plan to camp nearby for three nights.

To get to their territory, we had driven for weeks along rutted dirt tracks, slept in tents, peed behind bushes and showered under a bag that was slung over a tree. It was dry and hellishly hot country, and the few skeletal animals that had survived a recent drought stood about stupefied, staring at the stricken foliage.

While camping, we ate whatever we were served by our Amharic cooks, who had come with us from Addis Ababa. Omo Valley tribes subsisted on milk mixed with cow's blood, and maize meal smothered in a ground-up leaf, revoltingly devoid of any flavour and with the texture of sand. In the valley there would be no fresh supplies. We had to make do with what we had brought.

At breakfast, we ate bitter *injera* bread with a rationed layer of that ubiquitous peace offering to American travellers: peanut butter. Later in the day, the cooks would whip up some peculiar combination of spicy Ethiopian sauce, dried sausage, pasta and canned tomatoes. After four days, we had completely exhausted our supply of fresh fruit and vegetables.

By the time a week had passed, I became preoccupied by the thought of salad. Normally, I don't like salad much, and eat it merely to appease the health gods, but the image of a large bowl of lettuce with avocado began to obsess me in the same way I'd been obsessed with an unattainable boy named Steve when I was an ugly girl in middle school.

After two weeks, the thought of a salad and a piece of fruit, such pedestrian expectations in my regular life, became the Holy Grail. I tried to convince myself that this was a meaningful lesson in empathy with the millions of humans who experienced hunger and craving daily. On the other hand, I understood the message that hungry people often lob back at us: thanks for caring, but you can't eat empathy.

One hot afternoon in our third week, we finally entered Mursi country, although we had not yet seen any tribesmen. We set up camp and the rest of the group drove off to look for a Mursi encampment. I stayed back to take a shower.

As previously mentioned, a shower meant stripping off and standing under a polyurethane bag slung over a tree branch, which, for technical and safety reasons, needed to happen during daylight hours. While my fellow travellers had the good sense to make themselves scarce at such times, not so with the men of the Omo. Whatever tribe we had camped near, the males would inevitably hear that a white person was doing something very strange and a crowd would gather out of nowhere to watch me gyrate under a thin spray of tepid water.

I had begun by attempting to shoo them off, but seeing it was hopeless and realising that I was the interloper, I had abandoned all modesty. I would leisurely remove my traveller's garb – boots, safari shirt and trousers – and chuckle as the men inevitably expressed shock at the fact that I was, as perhaps one of them had wagered, a woman.

Given that Omo women did not wear anything other than an animal skin loincloth, sexual ambiguity was rare. When a flat-chested white person with long blonde hair rocked up wearing trousers and a shirt, there were questions that needed answers.

That afternoon as I performed my shower routine I was startled as a group of men, undeniably Mursi, gathered around me. They seemed more severe and taciturn than the other tribes we had visited, but they were magnificent warriors, muscular and gleaming, their hair shaved into a yarmulke-shaped circle, a leather headband with feathers in front and distended earlobes punched through with metal. They were totally naked but for their guns, their bodies painted with mineral dots and stripes. Absurdly, they had festooned their AK47s with fur, feathers and paint, making them look almost jolly.

I nodded an awkward greeting, to which they did not reply, finished my shower and dressed quickly, feeling a menace I had not felt before. I was alone in camp but for the cooks, who were even more terrified of the southern tribes than we were.

Trying to appear casual, I sat in the shade of a tree to read my book. The men did not disperse, but merely stood at a distance watching. Eventually one of them broke off and walked over, standing in front of me. Now that he had discovered I was a curious member of the opposite sex, his approach made me tense. So much for insouciance and strength.

I squinted up at him, doggedly trying to avoid staring at his penis, which was at eye level and extravagantly decorated with white waves and ochre dots. There was something in the man's hand but I could not make it out. He held it out to me and it took me a moment to recognise it as a mango. A *mango*!

It was a beautiful specimen of its kind: perfectly formed, ripe and resplendent in Rajneeshian yellows, oranges and reds. Even the omnipresent dust of the Omo had not sullied its luscious shine. I could smell it. I could smell all its hot sweetness and I wanted it perhaps more desperately than I had wanted anything in my life.

Perhaps the reader will now mistake my earlier foreshadowing of an ethical dilemma for an admission that I traded sexual favours for a mango. Naturally, I did wonder what the tribesman expected in return for this small miracle, but I was willing to chance it. I held out my hand and took the mango, and waited. Without a single sound, he turned and walked away. The mango was a gift. I smiled after him and called out, 'Thank you,' but he did not turn.

Now my ethical dilemma arose: not how to compensate for the fruit, but what to do with it once it was in my hands. In my own defence, I sat weighing my options for many minutes, the mango warm and pungent in my lap. I could wait until my five fellow travellers returned and then we could share this mango six ways. But there was our translator and the driver; they also deserved a slice, which would mean sharing it eight ways. And ought not we offer some to the cooks, who must also be missing fresh produce? Yes, I decided, sharing this mango ten ways was the noble thing to do. It was the *only* thing to do, given the circumstance of privation. Think of the happiness I would bestow. How grateful for my benevolence they would all be. We would remember this shared delicacy forever.

And then I ate it.

Amanda Jones

There was a small explosion in my mouth. I felt like I had taken a fast-acting, mind-bending drug, the pleasure was so intense, so otherworldly. Mangoes have a perfume, not just a fragrance, and embedded in every fleshy bite was that musky, floral scent. I peeled the skin off in strips with my teeth, allowing the juice to run in rivulets down my chin, down my forearms and onto my safari shirt. My taste buds did the rumba; they danced, hooted and wolf-whistled. I sucked at the seed until it was white and stringy, and gnawed on the skin until it became transparent and bitter. And then I buried the remains, washed my shirt and never mentioned it to my vitamin-C-deficient companions.

For all these years I have secretly harboured the memory of biting into that mango. And whenever I am asked about the best meal of my travelling life, I'll hesitate for a moment while I scan the many along the way, but it always comes back to the simple fruit gifted to me by a stark-naked man.

Adrift in French Guiana

MARK KURLANSKY

Mark Kurlansky spent fifteen years as a newspaper correspondent and since then has published twenty books, both fiction and nonfiction, including *Cod: The Biography of the Fish that Changed the World, Salt: A World History, 1968: The Year that Rocked the World* and *Nonviolence: The History of a Dangerous Idea*. He has won awards for food writing and science writing, and has also been awarded a peace prize. His newest books are *The Eastern Stars: How Baseball Changed the Dominican Town of San Pedro de Macorís* and *Edible Stories*, a collection of short stories. His story 'Vertical Administration', which appeared in a short fiction collection called *The White Man in the Tree and Other Stories*, is his only other published piece on the Guianas.

Guiana is not a word that is associated with success. I was sent on assignment to French Guiana – legally a *département* of France but lost on the northern coast of South America, squeezed between Brazil and Suriname – twice in the 1980s. The first was for the *New York Times Magazine* to cover the civil war, but the editor kept shouting at the assigning editor, 'Where is this place?' and finally killed the story. The second was for *National Geographic* magazine and they didn't run the story either because the photographer failed to produce pictures. In four centuries of history, almost all projects by outsiders here have failed.

But when I think of food adventures, French Guiana immediately comes to mind.

The restaurant scene in French Guiana was hard to understand. First, you had to consider who the customers might be. There weren't going to be tourists, since instead of beaches, the coastline had marshes inhabited by ferocious mosquitoes, caimans and vampire bats, and the rest of the country was a dense rainforest penetrable only in dugout canoes along the shallow, treacherous, rocky rivers. There was a lot of French administration, including, at that time, a *préfet,* who embarrassingly insisted on wearing the old-fashioned colonial white uniform of his office. And there were rocket scientists, literally, because Europe had set up its satellite-launching operation there.

The rockets had to be guarded, of course, so there was also the third division of the French Foreign Legion, a fit, skin-headed bunch, who marched through the forest every 14 September singing regimental songs to celebrate that day in 1918 when the regiment broke through the Hindenburg Line. That may have been their last victory; they went on to famous defeats in Algeria and Indochina, including the disaster at Dien Bien Phu. But this new generation was defeated only by nature, by the Guyanese forest that is literally known in French as 'the green hell' – *l'enfer vert.* While I was there they had a survival training exercise in which they went up the Maroni River and chopped down trees to float back to the coast. But all the trees were dense tropical hardwood and sank, and the troops had to be rescued by boat.

The locals didn't eat very much in the restaurants. They were mostly what was called Bush Negroes, descendants of slaves who escaped centuries ago into the rainforest and reinvented Africa with their own languages and religions. Then there were a variety of indigenous people, small in stature, steeped in traditions. They seldom left their territory, and the French government, which has tried to assimilate everyone in France and half of the rest of the world, protected them from assimilation. No restaurant customers there.

My favourite restaurant was in the wonderful, crumbling wooden capital of Cayenne. It specialised in the game of the forest: gamey little agoutis, succulent tapir stews, an occasional python or an iguana, foods you can't get in many places. The restaurant was dark and quiet and I couldn't understand why everyone else wasn't eating there too. In fact, I hardly ever saw anyone except for a rare adventurer from the Air France crews.

Why didn't anybody else like my restaurant? Instead, they crowded into French restaurants to eat northern foods ill-suited to the tropics, sweaty pâtés and gloppy sauces that languished in the heat – and later in your stomach. Well, I concluded, that is what the French are like – as with most cultures with good cuisines, completely hung up on their own.

But that didn't explain why the most popular restaurant in French Guiana was the Chinese restaurant in St Laurent du Maroni. St Laurent has always been an interesting outpost. Until the 1950s it was the centre of the infamous French penal colony, and until the last of them died off, the wasted survivors populated the town.

St Laurent is a jumping-off spot. Since it is at the mouth of the Maroni River, it is the last sight of civilisation – rustic but with electricity and even Chinese cuisine – before you slide into one of the most undeveloped rainforests in the world. Also it is a border. One riverbank is technically France and the other is Suriname, the politically unpredictable former Dutch Guiana. So it is Europe's most unstable border.

The first time I went to St Laurent, the Chinese restaurant was filled with dangerous, hard-looking men who spoke French with every accent in Europe. Some were arms merchants and others were mercenaries. A civil war had broken out in Suriname and the rebels were getting their weapons, ammunition, trainers and fighters. Deals were made under the ceiling fans over noodles, vegetables, shrimp and pork. Inexplicably, the mercenaries always ordered the duck, probably because it was the most expensive item. I would have rather had game, but I ordered the duck too, which came with a heavy sauce and some well-cut vegetables.

This was where I arranged to be taken up the Maroni to meet with the guerrillas. The guerrillas, however, soon tired of me and abandoned me on a rock mid-river. There I picked up a ride from an armed white man in a small dugout, who took me to a shirtless man with blue eyes and long hair who looked, as the British used to say, like he had been 'out too long'. He handed me an engraved card that indicated he was the local French official and said, 'Relax, *vous êtes en France*.' And then he arranged to have me dropped off at the Chinese restaurant.

———————⊨

The second time I was in St Laurent I had a bigger budget, but the war had ended and the diners were from the space centre, feasting on the only Chinese food available. The duck was still the big seller, though there were numerous noodlers as well. This trip lacked the clandestine intrigue of the first but made up for it with a freedom to travel. I even had permission from the French government to enter the Indian areas deep in the interior where the Maroni disappears near the Brazilian border. There is a continental divide where the jungle streams on one side run to the coast of the Guianas and on the other into the Amazon.

Travelling up the Maroni was the reverse of modern travel – and even more of a culinary adventure. Instead of removing your shoes, buckling the safety belt and surrendering all vestiges of both free will and responsibility, on the Maroni your survival depended on your own decisions. The trick was to make it back to the coast, to electricity and air-conditioning and beds and walls and Chinese food. It was said that an outsider could survive on his own for no more than 24 hours in the rainforest. So the first thing to do was to hire a good guide, two good boatmen and a solid pirogue.

I hired a French guide who seemed to speak every known language accept English, including about a dozen languages of the Maroni. The two tall, muscular and graceful boatmen were Ndjuka, a tribe of Bush Negroes known for their boating skills and well-made dugouts.

Into the twenty-foot-long, narrow pirogue, a single hollowed log from an angelique tree with sides built up with ebony boards, we loaded barrels of gasoline to keep the Yamaha 40 outboard on the back operating, and, to keep me operating, a case of white *agricole* rum made directly from fermented cane juice, a few bottles of cane syrup and a basket of fresh limes. These are the essential ingredients for the true Caribbean rum punch affectionately known in Creole as *ti punch*. This drink wards off tropical heat, fear and anxiety with a pleasant cloud of indifference. We also loaded a case of large Cuban Montecristo cigars, which would prove helpful – and a magazine photographer, a dubious luxury I hadn't had the first time around.

As the days went by, clothing seemed increasingly irrelevant. Shoes were the first thing to go. I was stepping into either the river or the riverbank, where I would sink a foot into mud and have to retrieve the shoe. We could never penetrate more than a dozen yards from the bank anyway. The shirt also seemed unnecessary.

The Bush Negro villages where we stayed were small communities of fewer than thirty people in wooden huts. The different carvings marked different tribal groups, each with slightly different languages. They lived on the river, or *libi,* which in their languages came from the word *liba,* which means life: they fished in it, travelled in it, washed in it, and the children played in it. The adults were reserved but the children were open and full of fun. They seemed very free and played in yard-long dugout canoes, developing boating skills that I could only dream of. They liked to find coves in the river with piranhas so they could plunge sticks into the water and watch the fish snap them in two.

As in Africa, whose societies they had imitated, it was important in the Bush Negro lands to act out very large displays of friendship to anyone encountered. Without this demonstration, you would arouse tremendous suspicion.

'*Fa weki!*' I would shout, my arms wide open, my face smiling.

The smile and gesture would be returned, larger than I could ever manage. '*Yu de?*'

'*Me de,*' I answered.

This conversation was repeated ten times in every village. How are you? – And you? – I'm fine.

At the centre of every Bush Negro village was a steel skillet more than a yard in diameter over a wooden fire. This was for making *couac.* It was made from bitter cassava root, the kind laced with a natural poison that indigenous people had used on arrow tips to shoot at intruders such as Christopher Columbus further up the island chain. The cassava root was soaked for a few days. Then it was grated and hung in a hemp press to squeeze out the poison. Dried into a flour, it was put in the skillet and gently stirred for a full day until it was reduced to little dry beige grains. *Couac* travelled well on the river and would keep for months. We ate it with every meal, absorbing the juices of whatever fish or game we cooked. I tried not to think how similar their use of *couac* was to the role of rice in Chinese food.

After dinner I would choose two trees to hang my hammock. Between snakes, lizards and mouse-size insects large enough to be spotted crossing a trail from twenty feet away, suspended from a tree was the only place I wanted to spend the night. Being on the equator, the Guianas have almost equal hours of daylight and darkness, meaning nights were very long – and very dark. The forest roared at night with birds, mammals and insects making so much noise that it seemed like one continuous scream. Since we camped by the riverbank, there was a break in the canopy and I could see up to a night sky so bejewelled with stars that it looked like mica schist in the sunlight. In bed with a bottle of rum and a cigar, I would gaze up at this wonder and feel content.

Next morning there would be *couac* for breakfast, sometimes with fish if anyone had caught one, then we would shove off in the first light of day. The river was the colour of satin-finished pewter, and trees on the opposite bank showed as black hulks above the thick white river mist. We left so early that by ten o'clock, when the sun had turned white hot, we had already been travelling for four hours and the guide would smile and announce, '*Uh, c'est l'heure du premier punch,*' and I would concur and fix everyone their first punch of the day. Sometimes we would drag lines and pick up a fish for lunch or we would trade with villagers. We had rum, which was of great value because it was used as an offering to the spirits at little stone and wood altars called *obiasanis* in every village.

Once a Bush Negro of the Boni tribe supplied a skinned iguana. Like most exotic animals, it had that predictable resemblance to chicken. And of course we ate it with *couac*.

The Ndjukas went fishing and hunting at night and I asked to go with them, which they politely agreed to, though it was easy to see that they weren't happy. They loaded a tiny two-man pirogue with fishing tackle and ammunition. These little dugouts shifted with every movement of your body. I knew I could not handle the large wooden-stocked antique rifle that fired with a kick like the right hook of a heavyweight champion. How, I wondered, could the rifle-bearer absorb that recoil and not capsize our unstable craft? It seemed hard enough to swing a lantern to find the reflection of eyes in the bush. I tried simply to land a small fish on a hand line and nearly capsized the three of us. After that they silently rowed back to camp and dropped me off – the rejected hunter.

They shot agouti; these small, cute rodents were too gamey in stews but their flavour was moderated by lots of *couac*. They also shot tapir, a delicious animal that tasted like pork in a rich stew with *couac* and was big enough to last for days. Tapir was an endangered species but we were eating a lot of endangered species – to people who live in the rainforest, they themselves are the only species that is in danger.

Along the river with its cooling breezes, fuchsia water hyacinth bloomed on the water's surface. The trees on the bank were flecked with yellow and blue from flitting butterflies, and the black ebony trees, known locally as *gringon fou* or wild fantasy tree, had bright yellow leaves that glowed in the distance. In the hot light it looked like a green fauvist canvas of dazzling beauty.

But when we pulled over to the shore, we entered a world of complete hostility. After we sank into the mud, stinging flies attacked us and butterfly-like creatures dropped stinging darts; the grass had razor-sharp edges that cut our legs and if you lost your balance and grabbed a branch, chances were it had sharp thorns or thistles or was covered with some type of aggressive insect. Everything seemed to single out the photographer for attack and he was becoming red-eyed, swollen, itchy and grumpy. Sooner or later, every outsider who ventures into the green hell, from Sir Walter Raleigh to escaping French political prisoners to curious European Union officials, cries out, 'Damn this place!'

The Ndjuka boatmen made their only mistake at Abounasanga falls, a treacherous stretch of white water and rocks. We had ventured beyond Ndjuka territory into the protected area of the

Vayana Indians, and at one point the pirogue was see-sawing on a pile of rocks in the middle of the river. We all jumped out into the shallow water. The dugout could not be rocked out of this situation because the log would split and that would be the end of our return ticket. So carefully and anxiously, following instructions from the two boatmen, we lifted it back into the water and were on our way. *'Danki, Danki!'* – Thank you! Thank you! – we gratefully cheered.

The Indians lived in thatched structures built above the ground on stilts. The grouchy swollen photographer, who did not like the Bush Negroes because they were camera shy, absolutely hated the Indians, who completely refused to be photographed. He cursed them and barked at them but they kept their faces hidden from his lenses.

Trading was more difficult here. Alcohol was forbidden by the French and devastating to the Indians. But I had my cigars. I traded a Montecristo for one of their hand-rolled leaf smokes, and we agreed that I had the worse of that trade. More cigars yielded some fish to cook up with the *couac* we had brought. When it was time to go, the four-foot chief spoke with a gentle, soft voice to the French guide, who translated for me. We could leave but they had decided to kill the photographer. With heartfelt candour I explained to him that they couldn't because I wanted to kill him myself, which the leader understood and we quickly shoved off.

As we headed swiftly downriver, the dark water rushing towards the Atlantic, my mind turned to dreams of banal things – a drink that had been chilled in a refrigerator, a bed to stretch out in, a shower, air-conditioning. I would not go to my favourite game restaurant in Cayenne. I was through with game. Instead, my fantasies turned to Chinese food in St Laurent. I would order the duck. With imported rice, not *couac*.

Speciality of the House

SIMON WINCHESTER

Simon Winchester is the author of twenty-three books, including *The Surgeon of Crowthorne* (also published as *The Professor and the Madman*), *Krakatoa, A Crack in the Edge of the World* and *The Map that Changed the World*. His most recent book is *The Man Who Loved China*. His *Atlantic: A Vast Ocean of a Million Stories* will be published in late 2010, and *The Alice Behind Wonderland* in early 2011. Simon was made Officer of the Order of the British Empire by Queen Elizabeth II in 2006. When not travelling, he divides his time between a farm in the Berkshire Hills of western Massachusetts and a flat in Chelsea, New York.

Seldom has anything that I have written over the years ever brought forth from readers a truly violent reaction. Of course, like any scrivener, I manage from time to time to get things wrong, and people have sent notes, couched in tones kindly or occasionally less charitable, to correct me. A few people get quite rude. And to be sure, once in a very long while, things have become a little more heated.

One book I wrote was so loathed by a particular critic that he said he wanted nothing more than to drop-kick it out of his back garden. And once I offended so many people in the Cayman Islands that a group called the Tradewinds wrote a calypso about me with a charmingly melodious chorus that included the words: 'If you get a dog call it Rover; if you get a cat name it Tabby; if you get a parrot call it Polly; but if it come to pass that you get a jackass, call it Simon Winchester'. (The calypso, by the way, got to Number Three in the Caymanian hit parade, and is still whistled at me by cheeky reception clerks when I check in to hotels in George Town.)

But, as I say, generally speaking, nothing truly awful, nothing violent. No hexes or public curses. No threats of enforced exile or public maiming.

Until, that is, one day in the early 1990s, when I wrote a perfectly innocent little essay about the time I ate a dog.

It was, as I recall, an unexceptional and not very pretty yellow dog, of the sort one sees in the outback of Australia. It might have been called a dingo, or a close relative of a dingo, and was not the sort of animal upon which one wished to heap affection. But I am getting ahead of myself here, so powerful is the memory. First things first.

I was in Korea, and it was a cold and rainy day in late March. I had been walking in the hills to the south of Seoul with a friend, a Mr Kim, who was at the time a similarly keen hiker. We had been up since before dawn, and were by now wet through and weary of the day, when my friend – a former soldier in the Korean army who was acting as my translator – suggested that we adjourn for a good and warming lunch. He said he knew a place.

189

So, after a further half-hour of walking, we turned down from the hills and emerged from the trees at the head of a narrow valley where there was a village, and beside its rain-swollen stream a small market. It was far from impressive: it was little more than a network of muddy lanes lined with stalls and display cabinets and with what appeared to be cages, all protected from the sheeting rain by sheets of plastic.

Eventually, after a minute or two of head-scratching, he found the inn that he had said he knew and liked. Its owner seemed to be a large and very boisterous and motherly woman, the kind you might find in a Dickensian grog shop, and the two of them beckoned to me to come to their stall, and to an entrance behind it. To get inside we dived behind some more sheets of dripping plastic, and then squeezed through a tiny entrance into what seemed to be a hidden room lined with walls made of plaited straw. It was quite dry here, and nicely warm. Three or four of the tables were occupied; it wasn't terribly noisy, just the normal buzz of amiable conversation. Most of the customers were men, and most were smoking. There was a cosy fug about the place, of a kind already faded into the recent past.

Two bottles of Korean beer had been placed waiting on the table, and as we sat down and started unlacing our walking boots and taking off our dripping anoraks and sou'westers, so the owner-lady, who was introduced with much smiling and bowing as Mrs Kim, inevitably, wafted in with two earthenware bowls of steaming soup. *'Poshin-tang!'* she declared, brightly, and gave us each one of the long narrow metal spoons that the Koreans like to use, and a pair of joined-up wooden chopsticks in a small red envelope. Another serving-wench, a lady as enormous and cheery as the first, then deposited a range of bowls and saucers with salt and beans and pickles and rice – and *kimchi,* of course – around the soup bowls, and retired to an ante-room as we tucked in.

And my word, what soup! Hot and spicy and as curiously strong as those mints. There were pieces of ginseng and sweet radish and onion and garlic and chunks of a rich meat that somehow out-beefed any beef I knew. The soup steamed and raged, almost bubbling with energy. After a few spoonfuls, all the chill of the drear outside retreated, and suddenly there was fire inside and I felt as though I had been plugged-in to some kind of battery charger and was in an instant just good and ready to hurl myself outside to take on the elements once again.

I chugged my beer and spooned down more and more soup, my insides now ablaze and my vitals back in full working order, and all the muscle aches vanished clear away. I must have become different in aspect too, because my soldier-guide Kim leaned over the table and remarked on the glow in my cheeks and said that he had just *known* I'd be happy in this place and that a bowl of *poshin-tang* would do the trick.

What was on earth was it? I asked him.

And he called out to Mrs Kim – who, no, was not so far as I was aware either his mother or his aunt or his wife, but just one of a host of five million Kims in a country that allows very few family names – and asked her to explain. At which point she opened a door in the straw wall of her little café, and there in the back was a cage, and in the cage was, of course, the aforementioned yellow dingo-type non-Australian dog.

I wish I could admit that I was shocked. But I wasn't, not at all. I am as much of a caninophile as the next Englishman. I had a beagle at the time, name of Biggles, and I adored him as if he were my own child, almost. The thought of eating a soup made of any relative of Biggles, however distant, was theoretically just beyond repugnant. Or at least, it had been, before this. But now I felt somehow altered, curious, different. Drugged, maybe.

And so as Mrs Kim was showing me the dog, *offering me the dog,* I thought it all out to myself, one point at a time. This is what they do here – they eat dogs, just as some of us eat cows or pigs. This lunch is actually pretty delicious. And besides, I'm a writer and I'm supposed to try anything and everything (subject to the usual codes of morals and decency, I feel I must add). So yes, Mrs Kim, I nodded at her – hit me with it. Yes, Mrs K. More, please! And she winked, went back out into the kitchen, did something I don't want to think about or ever imagine, and after a few moments returned grinning, and this time with an earthenware plate that was heaped with onions, rice and, layered on top of the mound, a dozen or so small oval slices of meat smothered in a richly aromatic gravy.

Medallions de chien Koreanoise. It could be nothing else. There must have been a moment's hesitation, but no more than that. I picked up my chopsticks, and with the two unrelated Kims beaming from the sidelines, tucked in happily, finished the plate in five minutes flat, licked chops and sticks with equal vigour and then said to myself: *I've just got to write about this.*

And so I promptly did, 800 crisp words, and I faxed it off (this was during that strange limbo period before the birth of email but after the death of telex, when foreign correspondents like me had the damndest time sending copy around the world) to a small magazine I knew in London. After which (except for the moment a week or so later when the cheque came in, and a month or so later when a copy of the magazine itself followed) I forgot all about it.

Except that the editor, a gentle and fragrant lady – not herself a dog-owner, but an Englishwoman of some sensitivity – rang me up one day not long after publication. The letters, she said.

You wouldn't believe it. Hundreds and hundreds of them! Sacks full of letters. Never seen anything like it. Every day! Twice a day, special deliveries. Torrents of them. And every single one abusive! The worst language imaginable. Threats! Taunts! Warnings! You have to come here and read them – it is just wild!

And so I travelled down to London on the train from Oxford, and found my poor benighted editor-friend sitting woefully amidst a Vesuvian pile of envelopes and cards and Royal Mail sacks, unopened. We laughed at the sight, as much in terror as in joy, and then spent the rest of our day ploughing through the mail and working hard to try to understand more fully the near mystical connection that apparently exists between the species *Homo not especially sapiens Britannicus* and *Canis familiaris.* I suspect you can imagine the tone of most of the correspondence: suffice to say, it could not in any way be described as *fan mail,* unless the fan was for fanning the flames of my funeral pyre.

Just one letter have I retained from this rather inglorious period of my journalistic career. It came from an elderly sounding gentleman in the seaside town of Bognor Regis, who signed himself both with his name and his army rank, which happened to be Major. Here it is, in full:

Dear Winchester:
I read your disgraceful article while on holiday in Spain. I have never in my life read or seen anything so dreadful. It caused me to vomit profusely. I had to end my holiday immediately and return to England.

I wish to tell you that I regard you, Sir, as a total scoundrel. If I ever encounter you in a street in London I promise you, Sir, that I will denounce you publicly and will then give you a sound thrashing with a horsewhip.
Major Ambrose Wilson.

His name I made up. The rest is true. I have happily never met the gentleman. But I have never eaten a dog since.

I did once eat a cat, though. Cat stew. It was given to me by a nun in West Africa. I wrote about that also. But no-one – not even the galloping Major – ever wrote in to complain.

Les Tendances Culinaires

DAVID LEBOVITZ

David Lebovitz is a pastry chef and baker from the San Francisco Bay Area, who worked at Chez Panisse in Berkeley for thirteen years. He is the author of five cookbooks, including *The Perfect Scoop,* a guide to making ice cream, and *Ready for Dessert,* a compendium of his all-time favourite desserts. He has been living in France for nearly a decade and penned a memoir (with recipes) called *The Sweet Life in Paris,* which chronicled his adjustment to living in a foreign land; the book was a finalist for an International Association of Culinary Professionals literary award. David also writes a popular blog, www.davidlebovitz.com, which features recipes, Paris travel tips and stories about coping with life in the world's most popular – and sometimes perplexing – city.

Where does one begin when it comes to the origins of French cuisine, often regarded as the pinnacle of high gastronomy? It might be with the biography of Antoine Carême, considered the patron saint of all chefs, who rose from being an abandoned child to cooking for French royalty, including baking the wedding

cake for Napoleon III. Carême was so committed to his craft that
he died for the cause – of carbon monoxide poisoning, the result
of a lifetime of cooking in unventilated kitchens.

A few decades later, *The Belly of Paris* was written by Emile
Zola. It's worth plodding through this sappy tale to read firsthand
accounts of the astounding market of Les Halles in all its
gastronomic *richesse,* where magnificent French cheeses,
charcuterie and produce converged from across the country,
creating what was the world's most thrilling marketplace in the
centre of Paris for nearly 1000 years.

Weighing in at over seven pounds, nearly twice what a jumbo
loaf of *pain* Poilâne clocks in at, *Larousse Gastronomique*
provides an encyclopedic overview of *l'art de la cuisine française.*
First published in 1938, it gave concrete definitions to French
cuisine. It's still in print and is considered the standard when it
comes to defining and explaining the myriad classic sauces,
techniques and culinary terms that are de rigueur for professional
cooks to know and master. If one has a question about a recipe or
technique, from whipping up a simple mayonnaise to mastering
a mousse-like *marquise au chocolat,* Larousse gets the final say.

All these are culinary classics, but change is in the air. Les
Halles was demolished in the 1970s and all the merchants were
moved to a grey, soulless warehouse out by the airport. The latest
edition of Larousse has blurbs by – *mon dieu!* – British cook
Jamie Oliver, potty-mouthed US chefs David Chang and
Anthony Bourdain, and American home cooks Martha Stewart
and Ina Garten. Even the two French chefs who lend their words
of praise, Jacques Pépin and Daniel Boulud, both live and work
across the Atlantic – in America.

The French have not completely turned their backs on their
treasured men in *toques,* however; in recent years, chefs Paul
Bocuse and Alain Ducasse have been honoured by the Musée
Grévin in Paris, which replicated their images in *la cire* (wax).

Still, unlike those *métro* tickets you're saving from your last trip to Paris, which will work for all of eternity, other things in France don't last forever, and when three-star chef Bernard Loiseau (who completed the trilogy of French chefs honoured at the waxworks museum) committed suicide in 2003, allegedly because of a rumour that he was going to lose his hard-earned third star, French chefs went on high alert that something had gone amiss. Although Michelin later revealed it had no intention of demoting Loiseau from his three-star status, his passing made many starred chefs question the point of doing what they were doing. All were spending enormous sums of money, racking up debts of hundreds of thousands of euros in the hope of getting, and guarding, that final star that sealed their success. Once anointed, they'd be considered *le top du top* in the culinary business, part of an exclusive club, a privileged handful selected annually by a roving band of anonymous inspectors who dined alone and never revealed their identities nor their exacting standards of inspection.

(This reminds me of my visa appointments, where they give you some vague idea of what documents you need to bring, but fail to provide a concrete list so you can properly prepare for it. I, too, have considered ending it all by plunging myself into the Seine after each of my annual appointments at Paris's fearsome *préfecture de police*.)

Even before the time of Loiseau's death – though many admitted the trend was accelerated because of his suicide – many French chefs were getting out of the *luxe* business, yanking the smooth linen tablecloths off the tables, trashing the whisper-thin wine glasses, and dressing down the waiters to jeans and T-shirts rather than constrictive tuxedos. Tables were set with stiff butcher's paper, wine was to be drunk out of supermarket-quality wine glasses and, perhaps most telling, the classic French bistro accoutrement, pots of Dijon mustard, were proudly back on the table.

The *bistro gastronomique* movement was born, and instead of paying €33 for a bowl of soup or a slice of cake, guests could eat quite well on a three- or four-course *prix-fixe* menu for less than the price of the long-cooked tomato dessert at L'Arpège – which might have you simmering too, when you found out it cost over €50. (Actually, two could dine for the price of one of those tomatoes, which seemed like a pretty good idea to me too.) The success of the *gastro bistros* that opened in Paris during the 1990s was proof that guests didn't care all that much about having a tufted Hermès stool brought to the table for their handbags, and that they preferred a meaty slab of *pâté de campagne* and a crock of cornichons to a team of waiters standing behind you monitoring your every mouthful, ready to pounce in case you needed a bit more bread or wanted guidance to the restroom.

It was a win-win situation: guests got to eat well, enjoying traditional French fare prepared with high-quality ingredients, served at reasonable prices. A lot of chefs were happy about it too; many noted that they were relieved of the stress of no longer having to have four cooks spend their entire shift peeling peas, or making sure the soap in the restrooms had perfectly shaved ninety-degree corners, lest the Michelin inspectors make a stop in the can. They could just prepare hearty French dishes, using inexpensive cuts of meat that benefited from long braising, and instead of stocking a wine *cave* filled with exceptional vintages, a hand-written chalkboard could make the daily announcement of which wines were on offer, sold inexpensively by the carafe. I happily ate in a lot of these restaurants, and except for how difficult it became to get a reservation, it was hard to find fault with them.

Well, apparently not everyone thought things were going well. In 2000 a movement with undoubtedly the most unfortunate name in French culinary history – or all culinary history, for that matter – was founded: Le Fooding. The idea seemed like a good one, I suppose, though I'm not so sure because no-one seemed to have a concrete idea of what Le Fooding was. Even the founders.

They issued a statement that they wanted to 'make a statement'. But as with many things the French do, it was hard to decipher the circular logic and figure out what the rationale was. What statement were they trying to make? The Spanish had come up with molecular gastronomy, Americans were embracing regional cooking, and British chefs were doing their best to erase unpleasant memories of boiled steaks and mushy grey peas.

What were the French doing? The only thing I could come up with was that the French love organising and categorising things, like the annual meetings we foreigners must endure at the *préfecture,* or city hall, where you need to show up with a minimum of seven *dossiers* that include the last five years of bank statements, photocopied in triplicate, proof that you've indeed been paying your electricity bill (because, lord knows, they don't want anyone not living with electricity) and your original sixth-grade report card, professionally translated and notarised back in your home country. No photocopies accepted.

The French also like 'movements'. A strike or demonstration is a *mouvement social,* which are those special times when the French get to exercise one-third of their national motto: *liberté, fraternité et égalité.* So they march in *fraternité* and in solidarity with their brethren down the boulevards of Paris, somehow forgetting about any *égalité* with their brethren when squashed together on the *métro,* packed so tightly that you'd better not get an itch on your nose because you can forget about making any sort of *mouvement* with your arms. And I know a few women who've told me that at times they'd like a little *liberté* when men have tried to become a little too *social* with them when the subway is that packed.

So an organisation and a movement was off and running, and a bunch of restaurants in Paris became part of the *Le Fooding*

Guide, an annual magazine that boasted *'864 restaurants de style'*. I was immediately leery because I've found that restaurants that boast 'style' usually mean they have attractive yet completely disinterested hostesses who greet you as if they'd rather be doing anything than checking to see if your name is in the reservation book. And you can be sure at such stylish establishments that at least one corner of each plate – square, of course – will be dusted with some sort of powder that may, or more likely may not, have anything to do with the dish.

Trying to stir things up, some of these chefs started to do all sorts of audacious things. Cumin became de rigueur. I remember sitting through a three-course meal at a stylish wine bar in the 5th *arrondissement* where each course had at least a tablespoon of it either mixed in or featured somewhere on the dish. One day, a package arrived with a generous sample of a French chocolate riddled with the stuff. When I pried the lid off the container and took a whiff, I had a true Proustian moment: I was transported right back to my high-school locker room, to the canvas bin where we tossed our stinky jock straps and gym socks after running around the sports field for a few hours. Peeling off those sweaty clothes was, I'll admit, a pleasant memory. But not necessarily one I wanted to recount over a bowl of steamy soup.

One chef in Paris, testing the limits of his imagination and our stomachs, held an event called 'Les Incorrects' and politically incorrectly served raw horsemeat pounded as carpaccio. Another cooked up a rabbit stew with *tagada*. If you're not French, *tagada* may sound like an exotic, elusive spice to you, which might go well with a lovely *plat du jour* of braised hare. Except *tagada* are bright red, artificially flavoured strawberry marshmallows, best appreciated by folks under the age of seven. The *cheval*-spurring chef dared guests to eat his horsemeat, announcing that people should stop thinking about where food comes from and just eat it. Oddly, this announcement was pretty much in contrast to the rest of the world, where many people had been taken ill because they hadn't sufficiently cared about where their food had come from, and as a result, food safety scares were becoming commonplace, prompting massive recalls of produce.

Around the same time, I tried horse milk, which I saw at the swank La Grande Épicerie supermarket. I reported about this on my website and then made a casual mention that because it's sold in France, I should probably give horsemeat a try as well. Almost immediately, someone who raises horses in North America, where the horsemeat in France comes from, strongly cautioned me that I should take a pass, as those horses aren't raised for consumption and are injected with all sorts of hormones and hazardous chemicals. In that case, pass the marshmallows.

The whole incident struck me as arrogant compared to what chefs elsewhere were doing, which was sourcing food locally and becoming more keenly focused on how food is grown and produced. Eating locally became popular and a vast network of farmer's markets flourished across America, including one in the middle of the most urban city in the world, Manhattan. Surrounded by skyscrapers, one could find dazzling vine-ripened heirloom tomatoes, clusters of organic grapes with the morning dew still clinging to them, and fantastic handcrafted candies made of just-tapped maple syrup, which would dissolve in your mouth, making you feel as if you were melting into a pool of buttery maple syrup.

Back in Paris, chefs were hunched over their countertops filling glasses called *verrines,* mixing things like soon-to-be-extinct bluefin tuna with popcorn, and baking up foie gras chocolate éclairs. In America, online foodies would have taken to task any chef who dared to mix strawberries, gelatine and rabbit parts. But where was the outrage in Paris? French chefs always waxed about how their cuisine was the best in the world. I heard not a peep of criticism. In protest, I cancelled my cable subscription to Cuisine.tv, France's food network, because I was tired of the focus being on *les tendances,* the trends, and seeing hyperactive women layering food into glasses and shrieking in delight at their cleverness, rather than promoting the beautiful cheeses, chocolate and charcuterie that France was known for.

(In their defence, change just doesn't come naturally, or easily, in France. The numerous bloody and violent revolutions over the course of French history can attest to that. Even today, anyone who has tried to get a shopkeeper or cashier to give them change for a €50 note knows that change still comes reluctantly to the French.)

Though already considered passé in Spain, foams had been discovered by French chefs, and it wasn't unusual to be served Caesar salad *bouchons* (mouthfuls) in one-bite portions on porcelain spoons. At this time, a reader – after dining around town on a trip to Paris – wrote to me, 'What the hell is up with all those little dishes they serve food in?' And I was sure that I'd missed the decree suddenly banishing bowls in France, since it appeared obligatory to serve soup in glasses, each serving invariably topped with a dab of crème fraîche and, uh oh, ground cumin.

I'm not against layering foods in glasses: things like tiramisu and spoonable desserts, custards and *gelées* are beautiful and easier to eat when served in a deep vessel. But the sudden proliferation of cookbooks in France with *nouveau*-style recipes for everything from soup to squid to spaghetti and meatballs meant no dish was off limits from being crammed into a glass. I imagine that if Carême had served Napoleon his wedding cake in a glass, he most likely would have met his fate a bit sooner, at the guillotine.

(One year during this period, I proposed to some French friends that I serve Thanksgiving dinner in a glass, stratifying layers of mashed potatoes, chestnut stuffing, chopped turkey and gravy in there, then topping it off with a mound of sweet potatoes. I stopped before I got to the part about finishing it with the classic, all-American topping of toasted marshmallows, because it wasn't obvious to them that I wasn't serious about putting it all in a *verrine* and they started nodding in agreement.)

I guess I've become more French than I thought, since I am proposing the once-again revolutionary idea of using drinking glasses for what they were intended. That is, for drinking. I'll take my salad back in a bowl, not a spoon. And call me a right-wing lunatic, but I'd like to propose a ban on cumin immigrating across the border from Mexico and North Africa into France.

But lest you think I'm joining the naysayers who say French culinary innovation is dead and there's no future for *la cuisine française,* I'm not counting the French out quite yet. I've lived in Paris for over a decade and have experienced a raw-milk *brie de Meaux* that was so good I was tempted to pass my American passport through a shredder. To my mind, the French have spent centuries perfecting their recipes and classic techniques, and once they figure something out, they should stick with it. Monsieur Ladurée put a dab of butter cream between two meringues and the Parisian macaroon was born; this dainty delight hasn't changed much in 150 years, and doesn't need to. I hope La Maison du Chocolat never changes their *Rigoletto noir:* dark chocolates filled with caramelised butter mousse.

Yet this doesn't mean the classics can't be updated. New flavours and sensations often delight by surprise. Consider the oval-shaped chocolates made by Jean-Charles Rochoux: they astound when you pop one into your mouth and the impossibly thin chocolate shell dissolves away, leaving you with a mouthful of minty, herbal Chartreuse liquor. Traditional caramels get a thoughtful update from Jacques Genin; his bite-size *pain d'épices* caramels each taste like a full stick of butter was reduced into a small rectangle, their richness offset by a mix of spices, which include star anise and cinnamon. And thankfully, no cumin.

Although nothing comes easy in France, I think change will happen. (Unless you're trying to break a €50 note. Good luck with that one.) When I moved to Paris in 2003, I shocked friends by wanting internet access in my apartment in Paris; it was nearly impossible to find service at that time. Now the city is completely wired, free Wi-Fi is available in all the public parks and government buildings, and iPhones and *le* Blackberry have become standard accoutrements along with those pots of mustard on dining tables. And like the shock of taking a bite of a Chartreuse-filled chocolate, Nicolas Sarkozy, one of the least-appealing men in France, surprised us all by marrying Italian model Carla Bruni just a few weeks after his ex-wife split for New York. The French continue to surprise and adapt.

Sure, France is the fastest growing market for McDonald's in the world, three cheeses disappear each year, and it's rumoured that some of the three-star restaurants are serving Starbucks because the French brew isn't up to snuff. (Apparently even snooty Michelin inspectors like their nonfat soy lattes, *non?*) And one might find it a little odd that the two most sought-after reservations in Paris at the moment are at Spring, which is owned by an American chef, and at Frenchie, owned by a French chef who named his restaurant after the nickname he was given during his culinary training – in New York.

But I'm confident that the next generation, the *génération coincée* of young, 'cornered' cooks who feel trapped by old culinary conventions, will see the light. Drinking glasses will go back to being used for drinking. You won't see any Seabiscuit steaks. And marshmallows will be used for what we Americans know they're supposed to be used for – topping puréed vegetables. *Bien sûr.*

Peanut Butter Summer

EMILY MATCHAR

Emily Matchar is a food and travel writer occasionally based in Chapel Hill, North Carolina. When she's not eating her way around the globe as an author for Lonely Planet guidebooks, she writes for magazines like *Men's Journal, Gourmet* and *BBC History*. She hopes her story will not be taken as a slight against peanut butter, which she actually adores.

Peter and I were young, adults only by technicality. It was summer. We were in love and in Europe.

The Europe trip had been long dreamed of, saved for through summers working in pizzerias and winters working in the campus library, feverishly anticipated with readings and re-readings of Hemingway and Henry Miller (like I said, we were young).

Finally, here we were, the two of us hopping from Paris to Madrid to Barcelona to Naples with nothing but our backpacks, our Eurorail passes and our sense of infinite possibility.

Oh, and a jar of peanut butter. Creamy Jiff, to be precise.

The peanut butter belonged to Peter. Back home in North Carolina, I'd rolled my eyes to see him tuck the economy-sized jar into his backpack alongside the Ziploc baggies of neatly rolled socks and underwear. After a year of nonstop togetherness, I knew well that Peter was a meat and potatoes guy, a veggie-hater whose idea of a salad was iceberg lettuce and shredded carrots. It had never bothered me much before – it was just another quirk to love, like his obsession with card tricks or his undying affection for spaghetti westerns. But we were going to Europe! People went to Europe just to eat the food, right? Why did we need peanut butter?

The peanut butter was only an emergency ration, Peter promised, something to munch on during long train rides or late at night in small town *pensiones* when no other food was available. But soon after we landed at Charles de Gaulle and set out for Basque country, it became clear that it would be much more than that.

I spotted Peter gobbling spoonfuls of peanut butter in a Spanish hostel kitchen as I changed for dinner one night. A few days later, I saw him spreading peanut butter on crackers before heading out for an afternoon at the Guggenheim in Bilbao.

'Don't you want to go find a little café or something?' I said. I was quickly falling in love with the region's *pintxos*, the Basque answer to tapas – chunks of sea-salty dried cod, smoky marinated peppers, hunks of rough bread with sheep's cheese and quince paste, all served on tiny plates in sepia-coloured bars full of noisy young men in football jerseys and noisy old men in black berets.

'Nah, I'm not hungry any more.'

For Peter, the peanut butter was a cheap and expedient way to avoid the hassle of searching for food. Hungry? Eat peanut butter. Problem solved.

But for me, seeking out interesting local foods was turning out to be a joy, a delight that grew deeper with each new city we visited – wandering Rome's old Jewish Quarter in pursuit of the neighbourhood's celebrated artichoke fritters, buying paper cups of fried sardines on the rocky beaches of Riomaggiore in Liguria, tasting spicy *merguez* sausages from Algerian street vendors in Paris.

In Madrid, I tasted my first lentil curry at a Pakistani restaurant in the La Ribera district. The interplay of rich, buttery legumes and the deep perfume of Silk Road spices made my hair stand on end. I'd never had anything like it.

Peter ate rubbery cheese pizza from the kids menu.

In the Loire Valley, I was captivated by the asparagus-shaped chocolates and jewel-bright glacé fruits at an old-fashioned chocolate shop, pointing and asking questions in my awful French.

Peter stood by the doorway, arms folded.

That night we had a fight outside a Lebanese takeaway restaurant. I wanted a kebab, and to chat with the friendly owners about their home country. Peter just wanted to go to sleep.

I turned to him and, without thinking, said, 'I'm not sure this relationship will last forever.'

I didn't even realise what I'd said until I saw the look of shock on his face. He told me to take it back. I took it back. We went back to our hotel and curled up in the middle of our sagging mattress. I held him tight as he fell asleep, my face pressed into the back of his neck.

But the canker was already in the rose. It wasn't that I cared about what Peter put in his stomach, not really. But I'd begun to see that his disinterest in food-related adventure had less to do with picky eating and more to do with other, larger personality traits.

As a deeply reserved person, he worried over the potential awkwardness of interacting with non-English-speaking store clerks and waiters, preferring to buy bread at the supermarket than risk getting stuck making conversation with an excitable

Italian baker. He didn't like getting lost, so long rambling walks in search of interesting local restaurants were not his idea of a good time. He hated spending money on things he considered unnecessary. By his rules, peanut butter was necessary. Gelato was unnecessary.

Gelato was not unnecessary to me. Gelato was crucial. In Italy that summer, the *gelateria* was the highlight of my afternoons. There were so many flavours to choose from, all piled in creamy mounds as luxurious as the cashmere scarves on display at the boutiques of Rome's Via Condotti.

I vowed never to have the same gelato twice. One day I'd have a cup of *stracciatella* and *frutti di bosco* berries; the next I'd be eating a double cone of *panna cotta* and *amarena* cherry; another day it would be a triple helping of hazelnut, *fior di latte* or Seville orange.

Peter liked lemon and coconut. In a cup.

Sure, he *might* like other flavours, he admitted. But he *knew* he liked lemon and coconut. Why waste money on 'might' when you've got a sure bet?

Why indeed?

Until that summer in Europe, Peter was my sure bet. He and I both loved horror movies. We both loved to read. We had the same dark sense of humour. He was the first guy who'd met my parents, who'd taken care of me when I was sick, who'd told me he loved me and really meant it. Even though I thought the idea of 'soul mate' was idiotic, I had secretly believed he might be mine.

But I was beginning to see that there were other flavours.

I broke up with Peter the following fall. It was my choice, but I still felt gutted. He wouldn't look me in the eye. I cried so hard it felt like I was suffocating. I couldn't eat for a week.

But then I could, and I did. In the following years, I ate and travelled so much that eating and travelling and writing about it became my career. Charred chunks of lamb and hillocks of greasy couscous at the Djemaa el Fna night market in Marrakesh. Roti bread, hand-stretched to the translucency of parchment paper, in the misty Cameron Highlands of peninsular Malaysia. Crunchy stacks of fresh-fried whitebait on the coast of New Zealand's South Island, grey waves pounding beneath the window. An austere chickpea stew at Gandhi's ashram in India. Green chilli cheeseburgers at New Mexico roadhouses.

There were other men. I ate tamales and shrimp ceviche in Mexico with an Australian cricketer, then followed him to Cuba to eat greasy *jamón* sandwiches in the twisted streets of Old Havana. I ate spaghetti *all'arrabbiata,* cooked for me by an Italian lover who fussed like a *nonna* over the poor quality of the red chilli flakes. I ate *entrecôte* and *tarte tatin* at a French restaurant in Vientiane, Laos, with an American philosophy professor on Christmas Eve.

It's been wonderful, all the travelling and eating, all the new places and new people. It's also been stressful, exhausting, and occasionally terrifying.

I haven't seen Peter in years. We'll write occasionally, and even though it's been so long, it always makes me feel ever so slightly unsettled to see an email from him in my inbox.

I sometimes wonder if people like Peter are happier because they know what they like and have no doubts. Would I be better off sitting at home with a peanut butter and jelly sandwich, knowing there's no place I'd rather be? Or am I lucky to be the way I am, always eager to see what's around the corner and always willing to believe that the next flavour will be even better than the last?

The Ways of Tea

NAOMI DUGUID

Naomi Duguid, traveller, writer and photographer, is often described as a culinary anthropologist. She is the co-author (with Jeffrey Alford) of six award-winning books of food and travel: *Flatbreads and Flavors*, *Hot Sour Salty Sweet: A Culinary Journey Through South-East Asia*, *Seductions of Rice*, *HomeBaking*, *Mangoes & Curry Leaves* and *Beyond the Great Wall: Recipes and Stories from the Other China*. In stories, recipes and photographs, the books explore daily home-cooked foods in their cultural context. Naomi is a contributing editor of *Saveur* magazine, gives photo-talks about food and travel, and conducts immersion food tours in northern Thailand each winter (www.immersethrough.com). She also writes a weekly blog (www.naomiduguid.blogspot.com). Her next book, celebrating the food cultures of Burma, will be published in 2012.

I'd made a promise to friends not to take risks. It was early March, and I was in the Solu Khumbu, above the village of Namche Bazaar, walking up the valley that leads to Gokyo, one valley west of Everest. I had a sleeping bag in my backpack, but no tent. I planned to stay each night in one of the villages, actually small hamlets, that looked from the map to be about three hours' walk apart. It seemed like a great plan, a chance to connect with people and to be out in a heart-stoppingly wonderful landscape. But when fat snowflakes started pouring down in the afternoon, blinding out the view, plastering the hillside, and making the path slippery, I thought of my promise.

So when I came to a branch in the trail, I opted to head downward, instead of on towards the next hamlet a good hour away. The small steep path led down to a rushing stream and a footbridge made of two logs. On the other side was a low stone hut. What a relief!

A Sherpa man in a rough woollen jacket came out to meet me. His wife and daughter were just lighting a fire in the hut that was used as a shelter when the herds moved up to summer pasture in the valley. I was lucky to find anyone there; the family was on a first springtime visit to open it. I asked if I could spend the night. The man gave a wide sweep of his arm and a smile to say, 'Yes, of course you can shelter here.' I was shivering with cold and damp (those snowflakes had melted onto me as I walked), but warmed up as I helped sweep the hut and carry in some wood for the fire.

The daughter made tea in the kettle, milky buttery tea, then poured it into three bowls in pale streams. She was shy, and could barely look at me as she handed me a bowl. I sat sipping slowly, breathing in the steam. There was a smell of wet wool from the Sherpas' clothing, and a whiff of wood smoke and butter from their hair and hands. I felt so grateful, so lucky to have stumbled into this timeless place. I could have been in a stone hut in medieval Europe or Japan … I fell into a kind of stoned, relieved, exhausted trance.

Suddenly, in from the snowy world outside walked five brightly clad men in hiking boots and down jackets, like a mirage of modernity. Their caps were coated with wet snow and their nylon and Gore-Tex clothing rustled as they moved. They were as surprised to see me as I was to see them. Four of them were Japanese, the fifth a Nepali, and all were mountaineers, part of a large joint Japanese–Nepali expedition to Cho Oyu, the spectacular 8000-metre peak five days' walk up the valley. When they learned that I was on my own, and planned to sleep in the hut for the night, they were a little appalled: 'No, no, come and stay with us. We have one woman climber and she is in a two-person tent. You can share with her.' I protested that we needed to ask her first, but they waved away my objections and insisted that I walk back with them to their camping place.

I put on my backpack and bowed my thanks to the Sherpa family. My gratitude was heartfelt, but seemed lame and inadequate. They'd rescued me so generously with their fire and their tea, but perhaps they were relieved when the climbers took me off with them, for then their responsibility to me was over.

We walked back across the log bridge, the rushing stream below us swollen with the still-falling snow, and made our way to the large level area the mountaineers had chosen for their campsite. The expedition's long train of laden yaks was still coming slowly down the trail, each animal picking its way carefully on the slippery, snowy ground. The men led me over to a small woman in a puffy red jacket and introduced me to her in careful English, 'Naomi-san, please meet Emiko-san.' They explained to her in Japanese that they'd offered me space in her tent. Emiko didn't seem at all put out; quite the opposite. She told me she was happy to see another woman, as her climbing partner had had to back out of the expedition at the last moment, which was why she found herself alone in a double tent.

The valley was already in shadow. As daylight faded, the snow stopped and it grew very cold. We set up Emiko's small blue sleeping tent and unrolled our sleeping bags, while the porters set up the cook tent, made fires and lit stoves. When night fell,

Emiko and I joined the climbers, about fifteen in all, for supper, a delicious blend of Nepali and Japanese food: dhal and rice and cooked green vegetables (classic Nepali *dal-baht-sabji*) and Japanese pickles and miso soup. The Nepalis told me they liked working with Japanese climbers because 'they eat rice, like we do. Much better than Western food!'

After supper Emiko and I joined five or six of the Japanese climbers in one of the larger, four-man tents. We left our boots at the tent door and sat crowded together in our thick jackets by the light of a lantern. They told stories, which one of the climbers translated for me; stories of getting lost in the mountains or happy triumphs in the Japanese Alps, tales of close calls on steep rock walls …

As the stories and laughter continued, one young climber quietly slipped on his boots and crouched his way out of the tent. He returned a minute later with a pot of cold water from the stream. He took a small camp stove from his day pack, lit it, then put the pot on to boil. Out from his day pack came a cloth-wrapped bundle: it was a beautiful porcelain bowl, wrapped in a silk scarf. He placed it carefully on a mat, then pulled out two small wooden boxes. In one was a graceful-looking bamboo whisk. He poured a little brilliantly green powdered tea from the other box into the bowl, then carefully put the tea box away. When the water came to a boil, he poured it into the bowl. The steam was thick in the cold air. He took the whisk from its box, put it into the bowl, and gently rolled it back and forth between his palms, whisking and blending the tea into the water until it foamed up a little, small bubbles forming in the greenness.

In the light of the lantern our faces glowed warmly as we watched, now as intent as the tea-maker, our breaths little puffs of mist. He lifted the bowl and passed it to his neighbour, who took a slow careful sip, then passed it on. The tea was astringent and bitter, a beautiful life-affirming green in the smooth elegant bowl, hot to the tongue. The bowl travelled around the circle twice, careful sip after careful sip, all of us sitting in a kind of focused appreciative silence. The only sounds were the hissing of the lantern and the steady rush of the stream outside. And then it was finished.

Carefully the tea-maker rinsed out the bowl, wiped it with the silk, wrapped it, and stowed it back in his pack along with the whisk. We headed out into the cold starry night, warmed from the inside, not only by the tea, but even more by the thread of companionship, the shared ritual of a tea ceremony conducted with grace and mindfulness, a momentary oasis of friendship and civilised care in the snowy Himalaya.

Breakfast Epiphanies

RUTH RABIN

Ruth Rabin discovered her love of writing a few years ago while dabbling in screenwriting and creative writing courses at De Anza College in Cupertino, California. Several of her pieces were published in *Red Wheelbarrow*, De Anza's literary magazine, and her story 'A Grandmother's Treasure' won second place in that magazine's nonfiction category. Ruth is currently enrolled in the MFA program in Creative Writing at San José State University. She has won the Bonita Cox Award for nonfiction and the James Phelan Award for fiction in SJSU's English Department's annual writing contest. Ruth teaches elementary school in her real life, and lives in the Bay Area with her two children.

There were only two tables inside the café and both were crowded with old men puffing away at nasty-smelling cigarettes. The ceiling fan turned so slowly that all it accomplished was tangling the thick smoke with the solid heat of the morning. The men stopped talking when I walked in. One of them stood up quickly and began to make room for me at one of the tables, clearing away ashtrays and gruffly shooing away a few of the others so I could sit down. Through wide smiles and effusive hand gestures, I indicated that I would be fine sitting outside and that they should not go to any trouble.

There were two tables outside. A man was sitting at one of them, so I went to the empty one, pulled out a chair and sat down.

Cairo in April. It was only spring, yet the city was already suffocatingly hot and dusty, and the streets were crammed. When men walked past me, they brushed their hands across my ass without once moving their eyes from some invisible spot in front of them.

'Coffee?' It was the old bossy man from inside.

'Min fadlak.' Yes, please.

I had been awoken at dawn by the muezzin's call to prayer, which is broadcast throughout the city from loudspeakers, the largest and loudest of which assuredly had been set up right outside my hotel window. So, yes, please, I'd love some coffee.

'And may I have a glass of ice water too?' He smiled politely, his few remaining teeth tobacco-stained and crooked, and gave a slight shrug. No English. That's okay, there was almost certainly no ice and I probably shouldn't be drinking the water anyway.

He came back quickly, carrying a large black tray. He placed an espresso-sized cup on a saucer and a *finjan,* a small copper pot with a long handle, in front of me. Then he set down several plates of food that I had not ordered.

'Excuse me, I'm sorry, I didn't order this,' I told him, pointing to the food and shaking my head. He smiled and bowed, and walked back inside the café.

Despite the heat, I put my face near the *finjan.* My skin absorbed the hot, fragrant steam that rose from it. It smelled like the desert, exotic and strange. It smelled like music I'd heard the night before while wandering the city. It smelled like something familiar that I recognised from a time and a place I'd never been. I knew that, forever after, this smell of coffee and cardamom, and not the diesel-filled air and fishy-smelling, stagnant Nile that crawled along at the end of this street, would mean Cairo to me. I took hold of the handle and poured. The liquid was thick and dark, and flowed like mud. I sipped. It scalded the roof of my mouth. It was so bitter I didn't know if I'd be able to swallow it, and when I finally did, it left small grounds of beans and seeds on my tongue.

'You must add a lot of sugar and let it all settle to the bottom before you pour,' said the man sitting at the other table. He took the sugar bowl from his table and brought it, along with his own cup of coffee, to mine, and helped himself to a seat. 'You must be patient,' he told me. 'Life is slow in the desert.' He dropped seemingly countless cubes of sugar into the *finjan*, then took hold of the handle and swirled it slowly in his hand, mixing the sugar, coffee and spices gently together. 'Now we let it sit for a few minutes.'

'We?'

He laughed. 'My name is Nasr.'

He was extremely good looking in that Omar Sharif way. His eyes were so dark that even the whites were a light shade of brown. His hair was wavy, grey at the edges, and even though it was still morning I could see he'd soon be ready for another shave.

I offered my hand, then pulled it away in case he wasn't allowed to touch a woman in public. He was a bit startled and must have thought I was an idiot.

'You are American?' he asked, gallantly pretending not to have noticed my quick hand trick.

'Yes,' I answered. American by way of Tel Aviv, where I had been living for the last year and a half, but that was not a detail worth mentioning right now. I had arrived yesterday evening after a long day's bus ride along the Mediterranean coast, past the Israeli towns of Ashdod and Ashkelon, past the very dreary and creepy Gaza Strip, through the Suez Canal, then west into Cairo.

'Please,' Nasr said, gesturing widely to the plates of food on the table, 'eat. Don't let me bother you.'

'This isn't mine; I didn't order it. And, besides, it's too hot out to eat.'

I looked over at Nasr. He wasn't even sweating.

'I think you have never eaten an Egyptian breakfast before,' he said. 'Am I right?' He didn't need an answer. 'I will help you. I will tell you what everything is, then you taste it and tell me if you like it, all right?' He took a deep whiff from the *finjan,* then poured us both another cup.

I wondered how many women this man had charmed, literally, out of their pants.

This was not the first time I had been given a tour of a meal; I had been hit on by Nasr's Israeli (and French and Italian) counterparts, men just as eager to strut around and puff out their tail feathers, men just as macho and just as handsome. But so what? If it made them happy, then who was I to say no? Who was I to deny this man the pleasure of explaining it all to me and why on earth would I deny myself the pleasure of watching him do so?

I liked being in this part of the world; it was refreshing to be in a place where the culture's ideal shape for a woman was the one I had. In the Middle East, you don't have to look like Barbie to find clothes that fit or men that look. The men here aren't looking for Barbie. Unless, of course, she puts out.

'I think you recognise this, yes?' He was pointing to a slightly cracked clay bowl.

I decided to sit back and let Nasr take my hand and be my guide, to journey through this breakfast and see it through his eyes.

The bowl Nasr was pointing to held a chopped salad loaded with fresh tomatoes, onions and cucumbers, and sprinkled with oregano, thyme, sesame seeds and salt. The whole thing was dressed with olive oil and lemon juice.

'This is *za'atar*,' he explained, indicating the mixture of dried herbs on the top. 'My father is Egyptian, my mother is from Lebanon. In Lebanon, the people believe that *za'atar* makes the mind alert and the body strong. For this reason, the children eat *za'atar* for breakfast before an important exam. I was not a very good student so my mother thought it was a good idea for me to eat it every morning, even when there was no exam.'

'Did it work?' I asked.

He grinned and patted his chest. 'As you can see.' His teeth were straight and even and the whiteness of them was almost, well, blinding in that dark face of his. He wore the smile well.

He heaped a large serving of salad onto my plate and leaned back in his chair to watch me eat.

The salad was stunning, a mixture of tangy, oily, salty and herby. It tasted like summer, the vegetables ripened on the vine by the desert sun.

'It's delicious,' I said and held out my plate. 'More, please.'

But he ignored my plea. 'You have to leave room for the other food.'

There was a tin bowl with designs hammered into it filled with large brown eggs. As I sat there with Nasr, it occurred to me that in all of my 'worldly experience', I had never actually eaten a brown egg. I had seen them, of course, here and there, but I had never tasted one. I was pleased that these were brown; they would only add to the unfolding mystery of the morning.

Nasr picked one up and rolled it in his hand.

'How do you know if this egg is raw or cooked?' he asked. He tossed it higher and higher in the air, catching it easily each time. He leaned towards me. 'Here, I will show you a trick. Watch. All

219

you have to do is spin the egg. If it spins tight and fast, then it is cooked. If it spins like a drunken camel, then it is raw.' He offered me the egg. 'Here, you try.'

I smiled. 'Or we can do it the old-fashioned way,' I said. I took the egg and tapped it not-so-gently on the table. 'We're in luck; it's cooked.' I started to pick the pieces of shell off the egg and was startled to find that the egg itself was not brown. I was confused and disappointed; I was expecting something more colourful, more interesting, something less … white.

'How come the egg's not brown?' I asked him, possibly a bit too accusingly.

He picked up another egg and held it in front of my face. 'But it *is* brown.'

'No, I mean on the inside. I thought it would be brown on the inside.'

'All eggs are white on the inside. At least, that is how it is in Egypt. I don't know what colour your eggs are in America.'

I felt like I was about to start rambling, but I went on anyway. 'Then why are they brown on the outside?'

'Why are they brown? Because they come from brown chickens. If you want white eggs, you have to have white chickens. But only on the outside are they different, on the inside they are always the same.'

Was that true? About the eggs and the chickens? How come I didn't know this? And did that mean it was true about brown cows giving chocolate milk? I had grown up in a small town and a lot of my friends and classmates had lived on farms, but I had never noticed whether there were any brown chickens around. The first boy I ever kissed, Robert P., lived on a big farm in the field behind my house, but kissing him was the closest I ever came to becoming a farmer's wife.

If what Nasr had said about chickens was true, I thought, then there must have been only white ones where I lived. Which, in retrospect, pretty much summed up the town as a whole. My family had added the only bit of ethnic flavour to the place, and my house had been a popular gathering spot – the food was so much better. Thanks to us, there were people in that hick town who had actually tasted matzo balls and gefilte fish. (But they had returned the favour: it was at their houses that I ate ham and cheese sandwiches with mayonnaise on that soft kind of white bread that you could roll into little balls.)

Nasr held an egg in his hand and looked directly into my eyes. 'They are like people, eh?'

'You mean different on the outside but alike on the inside?' It was so clichéd that it had to be true.

He continued looking at me, then abruptly looked away, but not before I noticed that even with skin as dark as Nasr's, a blush will show through.

'We're not done with our breakfast tour,' he said, recovering from his serious moment. I smiled and sat back and wondered what other treasures this man would reveal.

'Here. This. Do you know what this is?' He was pointing to a plate of flat doughy bread.

'Pita,' I answered.

Ah, pita. Delicious, hot pita, fresh from the oven. Small crumbs of guilt began to gather in my stomach. It was Passover, the commemoration of the exodus of the Jews from Egypt, and part of our tradition is that we do not eat bread during this holiday. I had made a reverse exodus: I had left Israel and come to Egypt, but only for a week. I figured it would not be a very gracious-guest-like-thing to mention to him that, at this exact moment, all over the world, *my* people were celebrating their freedom from slavery at the hands of *his* people. And I certainly wasn't about to start talking about the ten plagues that were set upon the Egyptians, or how the Red Sea parted, but only for the Jews. It would just be rude.

What the hell. I reached for the pita, but Nasr pulled it back and shook his head. 'Not yet.' He pulled a plateful of thick creamy beige paste towards him. It was topped with a swirl of a lighter paste and that was topped with another swirl of thick amber-coloured olive oil. Scattered over it all were pine nuts. I knew what it was, but I wanted to hear him tell me. He did not disappoint.

'This is hummus,' he informed me. 'It's made of chickpeas and sesame – very healthy.'

Nasr ripped off a piece of pita and used it to stir the pastes and oil and pine nuts together, then scooped up a large dollop and handed it to me.

I held it over the plate so it wouldn't drip onto my clothes.

He served himself a healthy dose, then went on. 'On top is tahini, sesame paste, and on top of that is olive oil, from right here.' He swept the air with his arm. 'From Cairo.'

Olive oil – the magic elixir. I could just imagine Nasr telling me about it: *Olive oil goes back to the beginning of this land and its people. It is believed to grant youth and strength. Olive branches are the symbol of peace and the reward for battle. Resistant to strong outside forces, bending with the never-ending winds, the trees symbolise this region. Nothing can destroy them.*

Or something like that.

But instead, he was telling me about the hummus. 'It is the most important food in the Middle East,' he said, 'and one of the oldest, but not everyone knows how to make it just right.'

'But you do.'

'Of course.' There was the grin – I could get used to that grin. He gestured to me to eat. I took a bite. I felt my eyes widen and I knew I must have looked like some American tourist who was tasting something for the first time that hadn't come from McDonald's, but I didn't care.

I had never thought of bread as a food that can melt in your mouth, but that's exactly what this pita did. It was one of the most delicious things I had ever tasted. The hummus was smooth and rich. I swallowed. Then I was punched by the after-kick. I gasped and my eyes began to water. I looked around frantically for the glass of water that had never arrived. I grabbed the *finjan* and poured myself a cup of what was left, which was pretty much nothing but sludge. I gulped it down anyway.

And in that tiny second, not only did my sinuses get clear, *everything* got clear and the answer to the whole problem came to me: the whole problem of the Jews and the Arabs and why it is so hard for us to understand each other. It's because we are like hummus – on the outside we are the same and on the inside we are the same (same dad, after all). But somewhere in between the outside and the inside, there is a thin layer where our spices got all mixed up into slightly different, distinct combinations – nothing really noticeable until you took a bite.

In this case, garlic, cumin and not a small dash of cayenne.

'So, you like it?' he laughed.

'I think I'm in love,' I answered as soon as I had recovered. I reached over and ripped off another bite of pita and scooped it through the hummus, gathering pine nuts as I went. 'Do you think this is fattening?' I asked through a mouthful, then, 'Who cares?'

'Later I will take you to my home and you will taste my mother's hummus. It is the best in Cairo. Maybe in all of Egypt.'

Take me home to Mother? Yeah, right.

'My wife has tried to learn, but it is never as good.'

Ah, there's a wife. Naturally.

'You're married?' I asked, trying to sound more interested than disappointed.

'Of course,' he answered.

Of course.

'Do you have any children?'

'Certainly.'

Certainly.

'I have five daughters.'

Five daughters. Yikes.

He said it with such pride that I thought the buttons on his shirt would burst. Then he put his hands in the air and added, 'I'm just like that man in the story.'

'What story?'

'The story about the man with five daughters. He is a Jew in Russia. He is always talking to God about his problems.'

Fiddler on the Roof?! I was so startled, I inhaled my pita and started to cough. Alarmed, Nasr stood up and signalled frantically to the men inside the café. Good. Maybe they'd bring water. They all came running out on each other's heels to see what kind of emergency was taking place. They had brought their cigarettes but had otherwise come empty-handed. Like magic, people in neighbouring shops, shopkeepers and customers and passers-by, began to appear. Everyone was speaking at once. Arguments broke out. There was a lot of shouting and arm flinging. Fingers were being wagged. One man's suggestion was shouted down by another, whose own suggestion was then dismissed by somebody else. The crowd grew as more and more concerned citizens joined in the excitement. They stood face to face and shook their heads at each other, and when one pointed emphatically down the street, another pointed just as emphatically *up* the street. When a man pointed to the right, a woman pointed to the left. Whatever they were arguing about, they seemed to be having a good time.

I suppose I should have been flattered to have been the centre of so much attention and I'm sure I would have been if anyone had bothered to notice me. For such a slow-moving country, they sure had forgotten about me quickly enough.

Their voices got louder and began to drown out the ear-numbing noise of nearby Ramses Street. They became a surprisingly pleasant alternative to the incessant blaring of horns and screeching of gears as the buses and taxis that sped down that wide, wild boulevard swerved and changed lanes and just barely avoided pedestrians who took their lives into their hands trying to cross to the other side.

There is no such thing as minding your own business in these passionate parts of the world. There are no words for 'elevator silence' in the Semitic languages. If you ask three people for advice, you will get four different opinions. Board a bus, ask the driver for directions, and by the time you reach your destination, every single passenger on the bus, from young schoolchildren to old grandmothers, will have piped up and given you different, 'better' directions to get you where you want to go. The warmth of the people is tangible; I have sat next to total strangers on a Friday-morning bus and found myself seated at their tables that same Friday evening sharing their home-cooked Sabbath dinners (and every single time, imagine that, there has been the host's unmarried son or grandson or cousin or brother or uncle also in attendance. Such a coincidence …).

If you are a shrinking violet, you will be trampled on. So, speak up, even if you have no idea what's going on.

Before too long the excitement started to wear off. The crowd began to wander back, talking and laughing, to their interrupted affairs. Nasr extracted his face from the face of an old man. The old man took hold of Nasr's hand and pulled him close. Then he wrapped his other arm around Nasr and hugged him tightly.

I had finished coughing and was fully recovered by the time Nasr returned to 'our' table. I asked him if he would mind bringing me a bottle of water. He went inside the café and returned a moment later with a full *finjan* instead. He was followed by the bossy old man who was carrying a large ceramic bowl overflowing with fruit and a small dish of oily green and black olives. He graciously put them on our table and began clearing some of the other dishes. I was no longer surprised by food appearing, unbidden, at my table, but I was surprised by the feeling of my never wanting this meal to end.

'*Shuchran,*' I told him. Thank you.

The old man turned and smiled and put his hands together like he was praying and bowed slightly. '*Afwan.*'

'You speak Arabic?' Nasr sounded impressed.

'No. Just the basics. Please, thank you, excuse me.'

Nasr looked at me with something like newfound respect, like perhaps I was not just a 'typical' American after all. Then he turned his attention to our dessert. The bowl was a dark cobalt blue, with a rough, unfinished surface. Figs, dates and grapes spilled over its rim. 'These fruits,' Nasr said, 'are among the sacred species of the desert. My people have eaten these same fruits since ancient times.' He put an olive into his mouth and spat the pit out onto his plate. The green olives were plump, the size of a thumbnail; the black ones were small and tightly wrinkled.

I took a fig from the bowl. It was purple-skinned and splitting apart at the seams. I could see its red and seedy insides. There was a drop of milk at the stem; it had been freshly twisted from the branch, probably from a tree in the café proprietor's own backyard. I brought it close to my face and inhaled. I filled my head with the smell of it. I tried to memorise the perfume of this fig. Nasr took it from my hand and when he split it easily in two, I shivered despite the heat. He handed me one half and put the other half into his mouth, eating the skin and the seeds, watching me. I bit into my half – the juice poured out and I laughed, suddenly shy, and wiped my chin. The seeds were tiny and they crunched softly as I chewed. Then he handed me a sticky brown date with an oblong pit that came out clean when I ate the fruit around it. The grapes were purple, so dark they looked almost black, and filled with seeds so big you could choke on them if you weren't careful.

I ate and ate.

'So, tell me,' he said in between an olive and a grape, 'do you have any children?'

I split open another fig and poked at the seeds with my fingers. 'I'm not married.'

He stopped suddenly, a grape halfway to his mouth. He looked so incredulous that I was afraid I had made a linguistic faux pas, which I often do.

'What's the matter?' I asked, fully prepared to apologise profusely for any offence I might have caused.

He stood up without a word, took out his wallet and placed some bills on the table. 'Come,' he said and looked at me expectantly.

I looked around furtively to see if I had missed something. The feeling of being in the middle of an inside joke was one that I often experienced out in the world (and, I hate to admit, at home as well). 'Where?' I asked.

'I want to show you Cairo,' he said, completely matter-of-factly, like it was the next logical step in our blossoming relationship. Would his wife come with us?

'Will your wife come with us?'

He ignored me. 'Perhaps you want to visit our souq – it is the best place to buy Egyptian souvenirs. It is not safe for a woman to go there alone. I will take you. Have you seen the Great Pyramid?' I shook my head. 'The Sphinx?' I shook my head again. 'I will show you. They are not far. I have a friend, he will take us on his boat on the Nile. Then tonight I will take you to my cousin's house. He is very nice. Don't worry, he is also very handsome. He will like you. He is not married. Like you.'

Ah ha. *Matchmaker, matchmaker …*

He was eyeing me carefully, doing the math; a few generations ago I might have fetched a good number of camels.

I fought the urge to say, 'Wha … ?' Instead, it occurred to me that he was serious and that I was actually considering his offer.

What could happen if I went with him? How bad could the cousin be? Who was I kidding – I've met people's cousins before; I know firsthand how bad they can be. I may not be shy, but I'm not stupid, either.

'Thank you for the offer. Really. And thank you for the wonderful breakfast. But I should go.' I gathered up my bag and started to stand up.

'Go?' he said, still standing. 'Go where?'

'Uh, I'm not sure, back to the hotel.' He wasn't going to get weird on me, was he?

'What is waiting for you back at the hotel? It's early. Come, before it gets hot.'

Before it gets hot? See – there were those crazy mixed-up spices again.

'Really, I need to get back.'

'As you want,' he said with a shrug. 'Enjoy your visit to Egypt.'

He turned to leave. 'If I go with you …' I caught myself just as I was about to reach out and grab his arm. He turned around. 'If I go with you, will you leave me all alone in the desert to die of thirst?' Alone in the desert to die of thirst?! Where did that come from? That was not even close to what I was thinking could happen.

He smiled slowly, the sun practically reflecting off his teeth, the way it does in corny cartoons. 'It is possible,' he said eventually. 'It is up to you.'

We stood looking at each other for a moment while I considered this, then I hefted my bag onto my shoulder and shook my head. 'I don't think so. But thank you.'

I watched him walk away into the dust and the heat, towards the river. He turned the corner and disappeared.

But, wait – I'd changed my mind. What were the chances that he really would leave me to die of thirst? Slim to none, and besides, I'd simply insist that we stay close to populated urban areas. I wouldn't wander far with him: a quick spin around the city, maybe a glimpse of the pyramids across the road in Giza, a leisurely cruise up the Nile just to see why Cleopatra would have ever wanted to be the queen of it. And then I remembered that time I'd met somebody's cousin and he hadn't been *that* horrible.

The old man came out to clear the table. I tossed a quick little bow and a smile his way and started to walk-run after Nasr. I turned the corner and at first I didn't see him. Then I spied him across the street. He was sitting at an outdoor table with two young women, blonde and fair as any Disney princesses, stirring sugar into their brass *finjan*.

I crossed over to get a better look. Nasr glanced up and gave me a wink. As I passed by their table, I heard him say to the women, 'Life is slow in the desert ...'

The Potion

JOHANNA GOHMANN

Johanna Gohmann is an American writer whose essays and articles have appeared on Salon.com, the *Chicago Sun-Times, Elle, Red* magazine, Babble.com, YourTango.com and the *Dubliner*. She is a frequent contributor to *Bust* magazine and the *Irish Independent*, and two of her essays were recently anthologised in *The Best Women's Travel Writing 2010* and *The Best Sex Writing 2010*. She lives with her husband in Dublin.

Venice wasn't beautiful. Quite the opposite, in fact. Venice was cold and slate grey, and the rain stung our faces like birdshot. The cloud-clogged skies turned the majestic palazzos into the gloomy, twisted castles of fairy-tale villains. Dark water swirled in the canals, the gondoliers' scarves snapped in the wind, and it was like the entire city had been carved from a giant block of dirty ice. My classmates and I, well, we were disappointed, to say the least.

We were also exhausted. It was 1995, my sophomore year of college, and I was doing the now standard 'study-abroad' semester that is so popular with American students. After five months of stomping around Europe in hiking boots, snapping photos of pigeons and pubs, my friends and I were worn out. Venice was the final trip of the semester, meant to be the highlight of our travels before we boarded planes to carry us back to our Midwestern university. However, it was the middle of December and Italy didn't really care if it was our last hurrah or not. It was winter, and that meant rain and sleet and fingers so cold they could barely grasp a soggy panini.

We were also broke, having blown all our cash on our previous jaunts around the continent. We'd already scooped up cheap souvenirs for our parents and ourselves. I'd bought my mom a sweater from Edinburgh, and for my dad, golf club covers shaped like cans of Guinness. For myself, I'd collected dozens of fabric patches bearing the names of the cities I'd visited. I imagined one day sewing these badges onto a coat, which I could then wear like I was some walking, stamped steamer trunk. Now, at age thirty-four, I come across these brightly coloured patches stuffed into a drawer, and I cringe slightly at my cheesiness. But I also smile. I was only nineteen, after all, and my study abroad semester was the furthest I'd ever been from my tiny Indiana town. Those swatches of material remind me of how exhilarated I was by my travels.

But by the time we hit Venice, my exhilaration had waned. The hostel where we were staying was damp and draughty, and I was sharing a room with two other girls. All three of us slept in a giant, lumpy bed that was covered by a pilled, threadbare bedspread. I remember feeling that no matter where we went in Venice, I simply couldn't get warm or fully dry. We'd get up in the morning, take a shower in the cold communal bathroom that trickled lukewarm water, then trudge downstairs to meet our professor, who would lead us through the damp to a museum or cathedral. I had seen so many cathedrals and religious paintings over the past five months that the Crucifixion had ceased to have any effect, and, like a grumpy child who needed a nap, I'd feel myself inwardly rolling my eyes at a Caravaggio. *All right already. He was nailed to a tree. It was gruesome. We GET IT.*

When our professor would release us from the scheduled itinerary to go explore Venice on our own, we'd stand in the rain, staring at our soaked maps, with not even enough money in our pockets to drown ourselves in a cheap carafe of merlot. We'd usually end up slinking off to some café to huddle together and share Americanos. Or else we'd wander into the countless tourist shops, staring at the famed stained-glass creations that seemed to glimmer from every window. I remember that stained glass being the only bit of colour we saw as we trudged those crooked streets. The reds and greens and blues winked at us, a teasing promise of the colour and beauty that the city secretly held … just not for us.

It felt horribly wrong to wish away time in Italy, and yet, that was what people began to do. 'Only three more days …' someone would mutter as we slipped plastic bags inside our boots to keep our socks dry. We were in what was supposedly one of the most beautiful cities in the world, and it felt like purgatory – a middle earth that hovered between the excitement we had just experienced on our other travels and what we knew lay ahead, the flatness and monotony of home. Of course, many of us were also dealing with a traveller's depression that had nothing to do with the awful weather. We were mourning the end of our European adventure, and the return to the reality of our everyday college life: house parties, chain restaurants, final exams … We were coming down from a five-month high of nonstop stimulation, and heading back to vast stretches of strip malls and lecture halls.

This feeling was compounded for me. For mixed in with my feelings of sadness was also a quiet nervousness that tremored just below the surface, like a dull thrum of anxiety. The year before I'd embarked on my semester abroad, my boyfriend – my first love – had died quite suddenly. Following his death, it was like someone had pulled a leaden blanket over me. Everything in my world dimmed as I tried to cope with the trauma. For months afterwards I'd felt like a zombie, wandering to my very first college classes, then driving home on the weekends to cry in my childhood bedroom. The safe bubble of my world had been punctured by tragedy, and I spent that first year struggling to make sense of it.

For me, the chance to study abroad wasn't just about the opportunity to see Notre Dame. It was also an escape hatch. If I got on that plane, I thought, I could get away from the images that reminded and rankled and sent my mind into shadowed corners. I was desperate to get away …

And while psychologists might have tsk-tsked my escapist strategy, being away from everything had indeed worked wonders. Once I arrived in Europe, the leaden blanket had been kicked to the floor. My young body began to prick to life with feeling again, as I laughed so hard with my new friends that my muscles ached. Being engulfed by this completely new landscape made anything possible. I had even dared to dip a toe back into the world of romance, and had engaged in an incredibly fun fling with a charming Englishman. He was twenty-six, which of course seemed both worldly and ancient at the time. He was also in the Royal Air Force, which sounded so exotic and sexy that my girlfriends practically drooled with jealousy.

I finally began to feel like myself again. Even scarier, I was allowing myself to feel hopeful. But I worried that this feeling was simply a spell cast by being under foreign skies. As the days ticked down to our return flight, I tried to quell the nervousness rising within me. Yes, I felt alive and renewed, but would I be able to hold onto these feelings once my feet hit Indiana soil?

Was I really different and strong now, or would the lights around me start to dim once more?

———————◅═

Our last morning in Venice happened to fall on my twentieth birthday. I awoke feeling such a strange mixture of sorrow and joy that I stared out at the grey skies, willing someone – God, Caravaggio, the Pope, anyone – to explain my emotions. At that age, there were still so many feelings that felt new to me, that were unexplainable, and frightening in their confusion.

It was 15 December 1995. My teenage years were now officially behind me. I was an adult now. Having already seen a bit of what the adult world could have in store, the thought was almost paralysing. It made me want to pull the pilled bedspread over my head and stay in that lumpy bed forever.

But the two friends I was sharing the bed with began to sit up and roll awake, and they croakily sang out birthday wishes. Despite the early hour, we rose and showered, and packed our things. My friends' faces shone with the excitement of heading home. I nervously smiled back at them as I tucked postcards of the Uffizi and Louvre into pockets of my suitcase, trying to quell the odd feeling that was roiling through my stomach.

None of the professors or other students were up and about yet, and the hostel was quiet. Hungry, the three of us headed downstairs to forage for some food. We made our way into the tiny, cramped quarters of the lobby, which allowed only for the clerk's desk. The clerk himself lazed behind it on a stool, like he was on a gondola, coasting through the city on a spring breeze. He had a rolled-up paperback in one hand, and he gave us a nod. He was maybe in his mid-twenties, and like so many of the Italian men I had seen, he was attractive in a way that seemed to say, 'Why would I be anything else, foolish girl?' His head was covered with shiny black curls, and his lips were almost embarrassing in their suggestive thickness. He looked like he had stepped from a Raphael canvas, like he didn't belong in the garish and bawdy world of the 1990s.

'The cafes will not yet be open,' he explained to us with a frown, 'but you may wait if you like.' He gestured to the stairs behind us like he was offering us a leather banquette to perch upon. We thanked him and, giggling nervously, shy under his handsome gaze, sat like ducks in a row, one behind the other on the steps. He put his book down and observed us, his brow furrowed.

'So. You are Americans, yes?' His accent no doubt made every female tourist he checked in have an inward, mini-swoon onto an imaginary fainting couch.

'Yes,' we echoed back in a chorus, as if our backpacks and JanSport raincoats didn't already answer the question for us.

'We actually return to America today,' my friend explained.

'Oh, that is too bad. The weather …' he gestured out to the swirling grey, 'it has not been good.'

We laughed in agreement, and for a moment we all stared out at the cold dawn light. There was a long pause, and to break the silence my friend, who was sitting behind me, clapped a hand on my shoulder. 'Today is her birthday!'

'Ah! It is?' And at this, his face finally melted into a smile. 'That is very nice, yes? How old are you?'

'I'm twenty,' I smiled back.

'Ahhh … twenty. That is a very good age.' His delicious mouth seemed to curl into a knowing smirk at this. 'Well, a happy birthday to you!'

'Thank you.' I could barely stand to stare into his black eyes, fearful they would make my cheeks blaze into a blush.

'Wait. I will return …' He smiled again, and disappeared behind a door. The second it clicked shut, my friend leaned forward to whisper hotly into my ear: 'Oh my God, he is freaking gorgeous!'

'I know …' I mouthed back. Our shoulders shuddered as we tried to suppress our laughter.

Suddenly the door opened, and there he stood again. He strode towards us, proudly holding something aloft.

'This is for you. For your birthday.' He grinned at me.

There in his hand wasn't a single rose plucked from a vase, or a tiny chocolate wrapped in gold foil, or even a shiny marble of Venetian glass. Rather, what he held out to me like a prize was a slender tumbler filled to the brim with orange juice.

'I'm afraid it is all I have.' He raised an eyebrow in apology.

I reached out and took the glass from him, our fingers brushing slightly. Both he and my friends watched as I raised the drink to my mouth. The first sip hit my lips, and I drank through a smile. I knew it to be, without a doubt, the best glass of orange juice I had ever had, or ever would have.

I stared at this stranger's old-world good looks, at his encouraging eyes. The cold sweetness tickled my throat, and I felt as though I had been handed some sort of magic potion. I would never tell my friends any of this, of course. To them, it was simply a glass of juice, probably from concentrate, at that. But to my mind, this clerk had become some sort of fairy-tale prince. I somehow felt he knew the dark thoughts clouding my eyes, and had slipped out of the Venetian shadows to specially hand me this potion – a potion that would buoy me, and see me out of my troubled teens and into my twenties. With his random act of kindness, some new knowledge wove its way into my brain. I gripped the pulp-smeared, empty glass, knowing that happiness and love would follow me back to America. To wherever I went. It might leave me again someday, but it would always return.

My friends, no doubt eyeing my glass of juice hungrily, left in search of an open café, but I stayed behind and went outside to smoke with the clerk. He shared his filter-less cigarettes with me, and in halting English told me about his struggles as a poet, trying to get published, trying to make enough money. I had no idea what he was talking about really, the authors he was referring to, his financial struggles, but I let his accent dance in my ears, the burn of the cigarette filling my chest with a pleasant ache.

Soon the hostel was buzzing to life as my professors and other classmates began to drag their suitcases downstairs. But the clerk did not leave me. We continued to smoke and talk, until finally my whole class was scurrying past me, hurrying to catch the bus that would carry us to the airport.

As the last student hurried past, she turned to yell to me, 'Jo, come on! It's time to go!'

And so it was. As I finally began to shrug on my backpack, the clerk grabbed one of my hands, as though we had been lovers for years and now were being ripped asunder by the fates. I almost had to bite my lip to keep from giggling at his urgency. 'Well, goodbye to you …' He clasped my fingers. 'Please …' he learned towards me. 'May I have just one kiss?'

And in one of my most foolish moments on this earth, I declined. I laugh at my innocence now, but the truth was I still felt loyal to my English boyfriend, who was probably on his way to Heathrow right at that very moment, waiting to greet me and clasp my hands in this exact same manner.

'No, I'm afraid I can't.' I smiled apologetically.

He shrugged, his face falling with sadness. 'Well, goodbye then, I guess …'

'Goodbye!' I shouted over my shoulder as I ran to catch up with my friends.

I've sipped sake under the cherry blossoms of Kyoto. I've drunk sangria in the sunshine of a Barcelona square. I've slugged cold beers on hot summer rooftops in Manhattan. But I will always remember that glass of orange juice. And always regret that I didn't give him 'just one kiss'. Perhaps the only thing more delicious than the tangy pulp of that gifted potion would have been sinking into the sweetness of the prince's lips.

Himalayan Potatoes

LARRY HABEGGER

Larry Habegger has been covering the world since his international travels began in the 1970s. As a freelance writer for thirty years and syndicated columnist since 1985, his work has appeared in many major newspapers and magazines, including the *Los Angeles Times, Chicago Tribune, Travel & Leisure* and *Outside*. In 1993 he founded the award-winning 'Travelers' Tales' books with James and Tim O'Reilly; he is currently executive editor. He is also editor-in-chief of Triporati.com, lead blogger for Cleared for Takeoff – the Triporati Blog, and a founder of the Prose Doctors, an editors' consortium of top editors for top writers (www.prose doctors.com). He regularly teaches the craft of travel writing at workshops and writers' conferences, and lives with his family on Telegraph Hill in San Francisco.

The Sherpa woman glared down from above the unmarked trail junction where I stood, uncertain which way to go. Her black eyes stared through me as if I were a ghost.

'*Keni hinang Nang? Lam ga Nang?*' I asked in phrasebook Sherpa and Tibetan, gesturing towards one trail and then the other. Then I tried Nepali: *'Kun bato Nang?'* Finally, English: 'Which way to Nang?'

Her look seemed full of some deeply rooted hostility that had finally found a place to rest. I had no idea if my attempts at the local languages and hand gestures were in any way comprehensible, but a shiver ran through me. She wasn't going to tell me which trail went to Nang. She was silent as rock, so immobile that I wondered if she was deaf or mute.

Travelling without a guide, my friend Neil and I had ventured off the most popular trekking route and were heading up a side valley to Mount Everest. We hadn't been concerned until now because the routes were clear and we knew we could get food along the way at the lodges or from locals happy to earn some money. But we were down to our last few scraps and we had a long way to go.

We shrugged, agreed on the lower trail, and went on our way. Despite the heavy pack on my back I couldn't shake the chill that had settled upon me, and the longer we walked away from the woman, the more I wondered if the chill was as much from the strange encounter with her as the clinging fog that had crept up the canyon. I began to mull stories my Nepali friends had told me of evil spirits that preyed on vulnerable beings, and wondered if I was vulnerable, if I'd done something to bring this ill omen into our path. I walked on, following Neil, cold, hungry, uneasy.

The trail gradually descended. Fog drifted around us like a shifting shroud. The sound of the river below had grown from a faint backdrop to a constant growling companion. More than an hour later we stopped and ate our final biscuits. We'd seen no-one since our encounter with the Sherpani.

'What did you make of that woman back there?' I asked Neil.

'Strange. Made me wonder if she even knew we were there.'

A puff of damp breeze penetrated my three layers of clothing. 'I felt like she saw us all right, but wanted nothing to do with us.'

'Could be,' Neil said. 'She probably has a hundred trekkers a day asking directions.'

'Yeah, maybe,' I said, but it felt deeper than that.

A moment later I struggled to rise, hardly noticing that Neil was already making his way down the trail. One foot in front of the other, I reminded myself, my mantra for trekking in Nepal. The fog clung to the trees, licking with an icy tongue, deepening my chill.

Soon we could see the river at the bottom of the chasm, a churning grey torrent, stripping the land and sweeping glacier dust from the flanks of Everest. Still we had seen no-one, nor any sign of human habitation except the trail that drew us silently on.

Abruptly, the trail broke off at the site of an enormous gash in the canyon, a landslide that had taken half a mountain with it. Neil was staring grimly at the near-vertical slope we had to cross when I caught up with him. My legs felt like lead, and by the look of things we had no choice but to turn back. My heart sank. We knew we'd find no food or shelter by going back. We'd walked too far and couldn't possibly climb out of the canyon before dark. But how could we proceed?

Neil surprised me by saying he thought we could make it across. 'Look, the hillside is soft, we can plant our feet. Take it slow and easy, and we'll make it.'

With a heavy pack to balance, I didn't see how I could, but I was too tired to dissent. One slip would mean a certain, fast slide down at least a hundred feet to the boulders and that roiling current. But we had little choice, and Neil set out.

He dug in his boot, then planted the next one in a timid step, then another, and another until he was moving slowly across the slide, leaving bootprints for me to follow.

Unsteadily, I took a step, then another. Pebbles dislodged and sluiced down the hillside to the rocks below, their sounds absorbed by the roar of the river. The weight of the pack bore down and I tried to keep it from shifting, certain that one misstep would send me tumbling along the same path as those pebbles. I glanced up to see Neil halfway across, fifty feet from me, and that gave me hope. I concentrated, wobbled once when my pack shifted, but caught myself with a flash of adrenalin. Sweat dripped from my brow, and my shoulders ached with the pressure from the pack. The delirium of the thin air made my head swim. But I kept moving, and an eternity later I looked up to see Neil standing on firm ground at the end of the slide, only twenty feet away.

A few more steps and I was across as well. I shed my pack and collapsed the instant I touched solid ground. I needed many minutes to regain my composure. Sweat soaked my whole body, stealing what little warmth I had. Down in this cold canyon, daylight was fading and we had to keep going to find shelter.

Neil urged me up and we set off again. I was woozy now, not sure why we were plodding along this way, even where we were and why. I'd spent enough time in the wilderness to know that the bony grip of hypothermia was latching onto me, and I tried to calm myself. Need food. Warmth. Rest.

Then Neil shouted. He'd spotted huts ahead. Two, three, perhaps a village, but certainly food and shelter. He rushed on and I kept up my mantra, step-by-step. When I arrived at the first stone hut, Neil's sullen look told me everything I needed to know. The place was deserted. Again I collapsed, this time against a cold stone wall, too tired to contemplate moving.

But then Neil shouted again. The third hut was open, we could get out of the fog. I dragged myself up and stumbled the few feet to the hut, where I dropped everything in a heap. Dim light edged in through tiny windows, but the place was dry, full of straw, and not nearly as cold as outside. We finished off our water, climbed into our sleeping bags, and lay down for the long wait till morning.

Sleeping at high altitude is never easy, and I spent hours shivering until my body generated enough heat to allow the down bag to warm me up. At some point I was aware that I wasn't freezing any more, and then I slept.

After some hours I woke to faint light that suggested a new day. My stomach ached, but not from the intestinal problems that afflict most trekkers in Nepal. I needed food.

Our maps revealed that we should have been much higher than we were, and we realised we must have taken the wrong trail and ended up in a summer herders' camp, abandoned now for the approaching winter. Would that mean that the villages ahead would be deserted as well? We needed to climb out of the canyon and keep going in the faith that we'd find the main trail, and someone still there who would sell us food.

With no other option, we began bushwhacking up the hillside. Eventually we found a trail that seemed to be leading us up, and as we trudged along, the track became clearer. Better yet, high above, the first rays of sunshine graced the hillside. Blue sky emerged where we'd seen only fog the day before.

We climbed out of the forest and steadily up. I kept looking ahead, hoping to see where the path would flatten out on the main trail. Then suddenly I thought I saw someone sitting on the rocks high above. With every step I looked again, trying to convince myself that yes, it was a person, but fearing the shattering disappointment if it turned out to be just a trick of the light. The sun was shining on it but it remained immobile, a gargoyle staring out into the canyon. We climbed, mule-like, and with every step what I saw continued to look like a person.

And then it moved. Yes! It was a man, resting on a stone wall in the glorious sunshine, watching our slow progress with amusement, anger, surprise, indifference? Who cared? He was salvation.

When we reached him, the old man slid off the wall as nimbly as a cat. Before we could speak he motioned for us to follow him, gesturing at his mouth and then to us to ask if we were hungry.

We didn't need to answer. We followed him through the sunshine to his stone hut ablaze with morning light.

He offered us seats on a bench covered with a Tibetan carpet. A fire burned in his earthen stove, sending wafts of smoke curling to the ceiling and out the thatched roof. Sunlight streamed through the window and threw halos around him that seemed to refract into rainbows. Deep lines carved his face into a mask of toil, but tranquillity shone in his eyes.

In a tin basin he washed his hands over and over, taking several minutes as if in a ritual cleansing, then he poured water into a black pot and put it on the stove. After that he took a bag of potatoes off the wall and gently removed them and put them on a tin plate. With a small brush he carefully scrubbed every speck of dirt off each potato, one by one, until they gleamed. The pile of potatoes glowing in the sunlight, and the care with which he handled this food, made me feel we were in a sanctified presence.

I watched every move he made, my hunger forgotten, marvelling at the precision with which he cleaned the cups into which he would pour our tea, the delicacy of his actions when slicing the potatoes, the patient care he took to polish every spoon and fork and plate before he placed them, just so, before us. Here was a man who treated hospitality – the preparation of a simple meal, the sharing of sustenance with guests – as a higher calling.

We sat for an hour or more in that warm hut, watching this patient yak herder prepare a simple dish of fried potatoes. When I took the first sip of tea, when I inhaled the first scent of those potatoes, when I tasted the first nibble of that life-saving meal, I discovered the true meaning of gratitude.

The sun beamed straight into the canyon when we finally rose to leave. Belly full, energy restored, I hoisted my pack to continue along the trail. And then I remembered the woman who had caused me so much anxiety the day before. She was our messenger as well as our nemesis, setting up our encounter with this man who'd taught me a lesson in kindness and the importance of every detail. He was the yang to her yin, the two of them the whole we all seek, the crazy mad jumble that is our humanity.

We all have our own doses of light and dark, and that thought, along with the memory of those simple but exquisite potatoes, left me feeling lighter than I had in days as we headed up the trail towards Everest.

Chai, Chillum and Chapati

SEAN McLACHLAN

Sean McLachlan is a freelance writer specialising in travel and history. He is the author of numerous books and regularly blogs at www.gadling.com. He has visited more than thirty countries, his favourites being India and Ethiopia, which never cease to amaze him. 'Chai, Chillum and Chapati' is adapted from his unpublished book, *The River Outside the Water: Wandering Through Kumbh Mela, India's Greatest Pilgrimage*. Sean divides his time between Spain, England and Missouri. You can learn more about him at midlistwriter.blogspot.com, where he talks about life as a prolific yet unknown writer, and his personal/ travel blog, grizzledoldtraveler.blogspot.com.

I and a million others have been walking since dawn. Walking to the Sangam, the confluence of the Yamuna and Ganges Rivers in northern India. Walking to immortality.

The crowd is immense yet unhurried. As far as I can see on the highway ahead and behind me is a vast, solid mass of pilgrims from all parts of India, converging here for this special time at this special place.

It is time for Kumbh Mela, when for the month of Magha the nectar of immortality flows through the Sangam, as it did when the earth was young. The planets are in an alignment seen only once every 144 years, making this the holiest pilgrimage India has seen since 1857.

North of the Sangam lies the broad sandy flood plain of the Ganges. During the monsoon the area is submerged, but now, in January of 2001, we're in the middle of the dry season and the Ganges has withered to a trickle. Most of the riverbed is dry, and it's here that the *mela* administration has built the main camp. Throughout the festival the pilgrims pray, eat and sleep within the sacred space of India's holiest river.

The government estimates seventy million people will wash away their sins by bathing in the Sangam. An estimated ten million will stay for the entire month of Magha to gain the same merits as an entire life lived as a Brahmin. It will be the largest gathering in recorded history.

But I'm not there yet. I'm in a different river, a river of people moving steadily towards the camp along a road lined with palm trees. The pace is unhurried, yet as relentless as the Ganges itself. I have not eaten breakfast and as I walk, the greasy tang of frying food wafts through the air to tempt me. To the left opens up a tamped dirt yard. Dozens of clay ovens give off the fragrance of chapatis and samosas, pulling in hungry pilgrims like a magnet. They crowd around ovens manned by sweating families serving up a hundred meals a minute, a desperate stirring, kneading, frying and stoking factory of food production. Money passes hands at a furious rate as customers scream for rice, bread, fried vegetables, while tiny child beggars pick through the lowing herd of adults, hands outstretched, little mouths watering, eyes impossibly big on filthy faces, or fight half-wild dogs for the scraps from overflowing trash bins.

I shuffle forward with the rest until I'm in front. The flitting workers, smoothly flowing back and forth like parts of some finely oiled machine, look calm and relaxed. The only sign of their hurry is their utter lack of curiosity at a sunburned face grunting out an order in bad Hindi. They shove food into my hands and toss me change almost before I've paid. The crowd flows in front of me and squirts me out its back like some amoebae ejecting a microscopic piece of indigestible flotsam. I tumble away from the mass, avoiding the swarm of newcomers, and weave my way to the curry-smeared safety of a wooden table, a greasy island of stability in a sea of movement.

The other diners watch as I use a chapati to scoop up dhal from a little leaf bowl held together with toothpicks. Their eyes follow my hand as I reach for a thin clay *miti* cup of steaming chai. They crowd around me and the questions start. 'Where are you from? 'Hello, what country?' 'What is your job?' 'What is your religion?'

I answer these questions politely but in haste. The frenetic energy of this place has me wolfing down my meal, eager to reach the *mela*. I've flown halfway around the world to see this greatest of pilgrimages, and almost being there has me anxious to continue.

My fast-food meal eaten, I move back into the solid mass of people headed towards the *mela* camp. There's no rushing or shoving; the frantic swirl around the food stalls is a lone eddy in a placid river of humanity. No-one cuts ahead or lags behind. We flow.

Up a hill and over into … something else.

Our view opens up on the long flat expanse of the Ganges riverbed and the *mela* grounds. Stretching below us is mile upon mile of tents, their dull brown canvas blending with the sand.

Here and there sprout the red, white and saffron pavilions of the great gurus and religious societies. The canvas spires of temporary temples rise above them. To the north the grey curve of a concrete overpass links one riverbank to another, and beyond that gleams the steel latticework of a railway bridge. In the distance are the slumbering bulks of the *yagna* pyramids, massive wicker constructions in which Brahmins are preparing a fire ritual as old as Hinduism itself.

Walking into the camp we enter a barren landscape. Featureless sand lies below an unchanging sky. I won't see a cloud for a month. The hard light brightens colours and puts people and tents into sharp relief, like figures etched on stained glass. The Hindus couldn't have picked a blanker canvas onto which to paint their picture of paradise.

I spot a sadhu, one of India's wandering holy men. He's no more than thirty, with hard muscles and rough skin from living outside, but the smooth belly hanging over his leopard-skin loincloth is evidence of a bit of luxury every now and then. His hair and beard are long and matted, dreadlocks reaching the small of his back.

'Hello, sir, what country?' he asks, fixing me with a bloodshot stare.

'Canada.'

'Your good name, sir?' His words are slurred.

'Sean. What's yours?'

'I am Dharamgiri. Come with me. We'll have chai.'

Dharamgiri is from the Juna Akhara, a Shiva-worshipping sect known for its large number of Naga Babas, warrior-saints who practise swordsmanship and go without clothes, dressed only in a fine layer of dust to protect them from the elements. They have a reputation for violent and erratic behaviour due to their frequent use of hashish. Dharamgiri doesn't look threatening, but it's obvious he's very, very stoned.

Dharamgiri leads me through the turreted gate of the Juna camp and down an alley hemmed by cloth barriers stretched between poles. Each cloth marks a compound of sadhus. They can be taken down when the sadhus want visitors, or left up when they wish to be alone. At Dharamgiri's compound the cloth is down. A little crowd of onlookers clusters in the alley, looking inside. Nobody dares cross the threshold. Dharamgiri ignores them as he pushes through. We remove our shoes and enter a small patch of sand ten feet to a side, enclosed by a cloth fence on which hang posters of the gods. Shiva meditates on a mountaintop, his skin blue from the funeral ashes with which he smears himself, the perfect sadhu. Krishna frolics with the milkmaids. Durga, the mother goddess, rides her tiger and brandishes weapons and objects of power in her sixteen hands. A tent takes up most of the space, its dark recesses hiding the slumbering forms of half a dozen sadhus. A young initiate rubs sleepy eyes and gazes at me with mild curiosity before turning over.

In front of the tent stands the hearth, a clay-lined square pit dug in alignment with the four directions. A heap of coals is always kept smouldering. An iron trident, the emblem of Shiva, stands with its shaft driven into the coals, its tines decorated with a garland of yellow flowers.

Two sadhus squat naked in the sand, their bodies whitened with ash. One is old, with deeply creased skin and a caved-in chest with the sagging, deflated breasts of a fat man gone thin. His ribs stick out like the bars of a cage. Dreadlocks are coiled into a bun on top of his head. He sucks on a chillum, a straight hash pipe. He shoots out the smoke in a series of wheezy hacks and hands it to his companion, a younger man with lean, hard limbs. The younger sadhu takes the chillum and sucks greedily, his corded neck muscles flattening and giving him a lizardy look.

Dharamgiri sits down by the fire and motions for me to sit next to him. The crowd outside grows, everyone wanting to see what would become a common scene at Kumbh Mela, the sadhu and his foreign guest. Dharamgiri calls out a name, and the sleepy-eyed initiate pops his head out of the tent.

'Get chai,' Dharamgiri orders.

The boy, his saffron robe looking out of place among so many bare bodies, emerges carrying a steel pot, sets it by my host and squats nearby, eyeing me with curiosity.

Dharamgiri takes the lid off the pot and pulls out a plastic satchel of milk, freshly bought from one of the camp's government dispensaries. Other bags follow and are arranged neatly beside him. He slices the packet with a blackened fingernail and holds it steady as milk burbles into the pot. Then he opens another bag and fishes out some ground ginger and cardamom, sprinkling them into the milk. A handful of black tea and heaps of sugar follow.

'Om Shiva,' the sadhu mutters as he blows the grey ashes from the coals. The older sadhu runs his hands through the ashes and rubs the grit along his arms and face. Dharamgiri continues blowing, and with each puff the coals redden and pulse like beating hearts. Heat shimmers between us. I see the wavering image of the old sadhu staring at me, his ash-whitened skin blending with the steam. His bloodshot eyes look like volcanoes on the moon.

Nobody speaks. We don't need to. It's a very Eastern trait, one I've seen from the deserts of Syria to the foothills of the Himalayas. Sit and absorb the feel of your company. Share a meal or some tea. Think of what you want to ask, then ask. If you don't share a language, you can always just sit and eat. Some of the best conversations don't require words.

Dharamgiri places the covered pot on top of the coals, grinding it a bit to set it in place. Moving into the lotus position, he inhales deeply through flaring nostrils. His eyes close. The old sadhu passes the chillum to his skinny friend, skipping the initiate. A tracery of smoke curls into the air.

I decide to join Dharamgiri. I close my eyes and drop my thoughts, slow my breathing and listen. Relax. Everyone is staring at me, but they've been doing that ever since I got to India, so it makes no difference. I hear the murmur of the pilgrims behind me. Across from me there's a slight crackle of the jute mat as the initiate shifts position. The coals of the campfire hiss and pop. There's a snap as one cracks and the pot settles with an almost silent rasp. The skinny sadhu is smoking again. The crackle of the burning hash and tobacco and the whistle of his breath through the tube sound loud in the enclosure.

I can't hear anything beyond what's happening here. The giant campground might as well not exist. I can't hear the people thronging the roads, or the honks of vehicles as they trundle along the main streets. I can't even hear the PA system, which gives announcements in a nonstop drone audible everywhere but here. The sadhus have created a *mela* hidden within the larger *mela,* an integral part of the festival but aloof from it.

A long, slow exhalation from my right tells me Dharamgiri is coming out of his trance state. I haven't gotten very deep in just a few minutes of meditation, but I feel more relaxed and more in tune with my new companions. I open my eyes. The two sadhus have finished the chillum. The old man sits with his eyes shut, meditating. The younger one and the initiate watch me. I look at Dharamgiri. He nods serenely, then turns to the staring crowd, grunts and waves his arm dismissively. They melt away like water.

The receding pilgrims part for a spry old sadhu clad only in a saffron loincloth. His dreadlocks are wrapped into a large bun, a single loose coil curving over his shoulder like a python.

Expressive eyes gaze forth from a broad face. He carries an old wallet of faded and cracked leather held together with duct tape.

Dharamgiri smiles.

'Come, sit down, we're making chai,' he says. He turns to me and adds, 'This is Mauni Baba. He hasn't spoken in twenty years.'

Mauni Baba beams me a grin that shows a row of yellow and uneven teeth. The deep creases on his face fold in on themselves like ripples on a pond. He looks like a yogic Cheshire cat. It's the expression of someone who has learned to speak without words. It's entirely open, welcoming, and makes me feel more at home than the chai or the chillum.

He sits at Dharamgiri's right hand and scrutinises me with a mixture of curiosity and unabashed delight. When you're the object of such unrestrained wonder, there's nothing to do but sit and smile back. After a few minutes of studying each other, he opens his wallet stuffed to bursting with bits of paper, stamps, photos, old envelopes, creased and faded postcards, even a boarding pass from a Swiss Air flight from 1989. Mauni Baba picks through the mess and pulls out a tiny map of the world printed in English. He hands it to me, points at my chest and then at the map. I point at Canada.

'You can ask him questions,' Dharamgiri says. 'He knows English.'

'How did you learn English?' I ask.

Mauni Baba elaborately pantomimes being hunched over a desk, typing furiously at an invisible typewriter, brow furrowed in intense concentration. Then he sits up and leafs through what can only be a newspaper, reading the imaginary lines with studied interest.

'He was a journalist?'

'Yes, eleven years in Delhi.'

'Why did you leave?' I ask.

Mauni Baba sits up in the lotus position, spine straight and eyes lightly closed. His features soften into such profound relaxation that I wonder if he's slipping into a trance, but a moment later he opens his searchlight eyes and places a finger on his abdomen. He raises his hand up his chest, touching all the chakra points up to the centre of his forehead, where he mimes the opening of his third eye by spreading out his fingers like a flower petal, eyes widening in wonder. He inhales sharply and seems to grow. He beats his fist against his chest. Power. Indicating the crowd that has once again clogged the alley, he thrusts his long arm out, bony fingers spread wide as if grasping, and pulls it towards himself. He turns and mimes pulling in people from all around, drawing a large circle in the air around him. Then he cocks his head and scowls at the crowd, brushing them away with a dismissive gesture one would use with a misbehaving child. The crowd breaks up even faster than it did for Dharamgiri. He turns to me and smiles triumphantly.

Dharamgiri pulls the lid off the pot and peers inside. A puff of steam envelops his face, followed by a sweet smell. He grasps a pair of iron tongs and lifts the pot off the coals, then pours the fragrant brown chai, speckled with blackened bits of ginger, through a sieve and into several steel cups lined up beside him.

'Om Shiva,' he intones, pouring a bit onto the fire. The coals hiss a reply.

'Babas must share their meal,' he explains. 'One quarter for Shiva, one quarter for guests. Two quarters for us.'

He passes the cups around, to me first, then Mauni Baba, the other sadhus, the initiate, and finally himself.

It's the best chai I've ever had, sweet and milky and strongly caffeinated. The poorer sadhus don't eat much, usually just round unleavened loaves called chapati, so they get most of their energy from endless rounds of chillum and chai. They say there are three C's in sadhu life: chai, chillum and chapati.

'So what's it like being a sadhu?' I ask Dharamgiri.

'Baba life good life, but very hard. Every morning I get up to do one hour yoga, one hour meditation. Then I go bathe in the river. The afternoon is the same.'

'Where were you before this?'

'At a monastery. Many Juna there. All the time smoking, all the time chillum.' He gives a chesty cough as if to emphasise his point. 'Too much smoking there, I'm not smoking so much at Kumbh Mela.'

'What will you do after this?'

'Go to the forest. Too many people here. All the time they come around to look at babas. All the time asking, "Baba give me *darshan*. Baba, tell me how to live my life." I go to the forest. Meditate. Be quiet. Rest.'

'Why did you become a baba?'

'I join the Juna when I was twelve. My parents brought me to Juna. I grow up a baba.'

'You must travel a lot.'

'I've been all over India. Down to Goa, down to Tamil Nadu. One time Sri Lanka. Goa was a good place. Lot of foreigners like you, very friendly. They want to meet the babas, smoke chillums. I've been to the Himalayas. Good place. No people.'

I catch Mauni Baba's eye as we both raise our cups of chai. He stops mid-sip and points to me, then extends his arm at a high angle, pointing to the far distance, and brings it palm downwards to the spot where we sit. He passes his hand to encompass our circle, points to the pot of chai, and gives me a smile of radiant joy. *Welcome to Kumbh Mela,* it says.

Welcome indeed.

The Icing on the Japanese Cake

STEFAN GATES

Stefan Gates is a food adventurer and award-winning writer/TV presenter renowned for his perceptive, witty and unconventional approach to food and cooking. He particularly loves wild culinary quests and extraordinary food adventures. His food and travel books and TV series have won many awards, including Best TV Series at the Bologna Food on Film Festival, and his documentaries have been shown in over thirty countries. Stefan wrote and presented *Cooking in the Danger Zone* for BBC2, presented the prime-time magazine show *Full on Food* and hundreds of episodes of the studio show *Food Uncut*. His food/travel series *Feasts* took him to the greatest feasts on earth. Stefan has just finished *E Numbers: An Edible Adventure*, a myth-busting food science series, and he has also written an accompanying book. He chairs events, performs cookery demos, writes for newspapers and magazines, and regularly appears on radio and TV shows as a guest. He has written five books, the latest of which is *The Extraordinary Cookbook*, on unforgettable food adventures. He is also the author of *Gastronaut, In the Danger Zone* and *101 Dishes to Eat Before You Die*.

It was never meant to be like this. Look at me: a bloodied, bedraggled waif staggering around a beautiful Shinto temple courtyard drunk as a skunk and soaked to the bone, bare bottom on display for all the world to see, only a thin strip of cotton hiding my genitals and above all else, desperately, *desperately* hungry.

In an unwise moment of blinding clarity, I catch sight of my reflection in a window and look deep inside my soul to ponder what brought me to this. Despite selling my soul to the evil gogglebox as a TV presenter five years earlier, I had, up until now, largely managed to preserve my dignity by sticking to serious documentaries, arcane food stories and explorations of the complex relationship between people and food. Sure, I had done a few wild things for TV, gone to war zones more dangerous than a food writer really needed to go, eaten bull's perineum for the thrill, and palm weevils for the flavour. But that had all been in the legitimate chase of knowledge and adventure rather than a good set of viewing figures. Now I stand at the top of my modest mountain of achievement, about to cast the whole shebang into the air to crash on the rocks of naked indignity. Worst of all, I know something extraordinarily important has just happened, but I have no idea what it all meant.

There is a valid(ish) reason for me being in this state of disarray. I am making a TV series for the BBC (the largest broadcaster in the world and, up until now, probably the most respected) called *Feasts,* which is about … well … feasts. I have been touring the world to find out why food has the power to bring people together, to channel grief, joy and God, and to see if I can use these feasts to get a deeper understanding of the world's more enigmatic people. I'll be honest with you: it had seemed like a cushy gig when I first suggested it. But now I have come to Japan, a country I have always loved but oddly never really felt a deep connection with, to see if I can dig deeper into the Japanese soul by joining in some of their more dramatic shared experiences.

The 1200-year-old Naked Man Festival is probably the most dramatic shared experience in the world, and it's also a Shinto ceremony that tells you all you need to know about repressed emotions (more of which later) and the Japanese obsession with superstition. Although Japan is often considered a Buddhist country, most Japanese people I know practise a pragmatic syncretism, combining elements of Buddhism and Shintoism (which is itself more of a philosophical path than a religion), neither of which require a traditional monotheistic profession of faith to allow you to be a believer.

If that sounds complicated, it is. Unless you're Japanese, in which case it's simple: most say that they aren't religious, but they often visit both Buddhist temples and Shinto shrines, picking whichever elements they feel they need. My friend Junko explains that she will drop into a Buddhist temple to show respect for her ancestors, but tie a wish ribbon at her Shinto shrine to ask for good luck with her driving test. She sees Buddhism as a faith for the afterlife, and Shintoism as a set of principles and superstitions that can affect everyday current life. But when I ask her if she's religious, she curls her nose up and squirms, 'Noooo!'

The Naked Man Festival is a thoroughly Shinto affair: an opportunity to banish bad luck for the year ahead, to make wishes for yourself and your family's health and happiness in a dynamic and dramatic way, and at the same time express your basest, most primal feelings by getting drunk, naked and violent. And it's all based around a cake. I've come to Nagoya, which throws the most spectacular version of the festival, to try to get to grips with the whole thing.

Let's start from the beginning: firstly a man is selected to be the Naked Man, or Shinotoko. He is kept in isolation for three days for spiritual purification, although this isolation includes his being regularly dragged out for display for TV cameras and meetings with local dignitaries and businessmen (he's not allowed to talk – apparently that keeps him pure). He's grateful for this period of relative calm, because in a few days he's going to be stripped naked and thrown into the arms of ten thousand drunken, semi-naked men desperate to slap him on the head or grab hold of an arm in order to pass all of their bad luck and evil deeds onto him, as he struggles to make his way back to the temple. It sounds like the very definition of bad karma.

During this period of isolation, local groups of people come together around the district to pound rice into flour and then use it to cook a series of vast rice cakes, the largest weighing in at around four tonnes. Because this cake is made using everyone's hard work and communal dedication, it begins to take on a spiritual power that is ratified and blessed upon delivery (by twenty-tonne hydraulic crane) to the main Shinto temple. The cake now has *intense* spiritual power.

Up to this point, all is well and calm and the festival is merely an interesting anthropological, socio-religious quirk, of which there are so many similar events around the world. Soon, though, the spiritual shit is destined to hit the fan in a big way.

———————◄═

There are lots of different theories about this festival's meaning, and many different versions around Japan. I don't want to offer the ultimate definition, as I don't think there is one, and in any case it's too complicated to pick apart, but this is my first-hand experience of the festival.

I meet an amiable elderly Japanese gentleman by the name of Kosaki-san, who has invited me to join him to celebrate the Naked Man Festival (this isn't the sort of gig that anyone, let alone a foreigner, should do on their own). Kosaki-san is small, formal, humble, smart and smiley. His wife is the same, but smaller. They invite me into their home for dinner and we spend a few days getting to know each other. They are prototypical Japanese straight from the cultural copybook: wonderful hosts, generous and kind, hard working and successful (Kosaki-san is an engineer with his own small but high-tech factory that makes lift parts) and, crucially, they seem chronically unable to express emotion. (Now, if you think I'm guilty of cultural stereotyping here, you're probably right. I'm sure there are plenty of expressive, emotional and argumentative Japanese; I just haven't met any of them. I nonetheless have a deep affection for my many wonderful but less expressive friends, Japanese or otherwise.)

After spending several days getting to know them and experiencing, amongst other things, an intriguing but painfully formal tea ceremony, I decide to break with convention and ask the Kosakis some difficult personal questions. I start by asking Mrs Kosaki if Japanese men hide their emotions. You could cut the atmosphere with a knife. Kosaki-san looks particularly ashen-faced.

'Yes, I think so.'

Has her husband ever told her that he loves her?

'No.' (They have been married for twenty years.) 'I think Japanese men find it difficult to say such things.'

Kosaki-san laughs nervously and says, 'I don't say it, but she knows it. She knows what's in my heart. The Japanese don't often thank their wives to their face. That's not to say we don't feel grateful. We just aren't very good at expressing that.'

Mrs Kosaki looks at me with her eyebrows raised and a 'What can you do?' expression on her face. She takes a breath before commenting judiciously, 'It would be nice if they could actually say thank you out loud.'

'Do you think it's a good idea for Kosaki-san to join in the Naked Man Festival?'

'I look at them and wonder what on earth makes them want to get naked with other men every year. The Naked Man Festival is all about men.' But she says this without malice, rather with the tenderness of a mother watching a toddler running happily around with a dustbin on his head. Kosaki-san looks intently at his feet.

I realise that I've probably crossed the line of formality and I'm in danger of upsetting my hosts and the rules of Japanese hospitality, so I take Kosaki-san up on his offer of dinner with some of his friends, bid goodnight to his lovely wife and we go out to get thoroughly, uproariously pissed.

The next day is the day of the festival itself. It's a freezing-cold, sunny morning and around twenty friends gather at Kosaki-san's house. I am feeling extremely anxious, but Kosaki-san is like a kid at Christmas, running around welcoming everyone and handing out cups of water. He hands me one and I take a large swig. I nearly spit it straight out: it's not water, it's *sake*. It's only 10am, for Christ's sake.

We gather cross-legged around a long low table to consume a small meal of sushi alongside a vast ocean of alcohol. Huge bottles of sake and smaller bottles of beer are passed around the table, and everyone drinks heavily. No-one is excused: the entire purpose of the next two hours is to get comprehensively, dangerously inebriated. 'You'll need this,' says Kosaki-san, 'otherwise you won't be able to join in.'

I tank down as much booze as I can, and watch as the men around me descend into giggling, slurring and staggering. Eventually, once we are all well pickled, Kosaki-san rouses us to get changed. The ladies withdraw and we all strip off and jump into Kosaki-san's ridiculously small bath to purify ourselves for the coming ritual. When we emerge, we dress each other in a long thin cotton cloth that wraps unflatteringly up our bum cracks and over our genitals, before being tied around our stomachs. Kosaki-san takes great pleasure in yanking mine up to give me what I can only describe as an excruciating wedgie, just for the fun of it. Ooooh, that smarts. Basically, we're wearing cloth G-strings that leave our flabby pink behinds poking out for all the world to see. But by now we're too drunk to care, and there's much cock-waving and arse-slapping before we're all ready.

One man collapses unconscious, too drunk to continue, and we drag him back to the sushi room to brew up his beastly hangover in relative safety. We write our wishes for health and happiness on strips of cloth and tie them to a long bamboo branch that Kosaki-san has found, and then a fat permanent marker appears and we all write mobile phone numbers on our arms in case of emergencies. I, for no good reason, decide to write in huge letters on everyone's back 'The BBC loves Japan'. Classy.

Fired up and staggering drunk, we set off at a terrifying running pace, holding our bamboo branch aloft as we head across the city to the Shinto shrine. At the same time, ten thousand other drunk men across Nagoya set off in groups of twenty or thirty to converge on the temple, and the city looks like a scene from a zombie porn movie. As I meet more and more semi-naked strangers, we slap each other's backs and share bottles of sake like old lost friends, and I engage in emotional conversations with people I've never met, discovering a deep connection with them, despite the fact that neither of us understands what the other is saying.

We arrive at the road in front of the temple and the ceremonial driveway is packed with men in the same inebriated half-naked state as us. We race along with our pole and run into the temple grounds to deposit it with the priests, nearly stabbing one of them as we throw it into the melee. We retire to the driveway to wait for the main event as tens of thousands of onlookers and umpteen TV camera crews, including my own team, head for safety onto rooftops and up trees. A voice comes over the loudspeaker warning that people are being crushed and collapsing from the stress. Kosaki-san and I have managed to get a prime position just outside the temple, and we are crammed in by hundreds of other men, buttock to sticky, sweaty buttock.

Suddenly there is a roar from afar. The Shinotoko has been released into the baying crowd, with all ten thousand men desperate to touch him. We all crush towards the noise, even though he is a kilometre away at the far end of the crowd, making his slow and painful way towards us. A great clamour breaks out from behind us as a team of men begin running with buckets of water through the crowds to douse the Shinotoko and his assailants to cool them down and reduce the danger of heat exhaustion. The water steams off the crowd as they scramble over one another, jumping on top of each other in desperation.

The epicentre of the crush comes slowly towards us as our anticipation rises, but the Shinotoko takes two more hours to get as far as the temple gates where I stand. The pressure becomes overpowering, and the mass of flesh sways and writhes, taking me along with it. I get trapped against a post, crushing my kidneys for what seems like ages until an enormously fat man yanks me free and shoves me back into the fray. I feel like I am part of a single huge, drunken, desperate fleshy beast, stinking of alcohol and filled with a toxic mixture of anxiety and anticipation.

The Shinotoko finally looms near and I am overcome by a desperate, primal urge to touch him. As I catch sight of his bloodied scalp, I lunge forward with all my might, at the same time as a surge from the men behind me. We shove through the crowd towards him, and I get within a metre when a bucket of freezing water hits me and a counter-surge from the opposite side stops me short, and I can only flail wildly at him. His guards shove him through the gates and, like a cork from a bottle, they propel him to the temple entrance where the priests and paramedics await him. He's raced through the crowd, and a priest crowd-dives into the melee, attached to the temple by a rope of rolled-up cotton strips. He grabs the Shinotoko by the head, and the other priests yank at the end of his rope and pull the two of them into the temple to ecstatic cries and wild cheering from the crowd. It's like a birth in reverse. Most of us are in tears at the wonderful, insane emotional outpouring of it all.

The crowd eventually stops cheering and people begin to leave, which is when I catch sight of my reflection and have a sudden moment of confused introspection, followed by a deepening sense of shame and indignity at everything I've done. I have been transported to a different place, felt a bizarre and unknowable connection to ten thousand strangers – but by what? By drunkenness and a primal propensity to violence as part of a baying mob? What was it all for?

I am bleeding from scratches all over my torso, I have bruises on my arms and legs, and my feet are bare and ragged. I'm shivering from cold and exhaustion and I've lost Kosaki-san and all of my new friends. After taking a moment to catch my breath, I head off in the direction of my host's house. It takes another hour for me to find my way there, and I walk in, desperate to get back into my clothes and go to a hotel. But I enter to a roar of welcome from my fellow Naked Men and their families.

A cascade of joy courses through me as they cheer me in, and they then help bathe and dress me with an extraordinary tenderness. I have never in my life felt so in need of this care and attention. They get me warm and safe, and then we sit down to share our experiences of the festival over a feast of the finest sushi and sake.

Kosaki-san assures me that getting close to the Shinotoko was enough: bad luck and guilt is transferred by my touching the men in front of me, and it travels like an electrical circuit to the Shinotoko. I try to believe him.

Meanwhile, back at the temple, the Shinotoko has the core of the four-tonne communal rice cake strapped to his back alongside some fireworks, then he races around the central temple and the bad luck is spiritually transferred to the cake, which is then unstrapped and buried in a secret location (I'm really not making any of this up), along with the bad luck and bad deeds of ten thousand men.

Back at Kosaki-san's, we feast on his hospitality, and I experience a revelation: I have made a deep, enigmatic, unspoken, barely explainable connection to Japan by sharing this bizarre experience. We all hug and carouse in a way that I never have before. I have experienced an intimacy with Kosaki-san and his crazy friends that I don't have with my closest friends. Okay, it's had a fair amount to do with the booze, the nakedness and the shared experience, but there is also an intense and palpable sense of hope and relief that's all packed into the bizarre cake at the centre of it all – a cake that no-one ever ate, but that ends up meaning so much.

As I drink even more sake, I luxuriate in the warmth of this new-found friendship, but I'm also aware that it will be but a memory tomorrow. I've had an extraordinary insight into how my Japanese friends' minds work, but come tomorrow they will return to their formal, less-expressive selves and the strictures and responsibilities of this tight-lipped society will throw its web over all these people again. But for tonight, they are free.

Outside in the hallway, I catch sight of Mrs Kosaki touching Kosaki-san's shoulder and giving him a light kiss on the lips. He smiles at her, then brings in more sushi.

The Abominable Trekker

JEFF GREENWALD

Jeff Greenwald is a resident of Oakland, California, and the author of several travel books, including *Shopping for Buddhas* and *The Size of the World*. He also serves as Executive Director of Ethical Traveler (www.ethicaltraveler.org), a global alliance of politically active travellers. Jeff's latest book, *Snake Lake*, was published in 2010.

The Arun Valley, slicing through eastern Nepal, is the world's deepest river gorge. Back in the 1980s, not many travellers bothered with that remote and undeveloped place. Trekking in Nepal was all about Everest, Annapurna and the Langtang Himal: places where the mountains had celebrity status, and a hungry hiker could find a good buckwheat pancake.

In the spring of 1984, I was living in Kathmandu on a Rotary fellowship. Having learned a bit of Nepali, and eager to test my mettle, I flew from Kathmandu to Tumlingtar, where our twin-engine plane shimmied to a stop on the grassy runway. From there I set off north, on foot, intent on tracing the Arun along the length of its gorge – all the way to the Tibetan border.

This was in April, and it had been a wet winter. Conditions could change in an instant, and my backpack was heavy with gear. After a few hours alone on the muddy, slippery trail, I realised I needed help.

Stopping in a wayside town, I was able to hire a porter: a friendly teenager named Norbu, which in Tibetan means 'wish-fulfilling gem'. Norbu was a Sherpa Spiderman: fleet of foot and incredibly fit. He shouldered my huge pack with ease, and we set off together towards the mountain snows.

The trail became drier, higher, and more beautiful, carpeted with brilliant red rhododendron petals. Norbu and I trekked up ridges and down verdant valleys, sharing tales. One brilliant morning, over breakfast, he shyly expressed a wish to visit a nearby village called Bala. His grandparents were the headman and headwoman of the hamlet. He hadn't seen them for several years. It would delight them, Norbu said, if we stopped in for a night.

I readily agreed, with one caveat: we couldn't allow ourselves to be a burden. Eastern Nepal has scant resources, and the long winter was just ending. Food would be scarce. We'd brought rations of noodles and dried meat, and would cook for ourselves.

'But they'll insist,' Norbu replied. 'You'll be an honoured guest, the first American to visit the village.'

'Well … Please make sure they don't overdo it.'

We arrived mid-afternoon. Bala was an oasis of tidy, mud-walled homes, nestled between terraced hills. Corn and chilli peppers hung from rafters. As predicted, Norbu was greeted like a returning moonwalker. I was the exotic alien he'd brought home. Kids ran over to stare at my nose, tug my beard, and pinch the strange fabric of my high-end expedition parka.

Jeff Greenwald

Despite my earnest and sincere protests, Norbu's grandparents – a wizened couple who lived in Bala's biggest house – insisted on preparing dinner. Norbu suggested, diplomatically, that I stay out of their way.

Supplied with a flask of the local millet *rakshi*, I climbed a nearby hill and watched the sun fall behind the foothills. The more I drank, the better I felt; soon I was feeling very good indeed. It was incredible that I should find myself in this remote Himalayan village, a guest of honour among the local tribespeople. Sometimes, on rare occasions, a traveller feels this way: that your entire life has conspired to bring you to this moment.

Time passed. I finished the *rakshi*. As the last rays of light scraped the clouds and faded from the sky, I heard the rhythmic ringing of a cowbell: the signal that dinner was ready. I picked my way down the hillside, followed a narrow lane between stone walls, and found the house.

There was no electricity. The large single room of Norbu's grandparents' home was illuminated with yak-butter lamps. Villagers filled the low wooden benches placed along the mud-plastered walls. In the centre of the swept dirt floor, facing the open-pit kitchen, was a single wooden chair, cushioned with a hand-loomed carpet: my place of honour.

I sat down, and the room fell silent. Norbu's grandmother, wearing her finest Tibetan *chuba*, turned from the hearth and approached me. She carried a large copper tray, a traditional Nepali wedding gift. Upon the tray was a mountain of rice, served with fragrant lentil stew. She'd prepared a side dish of *tarkari* – boiled greens and potatoes – as well as a small bowl of spicy *achaar* pickle. I detected hints of cumin and *timur,* the tongue-numbing Sichuan pepper. Atop this already bountiful offering was a fried egg, a rare treat in these subsistence villages. But my heart nearly broke when I saw the crowning touch: a

268

drumstick and thigh. The family had killed and roasted one of their few, precious chickens in our honour.

With great ceremony, Norbu's grandmother set the heavy tray on my lap. All eyes were upon me. I looked around, giddy from the *rakshi* and the altitude. A hundred thoughts raced through my head: self-consciousness, fascination, a childlike astonishment.

Norbu, seated beside his grandfather, grinned at me. I grinned back. My head felt large and warm. What a place to be. And what were my friends in California up to right now? Eating breakfast? Sleeping? Watching *Hill Street Blues*? That world seemed so far away … Distracted, without thinking, I crossed my legs.

The copper tray overturned, and crashed to the dirt floor.

For an infinite moment, time stood still. The room was a tableau of shocked faces – none more shocked than my own. Had this unspeakable thing actually happened? Had my entire life conspired to bring me to *this* moment? I leaped to my feet, incredulous, overcome with shame. *'Naraamro!'* I cried, staring down at the steaming mess. *'Maaph garnus!* This is terrible! I'm sorry!'

Norbu's grandfather stood up calmly, and walked towards me. He placed a firm hand on my shoulder, and turned towards his stunned guests. *'Ramro chaa,'* he stated calmly. 'It's fine. It's good. In fact … it's *wonderful*. Isn't it?' He scanned the room. *'Isn't it?'* Tentatively, heads nodded. The guests began to breathe again.

Suddenly, I understood. Here I was: a fabulously wealthy Westerner, an emissary from the most powerful country on earth. I had blundered into Bala, and been greeted with reverence – even awe. But in truth I was merely a pale-faced *kuhire*: a foreign klutz who couldn't hold his *rakshi*.

The Joan Osborne song echoed in my ears:
What if God was one of us / Just a slob like one of us …

With my oafish faux pas, I'd shattered the mystique. We were all equals now – no matter how much my Gore-Tex parka had cost.

I left the house, and found Norbu. 'What should I do? Do we leave now?'

'Are you crazy? Don't even think of leaving. Go to your tent,' he commanded. 'And wait. They're going to do it all over again.'

And they did – with one enormous difference. This time, we all ate together.

Italy in Seventeen Courses

LAURA FRASER

Laura Fraser is a San Francisco–based writer whose latest book, a travel memoir, is *All Over the Map*. Her last book, *An Italian Affair*, was a *New York Times* bestseller and translated into seven languages. She frequently writes about food, travel and culture, and maintains a blog at laurafraser.com/blog. Her work has appeared in such publications as the *New York Times*, *O, The Oprah Magazine*, *Afar*, Salon.com, *Gourmet*, *Tricycle*, *More* and many others.

Aperitivi
- *Stuzzichini, olives*

It is August in Sardinia, where Italian vacationers sleep late, down an espresso, then take off to the beaches, packing themselves together like slippery fish in a tin. I've been travelling for weeks in the less-touristed interior of the island, but today, like everyone else, I am splashing around and getting *abbronzata* at the beach. Historically, beach property was considered so worthless that only the girls inherited the spectacular cliffs and wide expanses of sand, for Sardinians – invaded frequently and from all sides – tended to cosy into the interior.

In the evening, the beachgoers gather at bars, laughing and teasing each other as only Sards can, with increasing drunkenness and daring, until nearly dawn. I'm visiting my friend Beppe, who brings me along to meet his friends, who seem to include everyone between eighteen and forty-five from Sassari to Sorso. He introduces me to Giovanna and Giuliano, a couple in their twenties with dark curls, and tells me they are getting married on Saturday. They kiss me on the cheeks and ask where I'm from. I say San Francisco, where Beppe is currently living, where friends called me in a panic several years ago because they needed someone to come speak Italian to this guy who had arrived to stay on their couch and cook spaghetti with seafood. Beppe explains that we became friends even though I am the most *napoletana* American he's ever met, by which he means conniving and ball-busting, but which I explain is because I make such good pizza.

Giovanna and Giuliano invite me to their wedding.

I'm startled. At home in the United States, people agonise over the guest list, counting every head at $120, cutting cousins and former colleagues, wondering who will be insulted and who will send a present anyway. They meet weeks in advance with caterers who will dole out four ounces of salmon for every guest, next to three baby rosemary potatoes, a dollop of spinach and one white roll. There is no inviting strangers to a wedding at the last minute. Brides, pocket-conscious parents, wedding planners, placecard-letterers – everyone would freak out.

'It would be a pleasure,' says Giovanna, with a smile that says she means it, and would even be sad if I were still in the country and didn't attend on Saturday.

'*Un gran piacere,*' I say, not only because they are such a charming couple, but because (being a little *napoletana*) I know a wedding meal in Sardinia – perhaps my most favourite destination among hundreds of favourite food destinations in Italy – will be the ultimate culinary pleasure.

The day of the wedding, I shop, because the only nice dress I brought is purple, and Beppe's mother informs me that purple brings bad luck to a wedding. She explains that today we'll have a light lunch, and a nap.

In the late afternoon, everyone drives from the beach up to the town of Sennori, high above the sea and overlooking the northwest part of the island, where the gathering cars begin to wind up the streets, honking. The procession stops first at the bride's house, where relatives serve finger sandwiches, and the small crowd waits for the bride to appear in her huge frothy dress to snap photos and accompany her to the church. Then Beppe asks me to come along to the groom's house to collect him. At the door, someone hands me a plate and Beppe tells me to smash it hard, or it'll bring bad fortune. I break it into smithereens, everyone claps, the parents offer us drinks and more snacks, and eventually we take the groom to the church, careening up narrow cobbled roads to the top of the hill.

The wedding is a traditional Mass, where all the men stand outside the church on the piazza smoking, taking turns scouting the ceremony so they can all rush in at the moment to hear the vows. The couple departs in a hail of confetti, and the guests make their way back, honking, down to a restaurant near the sea, to drink aperitifs while watching a Campari-coloured sunset. Waiters pass around olives and *stuzzichini* – Sardinian antipasti ('to pick') – with seafood, mozzarella and tomatoes, bruschetta, everything irresistible that almost everyone seems to be resisting.

Antipasti
- *Prosciutto crudo*
- *Antipasti di terra alla Sarda (salsiccia, olives, formaggio dolce)*

- *Antipasti di mare (insalata di mare, polpetti in agrodolce, cozze gratinate, capesante gratinate)*

We sit down to long rows of tables, maybe 300 guests, with the sea breeze wafting in from the terraces. There's a sense of giddy anticipation at the table, and I'm excited to be at my first Italian wedding feast.

The firstness of this meal reminds me of my first proper meal ever in Italy, twenty-five years before, when I was travelling the Mediterranean at age twenty-two, and landed in Florence to visit my cousin Tim. I would have been happy with any meal; I had just arrived from the Sinai desert, where I'd picked bugs out of pita bread to eat with tinned sardines. Previous to that, I'd spent four years eating college food, and had emerged from the suburbs of Colorado, where no-one was a good cook, and food was suspect anyway because it might make you fat. My mother doled out strips of flank steak with green bean casserole made with cream of mushroom soup and warned us against the bread. I took over the cooking in high school, turning out such delicacies as a Weight Watchers' recipe called 'Fish Delish', which involved catfish, canned red cabbage and mandarins in artificially sweetened syrup. Italian food where I come from meant Spaghetti-Os or big plates of soft pasta with bland tomato sauce and dusty parmesan cheese shaken from a green can.

My cousin Tim, on an academic semester in Italy, was staying with a modest family outside of Florence. I spoke no Italian, but the parents and two teenaged kids smiled when I said things in high school Spanish, and replied in musical chatter, which Tim tried to translate. We sat down at a simple wooden table with short drinking glasses of wine.

The mother brought out an appetiser dish: fried baby artichokes. I didn't touch them because not only is fried food fattening, but I'd tried vinegary artichokes from a can: no thank you. My cousin shot me a warning glance. I put an artichoke on my plate and tried a tiny bite. The crispy coating was as delicate and transparent as dragonfly wings. The artichokes tasted like green, like spring, completely tender. I took another bite, and another, finishing everything on my plate. The mama beamed when I said *'delicioso'*, which sounded Italian but was actually Spanish. Then she did something that neither Tim's parents, WASPy sticklers for table manners, nor my parents, WASPy guilty eaters, would ever have done: she took more artichokes off her plate with her fingers and insisted I eat them too. I did, to her relish, and mine.

———————⟨

At the wedding, waiters in short black jackets appear from all sides, carrying trays with overflowing plates. Here comes the traditional food from Sardinia's interior, the cured prosciutto and sausage, *salume,* that tastes of herbs and chestnuts, that has nothing to do with any deli cuts I've ever known, even in Italy. There are platters of olives and the world's best pecorino cheeses, delicately seasoned meatballs with a hint of sweetness, and some thin *carta da musica* – 'music paper' bread. I am content with this perfect feast before me. Then platters of antipasti arrive as if straight from the ocean: scallops in their shells *a gratin,* seafood salad, mussels. The table of food is like a map of Sardinia. Everything is here: the woods, the hills, the chestnut trees, the olive groves, the beaches, the stone villages, the wide Sardinian sea.

Primi
- *Lasagne al ragù*
- *Gnocchetti alla Sarda*
- *Risotto alla pescatora*

The waiters clear the appetiser plates and I realise that my perfect feast was just a prelude to the meal. It occurs to me that perhaps I've overdone it on the antipasti, the best-tasting little morsels in the world, but I'm not worried. I'm no longer someone who is neurotic about eating, as I was when I first went to Italy, someone who thought of food only in terms of 'good' or 'bad', with good meaning low-calorie – not fresh and prepared with centuries of heart and skill – and bad meaning fattening, like pasta. I'd starve on boring good food and binge on sugary bad food, then suffer heaped servings of guilt. Now, after fifteen years of frequent trips to Italy, I'm a different person, someone who may not have Italian blood, but at least has an Italian stomach.

This transformation began at that dinner in Florence. After the artichokes came the pasta, penne or rigatoni, who knows, with a simple tomato sauce. I was prepared for a canned Chef Boyardee taste. The pasta came into the room on wings of garlic, riding a waft of basil. The noodles weren't mushy, but chewy, a stand-up vehicle for the sauce, which was made from those rare tomatoes of summer that you grew in your own garden, the ones that had nothing to do with the square, watery variety in the supermarket; tomatoes of summer that tasted like the sun.

I savoured my plate of pasta and gave such dreamy looks around the table that everyone laughed. The mama tried to insist I have more, but I didn't want to spoil the perfection of the little plate I'd eaten. I was completely satisfied. I decided, right then, that I was going to have to forget everything I knew about eating and start over. I was going to have to learn to eat and speak Italian. 'How do you say delicious?' I asked my cousin.

'*Buono,*' he said.

'*Buonissimo!*'

The waiters arrive at the tables, choreographed on time, with several platters of wide, homemade noodles layered in a red sauce with creamy ricotta cheese. I think this is perhaps the perfect *primo* in the world, until I realise that the waiters are bringing two other dishes to the table. I put down a forkful of lasagne with regret. Can I skip the seafood risotto, with its calamari tendrils, rich saffron seafood broth, and little shellfish I can't even name? I cannot. Nor can I pass over the Sardinian *gnocchetti* in its red meat sauce; someone's *nonna* spent all day on those, and I'm never going to be here again. Just a bite. Or two.

Vini
- Rosso e bianco della casa

Everyone at the long banquet tables is starting to sigh, pausing to chat, taking a little break to light a cigarette on the terrace. The waiter refills my glass of red wine. I swirl, taking in the rich ruby colour, and sniff its blackberry aroma. It tastes like roses just past their peak, with still-soft petals, and a little bitter aftertaste, like fall is coming. It's undoubtedly a Cannonau, probably bottled within a mile of here.

The wine takes me off on another reverie, to a couple of days after my first meal in Florence, when I decided that I would have to learn something about Italian wine along with the food. All I knew then was that there was a wine called Chianti, which came in bottles with little baskets, so I found a bus to the town called Chianti.

When the bus dropped me off, I followed one of the lanes through the hilly vineyards to a stone winery and knocked on the tall wooden front door. An elderly man answered, and I made a gesture of tasting wine. He looked confused, then smiled and led me to a cool, dark cantina filled with thousands of bottles of dark red wine. I wondered how you knew where to start.

He pointed at me and asked something that sounded like the date I was born.

I shrugged, got out a notebook, and wrote down '1961'.

He shuffled into a back room, and came back with a bottle, which he wiped with a soft, clean cloth.

'*Millenovecento sessant'uno,*' he said, with relish.

'*Buono?*' I said.

'*Molto buono.*'

I smiled and pointed at him. He shook his head sadly.

'*Sono aceto,*' he said. I understood: I'm vinegar.

I asked the price of my birthday wine, which was expensive even then. I told him I was a student and would like his cheapest bottle.

He returned with another bottle, and wiped it with the same care. Then he brought two glasses and seemed to ask if I knew how to drink the wine properly. I shook my head no. With great style and ceremony he opened the bottle, sniffed the cork, and had me sniff it. Then he poured a small amount into the glass, lifted it by the stem to look at the colour in the light, then swirled, and dipped his long nose into the glass to smell.

I watched, fascinated. It had never occurred to me to do anything with wine but drink it down fast, since all I'd been exposed to was Boone's Farm strawberry wine. I followed his ritual and accidentally snorted some of the wine when I sniffed, since my nose is short.

He laughed and poured me a glass, and I gestured that he should pour himself one, too. The wine had so many flavours going on at once, woods and fruits and earth. The man picked up the bottle with his gnarled hands and placed it on a huge stone table with a view of the vineyards, and with few words, him gesturing occasionally to the birds and the sunflowers, that old vinegar man and I drank the whole bottle.

Secondi
- *Porchetto (maialetto) al mirto*
- *Arrosto di vitello con funghi*

Contorni
- *Patate al forno*
- *Verdura mista*

The pasta plates have been cleared, and the men are perking up: now the serious eating is about to begin. The meat.

Beppe's sister, next to me, tells me we are having a couple of traditional specialities: baby pork in *mirto,* the island's herbaceous liqueur, and roast veal with wild mushrooms. The rich aromas reach the table, awakening my already much-sated appetite.

There was a time when I wouldn't have dreamt of eating baby animal anything, or meat at all. I was a vegetarian for many of the years I visited Italy. In my late twenties, I went to Italy with my then-boyfriend, an Italian-American named Vince, to visit a woman who'd stayed in our place in San Francisco. The first evening we arrived, Renata fixed dinner: a Florentine steak *and* a roast. 'This is to make up for him having to live with a vegetarian,' she said as Vince tucked into the meat, his eyes glistening.

I sat there and swore I was content with just the pasta. We went out to eat another night, and I had celery with olive oil for my main course. I refused pancetta, roast rabbit, salty *bresaola* and carpaccio with capers. I said no to meat in Bologna. I turned down the prosciutto in Norcia. One evening in Fiesole, the chef brought out some homemade sausages as a special treat to the American guest, and I demurred, explaining I was a *vegetariana*. My Italian friends suddenly acted like they didn't know me.

I'd been a vegetarian for a lot of reasons, some having to do with health, and some philosophy, with not a small helping of moral righteousness. But at a certain point I realised that if I was to stop being neurotic about food and try to eat like an Italian – eating fresh food socially, with pleasure – then being a vegetarian just didn't fit with the plan. Nor did it make much sense to my friends that such an otherwise hedonistic woman had this one ascetic streak. Italians like to eat with people, and it happens that people are omnivores.

The veal almost melts in my mouth. It is so tender it reminds me of the paper-thin horse I'd tried at Beppe's house earlier in the week. And the baby pig in *mirto* I'd have at my last meal. It was worth coming to Sardinia just to eat that piglet.

The meat dishes come with *contorni*, side dishes of potatoes and greens. They look wonderfully cooked, but with all the splendid meat dishes, I don't see the point of the vegetables. I take a bite of greens for old time's sake.

- *Sorbetto al limone*

I think this is dessert and the meal has finally come to an end. That might not be so bad, because while it has been an enormous pleasure, it has also been an enormous quantity. I'm surprised they're just having a little dish of sorbet for dessert, though.

Then come the fish courses.

- *Gamberi alla vernaccia*
- *Aragosta alla catalana*
- *Pesce misto in bella vista (alla griglia)*
- *Monzette in teglia*

No-one cooks fish like Sardinians. Here, as in Sicily, still exist the remnants of *mattanza*, the great tuna kill, facilitated with a complicated structure of nets designed by the Arabs, and celebrated for weeks on end. Fish is life on these islands.

For the past few years, as a traveller through Italy, I have steadily gravitated towards the south. That's partly because the southern parts of Italy – Puglia, Sicily, Sardinia – still seem like Italy, with small stone villages where most people don't care about speaking English. It's also because the cuisine is fresher and lighter than in the north, based on olive oil, fresh vegetables – and fish. There's something so elemental about fish as food: it comes straight out of the ocean, still plentiful in these parts, you grill it, and it's delicious.

The platters arrive with lobster cooked *'alla catalana'* – recalling the Spanish who settled on the north-west part of the island – and shrimps, and quantities of plump, moist, steaming grilled fish. But I am so full that all I can do is stare at the fish, as if in an aquarium. Aren't they beautiful. *Non posso piu.* I just can't eat any more.

Then the plates of snails arrive, peeking out of their garlic caves, *monzette in teglia.* My eyes tear up because there is nothing I want more in the world than to eat these little snails. Everyone in my family, everyone I grew up with, would shudder at these slimy creatures. Everyone here will be at another Sardinian wedding in their lives, and will taste more of these *monzette.* I sigh, to see if there is room in my stomach, in some small corner, for a little snail. There is room only for my desire.

Frutta e desserts
- *Frutta mista*
- *Gelato*

The desserts arrive, then coffee, but everyone has pushed back from the table as the music starts. Everyone wants to move by now, and they crowd the dance floor, from ages sixteen to eighty.

We dance and dance around the couples, whose faces are glowing with pleasure, with the love of their huge community of friends and family, supported by the food they've made, the sustenance of their culture.

I dance until three in the morning, when suddenly a switch turns off and I can no longer understand a word of Italian, nor dance another step. Despite years of speaking and eating Italian, I've turned into an American up long past her bedtime.

Beppe accompanies me back to the house before returning to the party, to dance until dawn, and to down an espresso before heading to the beach.

Foraging with Pee

JEFFREY ALFORD

Between a farm in Canada and a farm in Thailand, Jeffrey Alford spends a lot of time these days with crickets, frogs, green manure and machetes. He is currently at work on a book tentatively titled *Eating Leaves: A Cookbook Memoir*. Together with Naomi Duguid he has co-authored two cookbooks (*Flatbreads and Flavors* and *Hot Sour Salty Sweet: A Culinary Journey Through South-East Asia*), both of which won the James Beard Cookbook of the Year Award. Alford thinks of himself as a writer, a photographer, a cook, but most of all, a traveller.

The other night I was across the street at Oie's playing with her one-month-old baby, Off. There were a bunch of us sitting together on a wooden platform under a roof made of simple thatch. We call it *ban off*, or 'house of Off'. Oie and her partner, Mai, built it one day a few weeks back, having nothing else to do on a hot late April day here in north-eastern Thailand, in a farm village named Kravan, just a stone's throw from Cambodia.

Suddenly from the pitch-black evening Tey, Oie's younger brother, aged thirteen, emerged with a flashlight attached to his head, the type that miners wear, only not so fancy. He threw a muslin bag down on the platform and then took the light from his head – turning it off in one quick, efficient movement. Still without saying a word, he opened the bag and pulled out a snake, approximately a metre and a half long, now dead. He reached further into the bag and brought out half a dozen large frogs. People around the table were impressed and told him so, but he'd saved the best for last. Out came a large plastic Coke container almost half-filled with crickets, *jinglets* as they are called here. He'd scored and he knew it.

Foraging is serious stuff here in Kravan. Pee, my partner, is one of the best in the village, and well known for it. 'Pee,' I asked one day, 'which do you like best, rainy or dry season?'

'Rainy season,' she shot back immediately, as she almost always does when she responds to what she considers to be yet another idiotic question. 'In rainy season I catch frogs every day, no problem.' Pee loves frogs, maybe even more than she loves crickets, although for most people here it's just the opposite. My theory is that she loves frogs more than crickets (though not to get me wrong, Pee loves crickets, too) because for cooking, frogs are more versatile. And Pee loves to cook, maybe even more than she loves frogs.

Pee wakes up almost every morning between four-thirty and five, the sun not coming up until well after six. She knows that I am deeply asleep, but still I hear her voice, as if in a dream: 'What you like for breakfast? You like frog? You want chicken?'

She gets out of bed and heads immediately down the steep wooden stairs of the traditional Khmer-style house, perched high on wooden stilts, finding her way in the dark to the three small earthenware stoves set up immediately in front between the house and the dirt road, just like every house in the village. She gets one fire going, maybe two. To light the charcoal, she first lights long, thin, resinous sticks, and when they're burning, she starts to stack the charcoal. All the charcoal is made household by household and 'cooked' in mud ovens that look like bread ovens using prunings from mango trees, jackfruit and tamarind; Kravan is intensely tropical.

Once the fires are started, Pee will take a shower or stroll across the street to chat with Oie or An. Early-morning life is very social in the village. By five o'clock I am generally the only person in the village not yet awake. When I first arrived here, I was accustomed to waking at nine o'clock, a good 'compromise' hour, not too early, not too late. Initially, Kravan was a big adjustment!

If Pee decides to cook chicken, she simply takes a slingshot hanging from a nail on the wall and finds a few stones, then, with deadly aim, targets a chicken that she's most likely had her eye on for a while. One afternoon, sitting on the large wooden platform in the shade of the overhang (where we spend most of every day here in the hot season), she scornfully nodded her head, a typical gesture in north-eastern Thailand, in the direction of one particular squawking chicken. 'Noisy chicken,' she said. 'Tomorrow, soup.'

Kravan, in Thai terms, is a poor village, as are most villages in this part of Thailand. Last year, before coming to Kravan, I lived for a year on a farm about an hour's drive west of here; I write cookbooks for a living, so *here* for me is both life and work, but the two have become increasingly indistinguishable these last few years. It was on the Yindichati farm where I lived previously that I first encountered the concept of 'free' food. Mae and Pa – the two incredible people who owned the farm, and who have knowledge and skills specific to the farm that no future generation can ever hope to have – would tell me at night to eat more rice: 'free food'. 'And eat more fish,' father would say, smiling. 'Free.'

Free food is the food that's grown, that's harvested, and it accounts for almost everything eaten. There's very little cash money, but there's food, unbelievable food.

When I first arrived in Kravan a few months back, everything felt wonderfully familiar, all life revolving around rice farming and subsistence agriculture. But in Kravan, I've found over time, there's actually much that's different. Kravan is ethnically Khmer. Everyone, when speaking together, speaks Khmer, a language absolutely not related to Thai or to Lao. When they speak with me, they speak Lao or even Thai, especially the children now learning Thai in school. Also, Kravan is an actual village, a very tight, intimate assemblage of houses, and the rice fields surround the village. The Yindichati farm, in contrast, is in a region primarily populated by people who speak Korat, a language somewhere in the middle between Lao and Thai. What they call 'the village' are individual farms set one after another in a two-mile stretch down a dirt road, like farms in the American Midwest.

Kravan, I am quickly coming to realise, is also considerably poorer than the Yindichati farm. People's landholdings here are tiny in comparison. Pee has four *rai*, or approximately 1.6 acres, while the Yindichati farm has 117 *rai*. Late one afternoon a few days back, I went to the farm with Pee to forage. The fields are deadly dry here in late April and early May, parched beyond description with the fierce heat of every day. We sat under a big tree talking about the weeks to come, about how we will plant the fields and what we must do to get them ready. At some point Pee got up to go, a plastic bag and her long narrow (and always razor-sharp) spade in hand. We headed off across the fields, Pee looking down, an eagle on a hunt. Mid-conversation she suddenly started to dig, fiercely, through the red lateritic soil now baked hard as clay brick.

'Maybe snake,' she told me matter-of-factly. 'A crab hole, but maybe a snake moved in.' The hole was long, and Pee kept digging, horizontally. Finally, nothing. So we moved on. Another hole, this one fruitful: a crab. Pee picked it up, put it into the bag, and we moved on again. Pee foraged for an hour, maybe more. She found crickets, more crabs. 'Everything goes under the ground now. It's too hot. Soon the rain will come and the frogs will come back.'

As early evening at last began to arrive and the heat finally began to give way, the towering coconut palms, the fifty-year-old mango trees, the *leucaena,* everything all around took on a soft tropical glow. Pee set down her spade and turned her attention to picking tree leaves. *'Khilek,* you know?'

'Yes,' I answered proudly, knowing it from the Yindichati farm. But unfortunately it was the *only* one that I did know. Pee moved from tree to tree, explaining as she picked the leaves what she'd use them for. Some are *kom,* or bitter, a common taste here in the wild foods that I am still trying to get used to. It's *yaa,* or medicine, people always explain to me when eating very bitter leaves. And I am sure they are right, but for me, bitter's still bitter.

Other leaves are for *nam prik,* a category of chilli pastes, or salsas, for lack of a better word. There are a million different *nam priks,* and most are complicated and labour intensive. They're the heart of the cuisine, the number-one sign of a cook's skill. Almost exclusively they're made in Thai-style mortar and pestles, the pestle being made from a hard tropical wood. The *nam prik* is made by pounding, pounding, pounding. Little red hot bird chillies will usually be the first ingredient pounded, followed by tiny garlic and small Asian shallots. But from then on there's infinite variety.

One of Pee's favourite ways to use tiny frogs (and I mean tiny, about an inch to two inches in length) is to grill them over charcoal in a metal grilling basket. Most of the grilled frogs get pounded into a *nam prik.* One of Pee's favourites is a combination of grilled frog and green mango, a *nam prik* so fiery hot you would not believe.

When I stagger down to breakfast, proud of myself at six in the morning, Pee is often grilling tiny frogs. I squat down to watch what she's doing; Pee will cook for an hour, squatting, never sitting. When the frogs start to crisp, she'll open up the grilling basket and give me two or three frogs to nibble on. They're hot and delicious.

'Lao khao?' Pee will inevitably ask.

'Sure,' I answer; the combination of rice whisky – mixed with a Chinese medicinal herbal drink – served with hot, freshly grilled frogs is impossible to turn down. It's the essence of morning in Kravan. A few weeks ago it dawned on me that I hadn't drunk a cup of coffee in months, and I'm a person who's been drinking coffee religiously for thirty-five years!

As we were about to leave the farm that day, dusk giving way to dark, Pee let out a scream. Up a tree she'd suddenly spotted a large red ant nest, the prize of the day. She found a long length of bamboo and tied her spade to the end of the bamboo, then dislodged the nest without having to climb the tree. She gathered the red ant eggs into her plastic bag and we happily rode the motorbike back home in the dark.

Red ant egg salad is my personal favourite, even better than crispy grilled tiny frog.

It's amazing how the rites and rhythms of life slip inside you here, out in the country. How one thing flows so easily into another, dawn to dusk, dry season to rainy season, frog to chicken to snake.

Yesterday Pee and I got married. Work merged into life.

The Best Meal I Ever Had

ANDREW McCARTHY

Andrew McCarthy has written for the *Atlantic, Slate, Men's Journal, Travel +
Leisure* and *Bon Appétit,* among others. He is a contributing editor at *National
Geographic Traveler.* He has also eaten his way around the world as an actor.

'What do the stars next to the numbers on the badges mean?'

'Those are the ones who give you a bath first.'

'Ah.'

'You want that.'

'Sure,' I said, my head nodding up and down.

We were looking through a large picture window at twenty or
so women sitting on tiered benches. They were dressed in evening
gowns. It was three thirty in the afternoon.

'This is where the politicians come, so you can relax,' David
said. I must have looked puzzled. 'So they're clean,' he went on. I
nodded some more – it was my first time in a bordello and I

guess it showed. 'Maybe we ought to have a beer first,' he suggested, and crossed into the empty bar.

David was an American photographer who had escaped to Southeast Asia years earlier. We had met in Saigon and agreed to hook up for a couple of nights of good clean fun in Thailand. But I hadn't had a drink in years and a whorehouse in Bangkok on a wet Tuesday afternoon didn't seem like the place to start.

'You know what, David, I think I'm gonna get that train up to Vientiane after all.' I had been considering a trip north, to Laos.

The northern Thai border with Laos had only recently been opened and there was a train from Bangkok every evening. It arrived in Nong Khai, on the bank of the Mekong River on the Laotian border, before dawn, where, I was to discover, entrepreneurs stormed the train, woke you from a sound sleep, grabbed your bag, and threw it on the back of their túk-túk as you gave chase through the pre-dawn mist. They then demanded a dollar, deposited you on a waiting bus that drove a few hundred yards and unloaded you on the Thai side of 'Freedom Bridge', which you walked across under the watchful eye of armed guards, after which you went through a version of customs and were released to fend for yourself among the eager capitalists of Laos at daybreak. But before I was to learn any of that, I first had to get out of the whorehouse in Bangkok.

I left David at the bar to mull over his options, hurriedly checked out of my hotel, crawled through the Thai traffic, and was at the train station with nearly an hour to spare. The short time spent in the brothel had depressed me. The more ladies the host had offered, the more lonely I felt. So as I sat back on a hard wooden bench in Hualamphong Station, watching the crowds mill anonymously by and listening to the tracks called out in a language that was indecipherable to me, I was glad to be getting out of town, glad to be on my own again. I began to take wilful pride in the fact that no-one I knew in the world could find me. I was a stranger in a foreign land. Alone. The relief of solitude masqueraded as contentment.

I was suddenly starving. An exhausted-looking conductor confirmed there would be no dinner on the train and a quick search of the terminal revealed one forlorn restaurant. I opened the door. The place was deserted except for a group of what seemed to be staff members sitting around a large bowl in the centre of a table. I took a seat on the other side of the room. A stout woman got up from the table, came over and conveyed to me in Thai that the place was closed. My head sunk. She touched my shoulder, said something I couldn't understand, and went back to her bowl with the others.

I gathered up my bags. As I shuffled towards the door, the woman waved me over to their table and an older man with thin white hair got up and dragged over a chair. The two younger ones slid their seats closer together to make room. I demurred. They insisted. One of the younger men handed the woman a bowl; she filled it and placed its steaming contents in front of me and they returned to the business at hand. The silence of a good meal being well eaten ensued and I realised I was sitting among three generations of a family at dinner.

Conversation eventually filled the table – words I could not understand followed by laughter I could. The large bowl in the centre of the table emptied. The last drops went to me. I finished my fish soup and looked at the faces around me, strangers no more.

Ten minutes later, walking down the platform, I found myself sad to be leaving Bangkok. I stepped onto the train and said aloud, to no-one in particular, 'That may have been the best meal I ever had.'

The Rooster's Head in the Soup

TIM CAHILL

Tim Cahill is the award-winning author of nine books, including *Jaguars Ripped My Flesh* and *Hold the Enlightenment*. He is the co-writer of three IMAX movies, two of which were nominated for Academy Awards. Cahill has also written for *National Geographic*, *Outside* and the *New York Times Book Review*, among other publications. He lives in Montana.

Do you eat the thing or what? It's a rooster's head and it's floating in the soup. You are in a dirt-floored hut, a two-room adobe family home up in what is called the Eyebrow of the Jungle, the Ceja de Selva, in the cloud forests of Peru. The Peruvian family has allowed you to camp on their little farm and now they've invited you to dinner. Out comes the first dish. It's a yellow soup. And there's a rooster's head floating in it. Skeletal thing: no skin or eyeballs. Nothing inside the cranial cavity at all.

That was the first time I asked myself the Question most avid travellers are presented with at one time or another. Are they making fun of me, or is the rooster's head really given to the honoured guest? Back then, I spent some moments wrestling with the implications. Ruminating, so to speak. Assumption #1: they are, in fact, making fun of me. Okay. What's the worst that can happen? I chomp down on the fragile bones of the skull and everyone bursts out laughing. Well, it wouldn't be the first time I was the object of hilarity. I can generally salvage that situation by simply laughing right along with everyone else. They might think I'm an imbecile, but no-one is going to be insulted.

Now assume that the rooster's head is, in fact, a local delicacy. If you treat it as a joke, there is a good chance you will alienate your hosts. You absolutely do not want to alienate your hosts. Not up here in the Eyebrow of the Jungle where the trails are steep and sometimes lead to a crumbling precipice over a 5000-foot drop. You don't want to alienate your hosts if you need them to tell you where the pre-Columbian ruins are. You don't want to alienate your hosts if you are going to camp in their vicinity for several days because you are, in fact, genuinely interested in the local culture. Finally, you don't want to alienate them because refusing a delicacy might be a mortal insult, to be avenged with machetes. Probably not, but why take the chance? Let them laugh instead.

So the Answer to the Question is simple enough: you eat what's put in front of you. It's a no-brainer. Just like that white avian skull, floating in the soup.

———————————⋲

The fowl tale I've recounted happened in Peru over three decades ago, but I've spent a lot of the intervening time travelling in the hinterlands of various countries, and something similar has happened to me on every continent, save Antarctica. Out in the back country, in those remote places where folks do not have much contact with the outside world, people tend to be generous with their food. Some kind family is always offering me something that, at first glance, does not seem to be 100 per cent palatable. Baked turtle lung. Sheep's eyeballs.

Smile and choke it down. That's my policy. If they have something vaguely alcoholic to drink – palm wine, corn beer – all the better. In central Africa, under the Virunga volcanoes, people make a kind of banana beer they call *pombe* that is served in one-litre brown glass bottles that once contained beer. *Pombe* simply means beer in Swahili, but I was cautioned about this banana variety: don't pour it into a glass, said the brewer himself; you don't want to actually see it. The *pombe* is best drunk with a wooden straw. This is because the fermenting bananas leave a thick layer of black sludge on the glass. I've since learned that, in the final brewing process, the beer can be filtered through a fine cloth. I'm thinking that my brewer may have found that process superfluous.

Banana *pombe* was the after-work libation for a couple of African guides who were taking me out to see a group of mountain gorillas. The animals lived low on the volcanoes, in the visually limited world of the bamboo forests, and care had to be taken not to blunder onto the gorillas and startle them. They could run away. Or charge. Neither situation was ideal.

So it was thirsty work, crawling through the bamboo along a gorilla path, trying not to make any noise. When we walked home in the evening, the guides always checked a certain home built of sturdy wooden slats. If there were flowers in a vase on the porch, it meant that the brewer who lived there had *pombe*. We were obliged to stop and help this gentleman dispose of the beer, which has about a 48-hour shelf life. It was our duty. Should the brewer have unsold bottles on his shelf he could, the guides informed me solemnly, simply stop making *pombe*.

The stuff was a titch sweet and seemed to contain as much alcohol, drop for drop, as anything brewed by Anheuser-Busch.

It was fine to sip beer through a straw after a sweaty day of crawling after primates. The way I saw it, I was helping the brewer and the community's beer drinkers, and learning all kinds of things about gorillas I might never have found out entirely sober.

While my policy is to eat what is put in front of me, I have tried, over the years, to reciprocate when I can. Usually I just have camp food, and if I have learned one thing, it is this: no-one on earth likes freeze-dried scrambled eggs.

I do recall a memorable meal I once cooked in Indonesia. I was visiting the Karowai, a clan of Papuans who live in tree houses. Some Karowai groups, especially those who live away from the river, are unaware of the outside world. The group I trekked through the swamp to meet had been contacted only the previous year. My travelling companions and I came upon this group in their tree house and we negotiated with them, standing in clouds of mosquitoes and shouting fifty feet up through the branches.

Eventually we were welcomed. The house was a large wooden platform, shaded by the tree itself. There were few mosquitoes and the wind was fresh. We met three men, two older, one younger. There were three women. The men, one couldn't help but notice, wrapped their penises with leaves. The women wore straw skirts.

There was a wooden wall and on it was the skeleton of a fish about the size of a trout. The remains of a fine meal? Just offset from the one wall were dozens of hardball-sized rocks arranged as a fire pit and the women placed something white and doughy-looking on the coals. It was, I was told, a staple starchy food made from powdered sago palm. After a short time, the women broke off a piece of the bread-like substance and handed it to me. It felt like a lighter version of Silly Putty and was so bland as to be almost tasteless. But, no, there was an unpleasant sour aftertaste.

I smiled brightly and nodded vigorously, a suggestion that this was a delicious treat. The Karowai stared at me in glum suspicion. They knew perfectly what it was. They ate it every day. Why did I climb fifty feet up a rickety ladder just to lie to them?

We stayed with the Karowai for several days and one night we asked if we might make the dinner. Rice was what we had. We doctored it with oil and bottled lemon juice and garlic salt. As the younger man ate, moisture formed in the corners of his eyes. He took another mouthful, eating with his fingers while tears coursed down his cheeks. Now what had I done?

Translating took a while, but in the fullness of time I learned that the man was crying because this rice was the best thing he'd ever eaten in his life. The other Karowai nodded in agreement. Never, I believe, has a chef been so complimented.

The next morning, overcome with an unwarranted confidence, I fixed freeze-dried scrambled eggs for everyone. The Karowai ate sparingly and stared at me, wan smiles on their faces. I recognised the expression. It was one I'd felt on my own face many times over the years. They were smiling the smile you smile when you've just eaten the rooster's head.